Ventures in Discipleship

Ventures in Discipleship

A Handbook for Groups or Individuals

John R. Martin

Foreword by Howard A. Snyder

HERALD PRESS
Scottdale, Pennsylvania
Kitchener, Ontario
1984

Library of Congress Cataloging in Publication Data

Martin, John R., 1928-
   Ventures in discipleship.
Bibliography: p.
   1. Christian life—Mennonite authors. 2. Anabaptists—
Doctrines. 3. Spiritual exercises. I. Title.
BV4501.2.M36435   1984   248.4'897   84-19140
ISBN 0-8361-3378-1 (pbk.)

VENTURES IN DISCIPLESHIP
Copyright © 1984 by Herald Press, Scottdale, Pa. 15683
   Published simultaneously in Canada by Herald Press,
   Kitchener, Ont. N2G 4M5. All rights reserved.
Library of Congress Catalog Card Number: 84-19140
International Standard Book Number: 0-8361-3378-1
Printed in the United States of America
Design by Gwen Stamm

90 89 88 87 86 85 84 10 9 8 7 6 5 4 3 2 1

To the students at
Eastern Mennonite Seminary
who were involved in the development
of this handbook, and to the
students who are preparing for
the ministry of discipling

Contents

Appendices

Foreword

What does it mean to live the life of the kingdom? Jesus made it plain that God's kingdom, with its righteousness and justice, should be the first quest of all who follow him (Mt. 6:33). Yet how little the church today, especially in North America, gives any concrete signs of taking Jesus' words seriously.

Ventures in Discipleship speaks to this need.

The key link between our lives and the kingdom of God is discipleship. What it means to live authentically as Jesus' disciples has been shown in flesh and with blood at various points in history. One of the most stirring examples is sixteenth-century Anabaptism. From the rich deposit of such leaders as Conrad Grebel, Pilgram Marpeck, and Menno Simons, author John Martin has drawn words of witness which speak directly to us in the twentieth-century church. Further, these insights are enriched by some of the best contemporary writing on discipleship and the church, particularly from Dietrich Bonhoeffer. I especially appreciate the way the book, though rooted in the Anabaptist heritage, draws freely on confirming insights from other branches of the church. Most of all, it is solidly based in Scripture.

This unique book promises to be profoundly useful for all who take it seriously. Merely to talk about what we should be doing is surely one form of cheap grace. This book provides concrete steps for making discipleship a way of life, not just a way of talk.

Ventures in Discipleship explores (1) biblical truth, with (2) Anabaptist insight, and (3) contemporary confirming content. It is strong in its built-in application to daily life, particularly through journaling and group process. The book is extraordinarily practical with its uncommon mix of doctrine and application, reflection and action, theological probing and challenge to commitment, basic discipleship and a broad range of specific disciplines. It strikes a healthy balance between the high standard of Christian discipleship and practical steps to get there. It both motivates and provides a path to follow.

Discipling material abounds today. Much of it is shallow or extremely narrow-gauge. Here, perhaps for the first time, is a resource grounded in a profound and costly understanding of discipleship which reflects the full biblical breadth and radicality of what it means to follow Jesus. And it is grounded in a tradition which has much to teach us about costly grace.

In light of the growing concern with discipleship, community, and the shape of the church today, Martin's book will be useful to serious Christians in all traditions. I especially commend it for cell groups, house churches, and other groups of believers who are willing to take their Christian faith as seriously as did the martyrs of the sixteenth century and other ages of the church.

No group of believers can use this book with serious intent and fail to move closer to real kingdom living, to genuine following of Jesus Christ.

—Howard A. Snyder
Chicago, Illinois

Author's Preface

God has given me a dream: a dream that discipleship will again become as central to our Christian lives as it was to the sixteenth-century Anabaptists; a dream that our discipleship will become contemporary and dynamic, requiring the power of the living Christ; a dream that spiritual disciplines will become vibrantly meaningful, undergirding our discipleship; a dream that many pastors and members will develop the skills of effective discipling; a dream that a fresh spirit of prayer will move upon the church, empowering vigorous activities in mission, education, and congregational life; a dream that we in the Anabaptist-Mennonite tradition will enlarge our view of spirituality by learning from other Christian traditions, and that we will contribute to Christendom in its search to understand Christianity as discipleship. This dream has motivated the development of this handbook.

Originally the handbook was prepared as a doctoral project at Lancaster Theological Seminary. I am especially indebted to Dr. Donald Freeman, project supervisor, for his valuable assistance and to Conrad C. Hoover, Washington, D.C., who aided in background studies in Christian spirituality and spiritual direction.

Throughout the process of research and writing, my family was most supportive by their interest and encouragement. Special thanks go to my wife, Marian, for typing the early stages of the project and to Lila Collins, who typed the final draft plus revisions for publication.

The faculty and staff at Eastern Mennonite Seminary have assisted with their counsel, participation, and cooperation. Many students at Eastern Mennonite Seminary have also contributed. Some have participated in facets of the study. Others have supported and encouraged the vision. Still others have undergirded the process with prayer. To all of these students I am most grateful.

Finally, a number of pastors and denominational leaders have supported and helped shape the project because of the potential they have seen for use in congregations. They have expanded my immediate vision beyond the seminary classroom to the denomination with its congregations and leadership training programs. Their influence on the study has truly been significant.

The wind of the Spirit is blowing on Christendom creating a hunger for a deeper spirituality and a more relevant discipleship. Christians from various theological orientations are learning from each other as books, articles, and retreats flow across denominational lines. I commit this book to the Lord of the church praying that it can be useful for any Christian who enters the venture of following Christ in daily life. And I invite small groups or individuals to read and ponder these discipleship studies.

—*John R. Martin*
Harrisonburg, Virginia

Introduction

Welcome to a venture in discipleship and discipling. If you have a serious interest in exploring the meaning of Christian discipleship and the process of discipling, this handbook is for you. The lessons will lead you through a process of study, reflection, sharing, and application. But before you begin the lessons, be sure to read this introduction carefully.

The primary purposes of this handbook are to help seminarians, pastors, and congregational leaders to articulate and personalize discipleship as understood in the Anabaptist tradition, to discover a biblical discipleship living, and to develop discipling skills. Plan to have your commitment to Christ strengthened, your obedience to Christ enlarged, and your understanding of discipleship stretched.

Definition of Terms

The term "Anabaptist" refers to a group of Christians in the sixteenth century who baptized again or practiced believer's baptism. In this handbook, the term refers primarily to the thought and life of the Swiss Brethren, the South and Central German Anabaptists, and the Dutch and Northwest German Anabaptists. It does not include the revolutionary Münsterites or the communitarian Hutterites, although they were related to the Anabaptist movement.

The term "discipleship" as used in this handbook refers to the Anabaptist concept of the Christian life as a daily following of

Christ by bringing the whole of one's life under his lordship. The Anabaptists used the German term *Nachfolge Christi,* "Following Christ," or "discipleship," which was central to their understanding of the Christian life and to their theology.

The term "discipling" refers to the process of helping Christian disciples understand and follow the call of Christ in their total lives as members of his body. While the Anabaptists did not have a "planned program" of discipling, the phenomenon took place through the intense form of their congregational and community life. (See Appendix 1 [pages 231-232] for expanded definitions.)

I recognize that the term "disciple" is a noun and that I am using it as a verb when I refer to discipling. My justification for this usage is based on both ancient and modern use. Dictionaries such as *Webster's Third New International Dictionary* and the *Oxford Dictionary* indicate an archaic use as a verb which meant "to make a disciple." Currently an increasing number of books are using the term "discipling" in their title and text. Two examples are *Discipling the Brother* by Marlin Jeschke[1] and a four-volume series entitled Discipling Resources by Larry Richards and Norm Wakefield.[2]

The term "discipler," as used in this handbook, refers to a Christian who attempts to help other Christians live a daily life of Christian discipleship.

Current Interest in Discipleship and Discipling

In recent years, there has been renewed interest in the Mennonite church in recapturing the concepts of discipleship and discipling. The writings of Harold S. Bender during the 1940s and 1950s brought the concept of discipleship into fresh awareness. During the 1970s, the concept of discipling began to emerge further in the form of Paul-Timothy programs and Discipleship Voluntary Service units.

In the broader Christian church, books and articles dealing with discipleship and discipling are appearing in increasing numbers. They represent a broad theological spectrum from evangelical to liturgical churches. A casual reading of these materials indicates that the terms "discipleship" and "discipling" mean many different things to many different people. It is for this reason that I feel the need to clarify the Anabaptist meaning of these terms or concepts. I am searching for an understanding and an application that is consistent with Anbaptist theology.

Some Meanings of Discipleship and Discipling
    In contemporary publications, the concepts of discipleship and discipling are given a variety of meanings and describe a variety of activities.
    Donald McGavran, originator of modern church growth theory, uses the terms "discipling" and "disciple making" almost synonymously with evangelism. For him, discipling is drawing or sweeping first-generation Christians into church membership. Later activity designed to build up the converts is called "perfecting."
    In *How to Grow a Church,* by Donald A. McGavran and Win Arn, McGavran states the following:

> Church-growth men use the word "discipling" to mean the initial step by which people come to Christ and become baptized believers. We go on and say that the second part of church growth is "perfecting" or growing in grace.[3]

In the same book, Arn describes discipleship as follows:

> True discipleship means that the disciple has the same goals and objectives as his Master. But being committed to discipleship has an additional dimension in growing churches. Discipleship suggests active involvement.[4]

    In his widely read book, *Understanding Church Growth,* McGavran states that "Christian mission is to disciple each unit out to its fringes."[5] He further states that "Matthew 28:19 instructs Christians to *disciple the tribes* ."[6]
    A second usage has been popularized by Juan Carlos Ortiz from Buenos Aires. His book *Disciple* has been translated into at least seven languages. He uses the term discipling to define an ap-

prentice relationship between a "young" and a "mature" Christian, in which the younger is the disciple of the older person. Discipling is helping another Christian mature through a relationship of submission. But the discipler must also be in submission to another Christian. It involves a "submission network." Ortiz states that "the person giving commandments to his disciples must be under the command of someone himself. He rebukes his disciple—who rebukes him? There is no submission if there is not submission at every level."[7]

A third usage originated with Dawson Trotman, founder of the Navigators. Discipling is the process of nurturing a new believer so that he or she can carry out the Great Commission, that is, win other believers. The approach to discipling is a one-to-one relationship between a "young" Christian and a "mature" Christian for a period of several years. This process does not directly involve life in a congregation. In fact, Trotman was not an active church person. The understanding of the Christian life is one's individual relationship to Christ as Savior and the calling to lead other individuals to that same experience. Two widely sold books reflecting this orientation are *The Lost Art of Disciple-Making* by Leroy Eims[8] and *Disciples Are Made—Not Born* by Walter A. Henrichsen.[9]

A number of persons have borrowed the Navigator program and adapted it to a congregational setting. The understanding of the Christian life has remained basically the same but the program is operated as a congregational ministry. Books representing this approach include *Successful Discipling* by Allen Hadidian,[10] *Multiplying Disciples: The New Testament Method for Church Growth* by Waylon Moore,[11] and *Discipleship* edited by Billie Hanks, Jr., and William A. Shell.[12]

Waldron Scott, in his excellent book, *Bring Forth Justice*,[13] takes many of the Navigator concepts of disciple making and relates them to a view of the Christian life which applies faith to one's public life, not merely one's private life.

Larry Richards and Norm Wakefield have developed a fourth approach in their Discipling Resources[14] series. Four booklets have been published and there are four yet to come. Each booklet outlines thirteen lessons which involve personal study and reflection along with a weekly small-group meeting where there is planned sharing and discussion. The context for use is the church. Discipleship is defined as "*doing* God's Word, *loving* one another, and *ministering* to each other."[15] The booklets are attractively designed and reflect a good grasp of educational principles. The approach and content of this series comes closer to Anabaptism than any of the other contemporary publications described above. However, none of these writings flow out of Anabaptist theology.

Rationale for the Handbook

What is the rationale for another handbook on discipleship and discipling considering the wealth of printed material already available? The answer lies in the distinctive definition of discipleship for the Anabaptists and in their distinctive approach to discipling.

For the Anabaptists, discipleship meant following Christ in daily life by bringing all of life under his lordship. Participation in a congregation was essential and there was a strong concern for personal and social ethics. Their approach to discipling related directly to their view of discipleship. The process involved helping believers understand discipleship and to follow Christ in daily life as members of his body. There was a strong corporate orientation.

Educational Approach

The educational approach reflected in the handbook has a number of features. First, the content relates to the three primary areas of seminary education: academic, professional, and formative. Material included for each session is drawn from biblical material, Anabaptist or discipleship themes, spiritual exercises, and skill development.

Second, there is a major focus on personalizing discipleship beliefs. Wilfred Cantwell Smith and James W. Fowler have identified the difference between faith and belief. Faith is defined as a person's way of responding to transcendent value. It is the orientation of a person to oneself, one's neighbor, and to God. Belief, according to Smith, is "the holding of certain ideas."[16] Belief can be ideas about God rather than trust in God.

It appears that some Mennonites hold discipleship as a belief (cluster of ideas) rather than as faith (the orientation of their lives). This handbook is intended to move discipleship from belief toward faith. In this process, there should be movement from what Fowler describes as stage 3, Synthetic-Conventional faith, toward stage 4, Individuative-Reflective faith. This would mean personally integrating the faith system of others in the community by reflectively adopting discipleship as one's own personal faith which involves individual response and consequent change in lifestyle.

Third, the approach combines individual reflection, group processing, and group member and group leader discipling relationships. The discipling process will take place between group members and between group members and group leaders.

Fourth, the discipling process contains the elements of commitment, accountability, interaction, and modeling. The persons in the group or class will commit themselves to each other and to the process; they will hold each other accountable to keep their commitments; there will be depth interaction between the group members; and the group leader will model the discipling process. The purpose is not to reproduce sixteenth-century Anabaptism. Rather, it is to discover the meaning of discipleship in the twentieth century.

Learning Objectives

The primary learning objectives are as follows:

1. To be able to articulate the Anabaptist understanding of discipleship.

2. To personalize discipleship themes giving them contemporary application.

3. To experience a variety of spiritual exercises that can undergird one's discipleship.

4. To develop the skills essential for effective discipling.

The secondary learning objectives are as follows:
1. To be able to converse freely with others about Christian discipleship.
2. To find in the concept of discipleship a center and focus for one's Christian life.
3. To experience spiritual renewal through meaningful spiritual disciplines and significant group sharing.

Handbook Content

Three types of material are included in the handbook. First, there is material related to Anabaptist or Discipleship themes. This material includes key biblical passages, selections from primary Anabaptist resources written between 1524 and 1560, writings of Anabaptist scholars, and contemporary writings from other theological traditions. Of necessity the material is brief. There is value in having two group leaders (disciplers) with backgrounds in different areas.

The major primary resources will be the writings of Conrad Grebel (c. 1498-1526), Michael Sattler (c. 1490-1527), Pilgram Marpeck (149?-1556), and Menno Simons (c. 1496-1561). Conrad Grebel was nurtured in the Zwinglian Reformation and became one of the founding Anabaptist leaders. Key second-generation leaders were Menno Simons in the North and Pilgram Marpeck in the South. Bridging the founding leaders and the second-generation leaders was Michael Sattler and the *Seven Articles of Schleitheim,* which provided the "transition between birth and consolidation."[17] (The Anabaptists are viewed herein as significant examples of faithfulness to Christ but not as perfect role models.)

Second, there are a variety of spiritual exercises which are intended to undergird one's life of discipleship. Third, there are readings and exercises intended to develop discipling skills.

Identifying the essential skills for effective discipling has been difficult because no one to my knowledge has attempted this task approaching it from an Anabaptist-Mennonite perspective.

In fact, the concept of discipling within the Anabaptist-Mennonite context is still being developed and defined.

In identifying skills for discipling, I have drawn from three major areas. The first has been the field of counseling. While discipling is not identical with peer counseling, it is certainly related in that the relationship between the persons is a major factor in the helping process. Also, the discipler needs to model the attitudes and qualities that are being encouraged.

The second area from which I have drawn has been Anabaptist faith and life. It is my conviction that discipling among Mennonites today should emerge from the Anabaptist concept of discipleship and touch on its various themes.

The third area from which I have drawn has been Protestant and Roman Catholic spirituality. I have found the concepts of spiritual discernment and spiritual disciplines to be vitally related to discipleship and discipling. Furthermore, these concepts seem to be compatible with Anabaptist spirituality. In scope, the concept of discipling relates to both spiritual direction (focusing on one's relationship to God) and spiritual formation (forming one in a spiritual tradition).

A summary of the discipling skills is as follows:

1. Relational skills: empathic listening, humble openness, constructive accountability.

2. Knowledge and practice of discipleship: personal aspects, corporate expressions, societal applications.

3. Spiritual discernment: Christian life, movement of God, spiritual disciplines.

Each lesson will focus on one of these skills by having either an exercise for development or a selected reading. An attempt will be made to select a skill that relates to the rest of the material in the lesson. Therefore, I will not follow the exact order as outlined above.

Lessons 1 through 8 focus on the personal aspects of discipleship. These include an understanding of discipleship and important aspects of the Christian life such as repentance, regeneration, obedience, holy living, and growth in Christlikeness. Lessons

9 through 16 deal with the corporate aspects of discipleship. Included are beliefs and practices related to the life of the congregation. The last seven lessons touch on the application of discipleship to society. Consideration is given to themes such as ethics, service, and the rejection of the sword. (The handbook design appears on the following page.)

Handbook Design

Title and Theme	Spiritual Exercise	Discipling Skill
Personal Aspects		
1. **Discipleship Is Following Jesus**	Group Commitment	Introduction
Christianity as Discipleship		
2. **A Disciple of Which Jesus?**	Journaling	Relating View of Jesus
Which Jesus Do You Follow?		to Discipleship
3. **Follow Me**	Spiritual Auto-	Identifying the
The Disciple, A Follower	biography	Movements of God
4. **Learn of Me**	Spiritual Auto-	Discovering God's
The Disciple, A Learner	biography	Dialogue
5. **Walking in the Resurrection**	Spiritual Auto-	
Repentance and Regeneration	biography	Empathic Listening
6. **The Obedience of Faith**	Spiritual Auto-	
Faith and Obedience	biography	Humble Openness
7. **Separated unto God**		Constructive
Holy Living	Bible Reading	Accountability
8. **Progressing Toward Perfection**		
Faithfulness, Growth, and	Bible Study	Relating Bible Study
Perfection		Methods and Needs
Corporate Expression		
9. **The Community of God's People**		Understanding
The Church, A Community of	Meditation	Meditation Methods
Believers		
10. **Christ Among His People**		Relating Meditation to
The Church, The Body of Christ	Meditation	Christ's Presence in
11. **Believer's Baptism**		His Body
Baptism as Commitment	Meditation	Teaching Meditation
12. **Communion and Community**		Teaching Others to
The Lord's Supper	Praying the Psalms	Pray the Psalms
13. **Admonish One Another**	Admonition and	Constructive
Fraternal Admonition	Accountability	Admonition
14. **Moral Discernment**	Discernment, Confess-	Moral Discernment and
Binding and Loosing	ion, Forgiveness	Forgiveness
15. **Brotherhood and Material Sharing**	Living into the	Accountability in
Mutual Aid	Scriptures	Brotherhood Sharing
16. **Gift Discernment**		
The Discovery and Exercise of	Discovering Gifts	Listening to Life
Gifts	and Vocations	
Societal Applications		
17. **Christianity and Ethics**	Discernment Through	Ethical Discernment
Separation from Evil	Presence	
18. **The Kingdom of God**	Discerning Kingdom	Personalizing the Two-
The Two Kingdoms	Orientation	Kingdom Concept
19. **The Cost of Discipleship**		Facing Costly
Bearing the Cross of Christ	Counting the Cost	Discipleship
20. **Children of Peace**	Discerning the	Relating to
Love and Nonresistance	Spiritual Battle	Spiritual Battles
21. **Ministry to Human Need**	Meditation and	
The Service of Charity	Service	Motivating for Service
22. **Discipleship and Evangelism**		
The Great Commission	Fasting	Fasting and Prayer
23. **The Motivation of Eschatology**	Living into the	Seeing the Present
The Return of Christ	Future	Through the Future

Handbook Use

This handbook can be used in several ways. First, it can be used individually for the purpose of increasing one's understanding of discipleship. Special attention should be given to the biblical, Anabaptist, and contemporary material in each lesson. Completing the journaling exercises and the spiritual exercises would aid in reflecting on this material. The primary benefit would be gaining a knowledge of discipleship.

Second, it can be used with a group for the purposes of increasing their understanding of discipleship and entering into the experience of discipling. The group members would study each lesson, complete the journaling exercises and spiritual exercises individually. They would then meet weekly for the discipling sessions. The ideal group size is from six to eight members plus the leader or leaders. The primary benefits would be growing in discipleship knowledge and application through the discipling experience.

Third, the handbook can be used with a group for the purposes of increasing their understanding of discipleship, entering the experience of discipling, and developing discipling skills. The group members would prepare each lesson individually and meet weekly for the discipling session which would include attention to developing discipling skills. Again, a group of from six to eight members plus leader(s) would be the ideal size. The primary benefits would be growing in discipleship knowledge, discipleship application, spiritual disciplines, and discipling skills. The leader is encouraged to meet individually with each group member every two to four weeks to deal with issues or concerns that were not covered in the discipling sessions. This also enables group members to observe discipling being modeled by the leader. The discipling experience involves a mutual relationship with another group member (see discipling session in Lesson 1), corporate relationships with the total group, and a modeling relationship with the group leader. The primary discipling relationship is mutuality in terms of function

Persons wanting to receive maximum benefit from the lessons should plan to spend at least 30 minutes a day, five days a week, completing the readings and journaling exercises. Groups wanting to receive maximum benefit from the lessons should plan to spend from one and one half to two hours each week completing each discipling session.

Recommendations for Use of the Handbook

Experience indicates that all persons wishing to lead others through the material and the discipling experience should first go through the material and the process themselves. This is because the handbook calls for a process, not merely a study of content.

Seminary faculty using the handbook with seminarians should keep a strong focus on the development of discipling skills because of the discipling role the students will likely exercise when they become pastors. The length of time given to the process should be a full academic year.

Pastors or leaders who wish to lead other pastors through the discipling process should likewise pay special attention to skill development. It is for this reason that an extended period of time is needed. Time is needed to grasp the concepts, experience the exercises, and test one's skills.

Pastors using the handbook with church members would likely place less emphasis on skill development and more on understanding and practicing discipleship. A particular concern would be developing the quality of life among the members.

For those who wish to expand their skills as disciplers, I recommend focusing on the three areas from which I drew in identifying skills; counseling, Anabaptist-Mennonite studies, and spirituality. The bibliography identifies relevant reading material. Beyond the reading is the value of experience itself. In fact, discipling with shared leadership can be valuable when working with a group. Either the leaders can complement each other by their various areas of strength or a person with less experience can learn from the leader with more experience.

It is well to remember that just as we continue to need the experience of being discipled, so we need to continue growing in discipling skills. The two are lifelong processes.

Ventures in Discipleship

Lesson 1

Discipleship Is Following Jesus

Discipleship Theme: Christianity as Discipleship

Welcome to a venture in discipleship. This is the first of twenty-three lessons. Each lesson will focus on a specific discipleship theme and all of the lessons will follow a similar format.

The theme will be developed by identifying appropriate biblical teachings, Anabaptist writings, and contemporary writings. Journaling exercises will help you reflect on these materials. A spiritual exercise will be described which is intended to help undergird your discipleship. Again there will be journaling exercises to help you relate the spiritual exercise and the discipleship theme. These activities will be done alone between class sessions. *The lesson design requires about thirty minutes a day, five days a week, for studying the material and interacting with it.*

The last part of each lesson will describe the discipling session. This is the activity for class interaction. The activities are to help you process and apply the material. Also, they are to help you develop discipling skills.

Biblical Teachings

The New Testament uses various concepts to describe the heart or essence of Christianity. Some concepts describe the believer's spiritual relationship to Jesus Christ. In the Gospel of John, Jesus describes this relationship with the phrase "abide in me." In the Epistles, Paul refers to the believer being "in Christ."

29

There are other concepts that describe the believer's social or physical relationship to Jesus Christ. Paul invited believers to "imitate Christ." Jesus' invitation was to "follow me." Those who followed were disciples, a term used at least 225 times in the Gospels. The concept of discipleship, which means following Christ, comes from the term disciple (*mathētēs*).

The Anabaptists selected the term and concept of discipleship as their way of understanding the essence of Christianity. To be a Christian meant following Jesus and following Jesus meant obeying his teachings.

A basic passage presenting the meaning of discipleship is Mark 1:16-20. Verse 17 is central: "And Jesus said to them, 'Follow me and I will make you become fishers of men.'" Several ideas are basic. Discipleship begins with a call from Jesus. Discipleship means following Jesus along with others whom he has called. The call involves a service task. The call is to a faith pilgrimage. None of the disciples knew what following the call would mean.

Another important discipleship passage is John 8:31-32: "Jesus then said to the Jews who had believed in him, 'If you continue in my word, you are truly my disciples, and you will know the truth, and the truth will make you free.'" To continue in Jesus' words is to obey his teachings. In so doing one knows the truth and experiences true freedom. This is a part of the meaning of following Jesus

Anabaptist Writings

In his article on "The Anabaptist Theology of Discipleship," Harold S. Bender described his perception of the centrality of discipleship for Anabaptism.

> Does it not seem that every time we have sought the essence of Anabaptism in one of the other major ideas, such as the Scripture, the church, or the principles of love, we are driven a step further into the ultimate relationship of the individual Christian to Christ? I would therefore propose that we pursue our search further down this road, for I believe that if we do so we shall find the answer in the concept of discipleship as the

most characteristic, most central, most essential and regulative concept in Anabaptist thought, which largely determines all else. We shall also find at this point the parting of the ways between various forms of Christianity, and various types of theology and ethics.[1]

Now the idea of discipleship is not unique with Anabaptism, for it has appeared in various forms through the Christian centuries, sometimes in almost identical form with that which it took in Anabaptism. It was the vision of the earliest Christians of the New Testament age. One of its purest expressions was in Peter Chelchitzki of Bohemia (1390-1460), spiritual father of the Unitas Fratrum. But though the ideal of "following Christ," "die Nachfolge Christi," or of "imitating" Him, has been a recurring creative idea all through Christian history, it was the mission of the Anabaptists to give expression in a powerful way to this idea at a creative moment in history, at the beginning of our modern age in such a way that this time it did not die shortly but was incorporated in a continuing group, and through manifold ways fertilized modern Protestantism. The tragedy is that the very group that professed this vision and seriously attempted to practice it lost its witnessing zeal and ultimately no small amount of the reality of this vision in its own practice, so that the discipleship (which its theology still holds), became flabby and diluted or shriveled and lost much of its vitality, though still retaining much of the pristine character.

In essence the discipleship which the Anabaptists proclaimed was simply the bringing of the whole of life under the Lordship of Christ, and the transformation of this life, both personal and social, after His image. From this point of view they subjected not only the church but the whole social and cultural order to criticism, rejected what they found to be contrary to Christ, and attempted to put into actual practice His teachings as they understood them both ethically and sociologically.

Now anyone who undertakes such a critical examination of his own world, must disengage himself from the contemporary culture in which he is immersed in order to clearly discern the discrepancies between this culture and the Christ whom he wishes to express. Fortunately, the Anabaptists succeeded in doing this to a considerable extent, though in varying degree. They did not always succeed so well in the creative application of Christ to their situation, since they were early deprived of many of their better trained and more capable leaders with the necessary equipment of mind and heart, as well as experience plus courage, to undertake this tremendous task.

The Anabaptist theology of discipleship can be better and more fully understood perhaps by comparing it with two closely related types of conception and practice in the matter of following Christ; the first of these is the type of *Nachfolge Christi* so powerfully and so beautifully set forth by Thomas á Kempis about a century earlier in the book which next to the Bible itself has reputedly had a greater circulation and influence than any other book, *The Imitation of Christ*. For all its effectiveness in urging upon the Christian disciple the imitation of the character of his master by the conquest of the human passions and the vices to which they lead, and the production of the virtues of Christ, this book is concerned primarily with the inner world of the soul, where the believer is to cultivate the garden of his spiritual life with his eye constantly upon his ultimate personal goal, heaven. Selfrenunciation and resignation are among the highest virtues. The reader is taught that only through suffering, by carrying his cross with him every day in imitation of Christ, can he reach the heavenly country. The goal of the disciple is purification of himself so that he can truly love God and Christ, and then also his neighbor. He is advised to avoid society as much as possible, to devote much time to contemplation, to read the "sacred writings" with one's mind freed from temporal cares, and with devotion. Basically this is mysticism mixed with asceticism. The social dimension is almost completely lacking, and criticism of the total social and cultural order with a view to the establishment of a full Christian order in the brotherhood and church of the living Christ in the midst of the present world is missing. This type of "following" Christ does not meet the fullness and richness of the New Testament concept, and is not at all the Anabaptist idea. Thomas á Kempis and all those many who follow in his train evade the conflict with the world, avoid the constructive labor of establishing the true church, and thus escape the real cross-bearing experience of true discipleship. There is more kinship between Thomas and the later Pietists than the Anabaptists.

Another type of discipleship comes still closer to the Anabaptists; it is that of the so-called Spiritualists of the Reformation, including Schwenkfeld and possibly even Hans Denk. These men caught the vision of full discipleship but decided to delay the practice of it until a more convenient season. At least this was the case with Schwenkfeld. He was very close to the Anabaptists but advised his followers to refrain from openly organizing a church, evidently because of the opposition and danger of persecution. Hans Denk at the end of his life regretted that he had baptized and would have merely preached the new faith without implementing it in an organization had he lived. Even Melchior Hofmann, when the going got hot, called for an armistice of two years with no baptizing. All these men shrank from the ultimate price of open discipleship in the crucial moment.

Now it is of the essence of discipleship in the Anabaptist concept that one openly take his stand for his Lord regardless of consequences. There was to be no crypto-discipleship.[2] Did not Jesus Himself say, "If you are ashamed of me, I shall be ashamed of you in that day"? What the Anabaptist accepted as truth that he put into practice in life forthwith. He came to grips directly with the world which is an enemy to God. It is this quality of what we moderns call "existentialism" which was deeply characteristic of the Anabaptist theology of discipleship, the inseparability of belief and practice, faith and life. To profess the new birth meant a new life. To take the name of Christ meant to take His spirit and His nature. To promise obedience to Him meant actually to live out and carry through His principles and do His works. To claim the cleansing and redemption from sin which baptism symbolized, meant to leave off the sins and lusts of the flesh and the spirit and to live a holy life. To take up the cross daily meant to go out into conflict with the world of sin and evil and fight the good fight of faith, taking gladly the blows and buffetings of the world. To be a disciple meant to teach and to observe all things whatsoever the Master had taught and commanded.[3]

Menno Simons described his view of the centrality of discipleship in his best-known work, "Foundation of Christian Doctrine." Notice his affirmation that the Christian must follow Christ or "walk as Christ walked."

> I confess my Saviour openly; I confess Him and dissemble not. If you repent not, and are not born of God, and become not one with Christ in Spirit, faith, life, and worship, then is the sentence of your condemnation on your poor souls already finished and prepared.
> All who teach you otherwise than we have here taught and confessed from the Scriptures deceive you. This is the narrow way through which we all must walk and must enter the strait gate, if we would be saved. Neither emperor nor king, duke nor count, knight nor nobleman, doctor nor licentiate, rich nor poor, man nor woman, is excepted. Whosoever boasts that he is a Christian, the same must walk as Christ walked. If any man have not the Spirit of Christ, he is none of His. Whosoever transgresseth and abideth not in the doctrine of Christ, hath not God. II John 1:9. He that committeth sin is of the devil. I John 3:8. Here neither baptism, Lord's Supper, confession, nor absolution will avail anything. These and other Scriptures stand immovable and judge all those who live outside the Spirit and Word of Christ and who mind earthly and carnal things. They shall never be overthrown, perverted, nor weakened by angel or devil.[4]

A further discussion of Christianity as discipleship is found in Appendix 1, pages 232-234.

Contemporary Writings

In the twentieth century, Dietrich Bonhoeffer has stated concepts similar to those of the Anabaptists in the sixteenth century. In his well-known book, *The Cost of Discipleship,* Bonhoeffer calls for a discipleship type of Christianity. Notice in the following quotation his appeal to obediently follow the commands of Jesus:

> When the Bible speaks of following Jesus, it is proclaiming a discipleship which will liberate mankind from all man-made dogmas, from every

burden and oppression, from every anxiety and torture which afflicts the conscience. If they follow Jesus, men escape from the hard yoke of their own laws, and submit to the kindly yoke of Jesus Christ. But does this mean that we ignore the seriousness of His commands? Far from it. We can only achieve perfect liberty and enjoy fellowship with Jesus when His command, His call to absolute discipleship, is appreciated in its entirety. Only the man who follows the command of Jesus without reserve, and submits unresistingly to His yoke, finds His burden easy, and under its gentle pressure receives the power to persevere in the right way. The command of Jesus is hard, unutterably hard, for those who try to resist it. But for those who willingly submit, the yoke is easy, and the burden is light. "His commandments are not grievous" (I John v. 3). The commandment of Jesus is not a sort of spiritual shock treatment. Jesus asks nothing of us without giving us the strength to perform it. His commandment never seeks to destroy life, but to foster, strengthen and heal it. But one question still troubles us. What can the call to discipleship mean to-day for the worker, the business man, the squire and the soldier? Does it not lead to an intolerable dichotomy between our lives as workers in the world and our lives as Christians? If Christianity means following Christ, is it not a religion for a small minority, a spiritual élite? Does it not mean the repudiation of the great mass of society, and a hearty contempt for the weak and the poor? Yet surely such an attitude is the exact opposite of the gracious mercy of Jesus Christ, who came to the publicans and sinners, the weak and the poor, the erring and the hopeless? Are those who belong to Jesus only a few, or are they many? He died on the cross alone, abandoned by His disciples. With Him were crucified, not two of His followers, but two murderers. But they all stood beneath the cross, enemies and believers, doubters and cowards, revilers and devoted followers. His prayer, "Father, forgive them," was meant for them all, and for all their sins. The mercy and love of God are at work even in the midst of His enemies. It is the same Jesus Christ, who of His grace calls us to follow Him, and whose grace saves the murderer who mocks Him on the cross in His last hour.

And if we answer the call to discipleship, where will it lead us? What decisions and partings will it demand? To answer this question we shall have to go to Him, for only He knows the answer. Only Jesus Christ, who bids us follow Him, knows the journey's end. But we do know that it will be a road of boundless mercy. Discipleship means joy.[5]

With penetrating freshness, Craig R. Dykstra has issued the following call to discipleship in our decade:

But Christians have historically understood the formation of the moral life as formation in discipleship. To be a disciple is to be an adherent of the way of Christ. It is to be a follower of his, and to have one's life formed through the strenuous discipline of going where he went, looking at things the way he did, trusting as he trusted, making ourselves vulnerable as he was vulnerable. If we believe that reality is revealed to us through the eyes of Christ and that our lives are transformed by being with him, then the way to grow morally is to undertake the discipline of becoming disciples.[r]

Journaling Focus

One objective of this study program is to help persons articulate discipleship as understood by the Anabaptists. Another objective is to help persons personalize discipleship themes giving them contemporary application. Each lesson will have a journaling focus designed to help achieve these objectives. You will interact with the material in writing. I recommend a notebook for this purpose. If your group is focusing on discipling skills, the person leading the study may ask you to turn in your notebook periodically so he or she can discover how well the process is going for you.

By journaling I am referring to the process of writing down your thoughts and feelings about a particular issue or something you have read. An enlarged discussion of journaling will appear in Lesson 2.

Day One: Reflect on the biblical teachings mentioned in this lesson. What message do they speak to you?

Day Two: Identify new insights concerning discipleship that you have gained from the Anabaptist and contemporary writings. Of the three types of discipleship described by Harold S. Bender, which type is nearest your present understanding? Explain your answer

Spiritual Exercise: Group Commitment

The Anabaptists adopted a level of discipleship that could be attained and maintained only through a vital corporate Christian life. Discipleship was undergirded by spiritual exercises. Spirituality was necessary for discipleship. Some of the spiritual exercises associated with ascetic theology (stress on moral virtue) in the sixteenth century were prayer, Bible study, worship, fasting, simplicity, poverty, footwashing, communal discipline, and deeds of charity.[7] Some of these were practiced by the Anabaptists.

Each lesson in this handbook will describe some spiritual exercise that you are to practice. The purposes are to nurture your own discipleship and to equip you to help others discover spiritual exercises that could be meaningful to them.

During the coming months as you meet together as a group, it is important that you be committed to one another and to your corporate pilgrimage. You will not attempt to be a congregation in the fullest sense of that reality, but you will "experience church" in numerous significant ways. The scope of your learnings and depth of your growth will be enhanced by the following commitments:

1. To reflect seriously on the readings and exercises in each lesson and to report your responses to one or more other persons.

2. To accept accountability in honestly searching for the meaning of discipleship in your own life and in faithfully following the path of obedience with God's help.

3. To pray daily for your discipling partner (see discipling session) and regularly for each group member that life with Christ and with the people of God will be deepened and strengthened.

Day Three: Describe the level and scope of commitment you are willing to make to the group in your discipleship-discipling venture.

Day Four: Identify group commitments you have made in the past. Evaluate your experience with those commitments.

Day Five: As you contemplate beginning this study, what do you anticipate? What do you fear?

Discipling Session

For the discipling sessions, you will normally meet first in groups of two and then as a total group. At this first meeting, each group member should be paired with a discipling partner. These small groupings of two persons each will function as discipling partners throughout the discipling program. The group leader may want to suggest possible groupings. Each person should have a voice in the groupings so that every person feels comfortable with his or her partner.

1. Share with your discipling partner your response to the exercise for *Day One* and *Day Two*.

2. Share with the total group your response to *Day Four* and *Day Five*

3. As a total group, clarify questions you may have about the group commitment. Then share with the group the commitment you are making to them.

4. Desired Discipling Skill: ability to enter into and maintain group commitment.

Lesson 2

A Disciple of Which Jesus?

Discipleship Theme: Which Jesus Do You Follow?

Biblical Teachings

Historically there was only one Jesus, the eternal Son of God who became incarnate, who both lived and taught the good news, who invited all men and women to follow him, who died, arose, and ascended to the Father, and whose life and message are recorded in the Gospels.

However, people in Jesus' day had various understandings of who Jesus really was and these understandings resulted in varying responses to him and his message, even among his followers. This same pattern of different understandings and varied responses has continued to the present time.

But not only are there various understandings and responses, there appears to be a direct relationship between one's understanding of who Jesus is and one's response to him. In fact, much of the variety within Christendom at the time of the Reformation and continuing to the present time is a reflection of the variety of answers Christians gave and still give to the question, Who is Jesus?

During Jesus' own ministry, he questioned his followers about his identity. Matthew 16:13-16 records questions of Jesus to his disciples about himself. The first question was general, "Who do men say that the Son of man is?" The answer reflected a variety of opinions from a recent national hero to a predicted prophet. The second question was specific, "But who do you say that I am?" Peter's confession, which apparently reflected the thinking of the other disciples, recognized Jesus as the Christ.

However, when Jesus began speaking about his own cross and the cross of his followers (vv. 21-25), it became clear that Peter's view of the Messiah and Jesus' view of himself were different. These views were reflected by the various life expectations for Jesus' followers. Jesus and Peter had two different views of discipleship. For both of them, their view of the Christian life and discipleship was determined by their view of Jesus.

While our view of Jesus will always be limited by our humanity, we do need to continually search for a more complete understanding, to be alert to various understandings, and to be aware of the direct relationship between our view of Jesus and our view of the Christian life.

In Colossians 1:15-23, Paul closely links his view of Christ and his view of the Christian life.

The message of 1 John also illustrates this principle. False prophets denied that Jesus Christ had come in the flesh (1 Jn. 4:1-3). To claim that Jesus was God but not man took away his role as Savior and took away the basis for moral living. John found it necessary to appeal to his readers to stop practicing sin because the humanity of Jesus called for holy living (1 Jn. 3:4-10). In this book one's view of Jesus directly affects one's view of ethics and morality.[1]

Anabaptist Writings

In the article "The Anabaptist Theology of Discipleship," referred to in Lesson 1, Harold S. Bender also reflected on various views of Jesus which were common during the Reformation as well as today, and the implications of these views for one's Christian life. Bender's discussion reads as follows:

> What think ye of Christ? The limits of this paper will not admit of a comprehensive review of all the answers which have been given in Christian history and theology to this question. May I briefly sketch the major types of answers and then proceed to delineate the major features of the Anabaptist theology of discipleship.

First, there are those who think of Christ primarily as a prophe
moral teacher, one who brings intellectual truth out of which to builu a
system of thought, theological or ethical, with answers to the meaning of
life or existence. For such Christ remains primarily an object of thought and
reflection, about whom one intellectualizes. It goes with a certain attitude
toward life in which all too often speculation, whether philosophical or
theological, becomes the technique by which life is mastered. The actual
processes of life are carried on often quite apart from the ideal of truth
which Christ brings, and intellectualization or rationalization is used to close
the gap or to conceal the disparity between the comprehended ideal of
Christ and the disobedient practice of the actual life. This is the peculiar
danger of classic Protestant theology, particularly of Calvinism.

Another answer is to think of Christ primarily as a being to be
worshiped. The most orthodox theology of His person as a member of the
Trinity, is combined with a high liturgy of praise and symbolic representa-
tions in sacrament, in art, and in literature, which call forth the ultimate in
adoration. This type may eventuate in a Christ-mysticism, or in a refined
theological dialectics, or in sensualized liturgy and routine formalism. In
any case Christ remains remote from the actual daily practice of life. This is
the peculiar danger of Catholicism, Greek and Roman.

A third answer to Christ is to think of Him and use Him exclusively as
Saviour. Now in the true ultimate and comprehensive meaning of salvation
this answer would lead us into the heart of the Anabaptist theology of discipleship. Actually it often stops far short of that, for Christ becomes only
the sin-bearer, who by His atoning death on the cross delivers from the guilt
of sin, and by forgiveness and justification reconciles the sinner to God and
brings peace. This marvelous and wholly necessary experience of the forgiving and cleansing grace of God in Christ, both for the past sinful life and for
the inevitable sins of believers, is intended in God's plan of salvation to be
only the initial step in Christian experience as well as the constant carrying
foundation for the daily life, not the whole of the Christian experience nor
even its end goal. But the joy and blessing of this experience with the access
it brings to God and the blessedness of the fellowship with Christ is so great,
that all too often it becomes the essence and the whole of the Christian
experience, beside which other things become relatively unimportant. Justification by faith becomes so great and so wonderful, that sanctification of
life and obedience to Christ, and transformation after His image, are in effect minimized and neglected. The Lordship of Christ is in effect set aside.
This has been the peculiar danger of historic Lutheranism and remains the
besetting temptation of modern Fundamentalism. Dispensationalism even
goes so far as to relegate the Lordship, or let us say, the Kingship of Christ
to a later age beyond the scope and ken of our present Christian practice.

Then there is the final answer to Christ which takes Him as
everything, Prophet, Saviour, *and Lord,* and makes the believer His disciple. This answer basically believes that Christ is to be translated in the life-
expression of the disciple, or in the words of the Apostle Paul, Christ is to be

"formed" in him, and He is to be Lord of all his life. This is the Anabaptist answer to Christ, and out of the understanding of the meaning of this answer derive all the major ideas of Anabaptism. (It has been also in some sense the answer of other movements in the history of the church, including even Methodism and Pietism in its best form.)[2]

(In this quotation as well as later quotations, Bender reflects the polemical atmosphere in which Anabaptism emerged.)

Pilgram Marpeck saw very clearly the importance of Christology and it emerged as one of his central concerns. He emphasized the fact that Christ was both Son of God and Son of Man. However, particular stress was placed on the humanity of Christ and its implications for the Christian life and congregational life. Toward the end of Marpeck's life, he wrote a letter entitled "Concerning the Humanity of Christ." The letter begins with this theme but soon moves to a discussion of two types of obedience and how to tell whether we are being led by the Spirit. Marpeck's view of Christ found immediate expression in the Christian life. The first part of the letter states that Christ, being human, has been made Lord, Ruler, Judge and Director of the saints. His humanity calls for obedient following.

This epistle deals with the humanity of Christ and the Son of Man, etc., also with the Christian life and calling, etc., and the difference between servants and children, etc.

Grace and peace from God, our heavenly Father, and from the Lord Jesus Christ His beloved Son, abide with us and all who love and seek Christ with a pure heart. Amen.

Dearly beloved, loved in God the Father and in Christ. First we thank God for the bestowal of all His graces, which He, through Jesus Christ, and for the sake of Christ, indeed, the Lord Jesus Christ Himself working in us, does and accomplishes, ruling, directing, and leading us through His Holy Spirit in all truth of His divine will and good pleasure; namely, in all who love and seek Christ Jesus with pure heart, in them He accomplishes the good pleasure of our heavenly Father. Therefore no one (indeed no creature, in heaven or on earth) is accounted as anything before the Father, but alone the Son of man, who was born of Him of the virgin of the tribe of Judah, and of the seed of David. This Son of Man (I say "Son of Man") is appointed a Lord and Ruler of all things; yes indeed humanity is taken up into God the Father and God the Father into the Son, who from eternity has been one essence, Spirit, and God. Indeed, He has been the true way, the truth, and the life in true humanity by nature and kind, born of the generation of men in and of Mary, the pure virgin, a true, pure, immutable Man. In Him alone the fullness of the Godhead dwells bodily. From the fullness of the Son of God, all true believers are filled with the Holy Spirit, so that they may not speak anything unless Christ (the Son of God and of man) works, completes, acts, and rules in them Himself (Rom. 15:18). . . .

For the very reason that He is the Son of Man He will be a Judge and not for the reason that He is also the Son of God, one essence with the Father. The Spirit of the Father and the Son are judges apart from and prior to that. The transfer [of power] which took place, took place for the sake of the humanity of Christ, that it might be honored like the Father as essentially true Son of God and of man. He, the Man Jesus Christ (who alone accomplishes in the believers the good pleasure of the Father), He, the Lord, a true Son of Man, is Lord, Ruler, Leader, and Director of His saints.[3]

Contemporary Writings

Dietrich Bonhoeffer also saw the importance of one's view of Christ, and of the relationship between Christ's humanity and our discipleship. In Bonhoeffer's chapter on "The Call to Discipleship," he states the following:

Discipleship means adherence to Christ, and, because Christ is the object of that adherence, it must take the form of discipleship. An abstract Christology, a doctrinal system, a general religious knowledge on the subject of grace or on the forgiveness of sins, render discipleship superfluous, and in fact they positively exclude any idea of discipleship whatever, and are essentially inimical to the whole conception of following Christ. With an abstract idea it is possible to enter into a relation of formal knowledge, to become enthusiastic about it, and perhaps even to put it into practice; but it can never be followed in personal obedience. Christianity without the living Christ is inevitably Christianity without discipleship, and Christianity without discipleship is always Christianity without Christ. It remains an abstract idea, a myth which has a place for the Fatherhood of God, but omits Christ as the living Son. And a Christianity of that kind is nothing more nor less than the end of discipleship. In such a religion there is trust in God, but no following of Christ. Because the Son of God became Man, because He is the Mediator, for that reason alone the only true relation we can have with Him is to follow Him. Discipleship is bound to Christ as the Mediator, and where it is properly understood, it necessarily implies faith in the Son of God as the Mediator. Only the Mediator, the God-Man, can call men to follow Him.

Discipleship without Jesus Christ is a way of our own choosing. It may be the ideal way, it may even lead to martyrdom, but it is devoid of all promise. Jesus will certainly reject it.[4]

All of these writers, both Anabaptist and contemporary, suggest that seeing Jesus as both divine and human calls for a response of worship and discipleship. An additional discussion of this theme is found in Appendix 1, pages 234-235

Journaling Focus

Day One: Reflect on the passages in Matthew 16, Colossians 1 and 1 John 4. What changes do these passages cause in your view of Jesus and of the Christian life?

Day Two: Which view of Christ, as described by Harold Bender, is nearest to your understanding? What new insights have you gained from the Anabaptist and contemporary writings?

Spiritual Exercise: Journaling

In Lesson 1 there was a brief explanation of journaling as it related to the daily exercises. Writing your reflections and beliefs helps to clarify your thoughts and personalize the truths.

Many Christians practice journaling for their own enrichment, apart from a study such as you are now following. For them journaling has a different purpose.

Each lesson will have four journaling exercises related to the lesson material. In addition there will be one journaling exercise each week when you will be asked to journal about what is going on in your life at the moment. This journaling does not need to be related to the theme of the lesson, although it can be. This journaling is for your own benefit and does not need to be shared with any other person unless you choose to. The following suggestions are intended to help you in all of your journaling.

Journaling is done for a number of reasons. For some the purpose is selfactualization. Their journal becomes an instrument for expressing their creative urges and emerging life goals. For others the purpose is self-discovery. They record dreams, emotions, or insights. Their journal becomes a mirror of themselves.

Still others use a journal to help them better understand their relationship to God. They record highlights of their walk with God and express their praise and aspirations through written prayers. You may wish to reflect on your walk in discipleship. (For an enlarged discussion of journaling see *Adventure Inward* by Morton T. Kelsey.[5])

Here are some general suggestions for journaling.

1. Use a loose-leaf notebook so that you can remove or rearrange the pages

2. Date each entry with day, month, and year. This helps orient you to the present moment and makes your entries more useful at some future date when you reflect back over your past pilgrimage. Remember, your entries are for *your* benefit, not for others to read unless you choose to share something you have written.

3. Write whatever is on your mind, especially regarding your walk in discipleship, such as:
   •past steps of faithfulness to Christ that you have discontinued;
   •present steps of faithfulness to Christ that are especially difficult;
   •new steps of faithfulness to Christ that are emerging;
   •special moments when you experience the presence of Christ;
   •special moments when you uniquely experience the body of Christ;
   •a prayer of praise, confession, petition, or commitment.

4. Write in your journal as frequently as you choose. Some persons prefer a daily entry; others prefer entries several times a week. Many include journaling as a part of their devotional time of Bible reading, meditation, reflection, and prayer.

5. Values of journaling include:
   •clarification of impressions, urges, or feelings;
   •comparison of present life issues with those of the past;
   •a mirror of one's spiritual health and direction.

Day Three: Practice what you have just read by journaling

what is happening in your life today. This will help you become aware of your own feelings and concerns.

Day Four: In this lesson you are reflecting on the relationship between one's view of Christ and the way one lives. Identify and describe a recent example in your own life where you experienced this principle at work.

Day Five: Read the section below called Discipling Session. Notice the progression of the lessons from personal aspects of discipleship to corporate expressions to applications in society. Journal your feelings about this type of pilgrimage.

Discipling Session

Jesus began his ministry by calling disciples. A major part of his ministry focused on training those disciples. At the conclusion of his ministry, he commanded his disciples to go forth and make more disciples (Mt. 28:18-20). It is significant to notice that Christ did not give them the Great Commission until they had already been discipled. They learned the meaning of discipleship and the method of discipling by being discipled.

During the coming weeks and months, you'll learn the content of discipleship as a part of your preparation for discipling. Each of the twenty-three lessons contains a discipleship theme. The first eight lessons focus on personal aspects of discipleship, the second eight deal with corporate expressions of discipleship, and the last seven touch on applications of discipleship in society.

As you study and reflect on the first eight lessons, you will want to keep in mind that the Christian life for the Anabaptists was not individualistic, but it was very personal. Sharing their new life with others was very important but they first needed a new life to share. For them discipleship began with repentance of personal sins, conversion through the work of the Holy Spirit, and a commitment to walk in obedience to the teachings and examples of Jesus and the apostles.

As you study about the Christian life, reflect on your own

life, and learn about the life experiences of others, you will be developing a discipling skill. You will be learning about the type of Christian life you will encourage others to experience, if they are serious about discipleship.

1. Share with your discipling partner important insights that emerged from the journaling on *Day One* and *Day Four.*

2. Discuss as a group the journaling on *Day Two* and *Day Five.* What view of Christ do you hold? How does this view influence your attitude toward discipleship?

3. Desired Discipling Skill: awareness of relationship between the view of Jesus and the view of Christian life. Listen carefully and reflectively as each member shares in the group meeting.

Lesson 3

Follow Me

Discipleship Theme: The Disciple, A Follower

Biblical Teachings

There are several New Testament words associated with discipleship which apply to those who follow Jesus in a life of faith. *Akoloutheō* (follow) speaks of answering the call of Jesus to a new life of obedience. This term is used in Mark 1:18 to describe the response of those called by Jesus. They "followed him." A person who hears the call of Jesus and joins him is a *mathētēs* (disciple). The behavior of modeling Jesus is *mimeomai* (imitate). In this lesson, we will examine more closely what it means to follow Jesus and will touch on the concept of the imitation of Christ.

In his discussion of *akoloutheō*, in *The New International Dictionary of New Testament Theology* (Vol. 1), Christian Blendinger provides helpful insight into the New Testament meaning of following Jesus. I will summarize those insights that relate most directly to this study.

In post-exilic Judaism the term was used to describe the relationship of a pupil to a teacher of the Torah. The pupil followed the rabbi everywhere he went, learning from him and serving him. The goal was complete knowledge of the Torah and the ability to practice it in all situations.

In the New Testament, *akoloutheō* appears primarily in the Gospels (60 times). It appears only 10 times in the rest of the New Testament. Blendinger notes that it "is always the call to decisive and intimate discipleship of the earthly Jesus. It always points to the beginning of discipleship."[1]

In his theological analysis, Blendinger points out two important observations. The term is almost always used to refer to the teacher-pupil relationship of the rabbis as was noted earlier. However, there are also important differences between the disciples of Jesus and those of the rabbis.

First, Jesus called disciples as God had called the prophets. He did not wait for voluntary followers which was the practice of the rabbis.

Second, Jesus did not call his followers to "master traditional modes of conduct." Rather, he pointed them toward the kingdom of God (Lk. 9:59f.) and to service in the kingdom which was at hand (Mk. 1:15). They shared in Jesus' authority and were sent out with the same message.

Third, the person who took up the new "calling" generally gave up the old one. (The so-called rich young ruler failed at this point.) However, the disciples needed to stay open to new calls of obedience (Mt. 8:21f.).

Fourth, the disciple needed to accept the same future as his master. The expectation of suffering became a part of discipleship (Mt. 10:38). "But readiness to suffer is only made possible through the 'self-denial' which consists in freedom from oneself and all forms of personal security. Such self-denial is possible only when man gives himself to God in unconditional discipleship."[2]

In the Gospel of John there is a transition from the synoptic Gospels to the Epistles. John sees following Jesus as believing acceptance of the new revelation of God in Jesus Christ. "To follow the call of the Shepherd (10:4, 27) means both safety in Christ and fellowship in suffering with him (12:26) which in turn means 'exaltation' with him (12:32)."[3] The call to discipleship has within it both invitation and promise.

In concluding this discussion, the insight of Jack Kingsbury offers additional understanding. Kingsbury points out that Matthew uses the verb *akolouthein* ("to follow") in both a literal and metaphorical manner. The literal sense refers to going after a person while the metaphorical sense refers to going after a person as his disciple. When Matthew uses the term in a metaphorical manner, it carries with it the factors of "personal commitment" and "cost." There is the summons to follow and the note of personal sacrifice.[4]

A related concept to following Jesus is the concept of imitation of Christ or to imitate (*mimeomai*) Christ. The concept is found only in the Epistles. Wolfgang Bauder has a helpful discussion of this concept in *The New International Dictionary of New Testament Theology* (Vol. 1). He points out that when Paul uses the term in (1 Cor. 4:16; 11:1; Phil. 3:17; 2 Thess. 3:7, 9), he is not calling for an imitation of himself. Rather he is calling his hearers to lay hold on Christ and to let their lives (ethical conduct) be continually remolded by Christ. The ultimate call is for believers to imitate Christ's obedience to the Father. Bauder has the following summary to his discussion:

> 'Imitation' in the NT is consequently not conceived as the reproduction of a given pattern. It is the way of life of the man who derives his being from the forgiveness of God. . . . The summons to discipleship can only be fulfilled, when a man is grasped by Christ and undergoes the transformation which existence under the Lordship of Christ involves.[5]

Anabaptist Writings

In light of the insights provided by Blendinger and Kingsbury on following Jesus, it is easy to understand why 1 Peter 2:21 was a Scripture frequently quoted by the Anabaptists. It brings together the themes of following and suffering.

One example is an excerpt from "A Letter to the Church at Rattenberg," written by Leonhard Schiemer in 1527. It reads as follows:

> As soon as a man wants to begin to live as a Christian he will experience exactly those things that Christ experienced. : . . That is the lot of all Christians for the disciple is no greater than the master. For it is grace if someone for the sake of conscience suffers godly sorrow. . . . For it is grace with God when you patiently suffer for doing good. For to this you were called, since Christ also suffered for us and left us an example that you

should follow in his footsteps. He committed no sins neither was deceit found in his mouth. Christ suffered in the flesh. Arm yourselves with the thought that whoever suffers in the flesh ceases from sin.... It is given to you that you not only believe in Christ but also suffer for him and fight the same battle. Paul says that you are heirs of God and joint heirs with Christ if you suffer with him in order that you may be exalted with him in glory. For we must be conformed to the image of his Son.... It is true, Christ's suffering destroys sin but only if he suffers in man. For as the water does not quench my thirst unless I drink it, and as the bread does not drive away my hunger unless I eat it, even so Christ's suffering does not prevent me from sinning until he suffers in me.[6]

(A similar emphasis can be seen in Menno Simons' "Hymn of Discipleship" found in Appendix 3.)

The insights of Bauder are in harmony with Anabaptist spirituality at its best. They viewed following Christ or imitating Christ in a holistic and dynamic sense. These concepts were used by others at the time of the Reformation (see Appendix 1, pages 251-253), but the Anabaptists created their own unique meaning.

The Desert Fathers[7] had focused on imitating Christ in his death or the concept of spiritual martyrdom. This concept lay behind their desire to mortify the senses and be detached from family ties. The Brethren of the Common Life experienced the imitation of Christ through individual mysticism. The Anabaptists used the term to express their desire to outwardly follow Christ in their total lives.

Contemporary Writings

Dietrich Bonhoeffer wrote the following reflection on the call of Jesus to Levi (Mk. 2:14). It speaks a similar message.

And what does the text inform us about the content of discipleship? Follow me, run along behind me! That is all. To follow in His steps is something which is void of all content. It gives us no intelligible programme for a way of life, no goal or ideal to strive after. It is not a cause which human calculation might deem worthy of our devotion, even the devotion of ourselves. What happens? At the call, Levi leaves all that he has—but not because he thinks that he might be doing something worth while, but simply for the sake of the call. Otherwise he cannot follow in the steps of Jesus. This act on Levi's part has not the slightest value in itself, it is quite devoid of significance and unworthy of consideration. The disciple simply burns his boats and goes ahead. He is called out, and has to forsake his old life in order that he may "exist" in the strictest sense of the word. The old life is left behind, and completely surrendered. The disciple is dragged out of his relative security into a life of absolute insecurity, from a life which is observable and calculable into a life where everything is unobservable and fortuitous, out of the realm of finite, and into the real of infinite possibilities. Once again, the new life is not a law, not a set of principles, a programme, or an ideal. Discipleship means Jesus Christ, and Him alone. It cannot consist of anything more than that.

When we are called to follow Christ, we are summoned to an exclusive attachment to His person. The grace of His call bursts all the bonds of legalism. It is a gracious call, a gracious commandment. It transcends the difference between the law and the gospel. Christ calls, the disciple follows: that is grace and commandment in one. "I will walk at liberty, for I seek thy commandments" (Ps. cxix. 45).[8]

Journaling Focus

Day One: As you reflect on the Anabaptist and contemporary readings, what new insights have you received?

Day Two: Of the two terms, following Jesus and imitating Christ, which best describes your approach to discipleship. Explain your answer. Also, identify new understandings found in the biblical teachings.

Spiritual Exercise: Spiritual Autobiography

The spiritual exercises are designed for spiritual enrichment. It is enriching to gain a clearer awareness of one's own spiritual life. It is also enriching to become aware of the spiritual lives of other persons. However, the spiritual exercises are also designed to assist the discipling process.

A spiritual exercise that relates to all of these areas is writing and sharing your spiritual autobiography. Morton T. Kelsey provides some helpful insights on autobiographical reflections.

It is nearly impossible to see the way ahead unless one has stopped and reflected on the way one has come. Many professional schools require applicants to write a short autobiography as part of their entrance requirements.

They want to see the desire for professional training in the context of the whole of a person's life. It is strange how seldom we stop and look over the general pattern of our journey. Like so many aspects of our depths, the more time we spend reflecting on our past days and hours the more we are likely to remember. One's picture of the past is never completed until one dies (and perhaps not even then), for new experiences and new insights open up the locked doors of memory and give new understandings of the thread of meaning in one's life. One's autobiography is never completed. Only God knows the full meaning of my life, and only as I bring my life before the divine lover and listen will I find its ultimate significance.

There are many ways to begin an autobiography. I can simply set aside some time and try to write four to ten pages about my life and its meaning. Or I can start on one aspect of my life, my religious experience, my professional life, my hobbies, my family life, my relation to my body and sports, my sexuality.... The list is endless. In his book *At a Journal Workshop* Ira Progoff suggests starting with the *now*. One takes a look at the period (or general situation) in which one finds oneself. How do I feel about my life and work, about my achievements, my hopes? What are my fears and ambitions, my joys and satisfactions? The best beginning for an autobiography is knowing where I am and what I am looking for. I have found that one of the best ways to get people to start in the now is to ask them to take an hour and write the ten deepest hungers of their hearts, and then to write the ten most disturbing doubts about their faith and meaning. This opens many people to greater inner searching.[9]

Please write an autobiography of your spiritual life by identifying the times when God seemed to break through and touch your life. This would include times when God seemed especially near, times when you heard the call "follow me." Your autobiography should be written so that it can be read by your group leader.

Day Three: Begin an autobiography of your spiritual life by listing the times when God seemed especially near, times when you heard the call "follow me." Reflect on those "times" and their significance for you.

Day Four: Write your spiritual autobiography in essay form so that it is clear to you and can be read by your group leader. Remember, this is a spiritual autobiography, not a complete story of your life.

Day Five: Today you are to do general journaling focusing on the present important issues in your life.

Discipling Session

Discipling relates in a very direct way to one's spiritual life. A discipler should understand and be able to discern the way God works with his people. God does work uniquely with each person. We have our own story, and our story is unfinished. A discipler should help persons become aware of the past movements of God in their lives and the directions of the present. Seeing the footsteps of God in the past helps persons discover them in the present and also helps them sense a direction for the future. This is a part of the discipling process.

1. Share with your discipling partner your responses to the journaling exercises from *Day One* and *Day Two*.

2. Have one or two persons share their spiritual auto-biography. Listen especially for the "God moments" in their lives, any message God may have spoken, and any pattern of movement or direction. This will be important when you reflect on their vocational direction in connection with some future lessons.

There are several approaches to sharing the spiritual autobiographies. They may be shared during the regular weekly discipling sessions. Four lessons, 3-6, designate time for this sharing so if there are eight persons in the group, two persons should share at each meeting. If there are more than eight persons in the group, some sessions could be devoted totally to sharing autobiographies thus lengthening the total study. Or the group may want to spend an extended period of time together so that all of the autobiographies can be heard in one setting. A weekend retreat could be an excellent experience for the group.

3. Desired Discipling Skill: ability to discern God's movement in persons' lives.

Lesson 4

Learn of Me

Discipleship Theme: The Disciple, A Learner

In Lesson 3, we noticed that a person who responded to the call of Jesus and joined him was called a *mathētēs* (disciple or learner). The verb *manthanō* means to learn, so a disciple can be called a learner as well as a follower. In this lesson, we will examine further the meaning of discipleship as learning of Christ.

Biblical Teachings

In *The New International Dictionary of New Testament Theology* (Vol. 1), Dietrich Müller provides a helpful discussion of the term *mathētēs*. The following insights relate to this study.

In the Old Testament, the equivalent term in the Hebrew was *lāmad*. This meant to reflect on past experiences of God's love and to learn from them obedience to God's law (Deut. 4:14). It meant to learn from God's special acts for Israel in the past and to then accept God's will for the present (Deut. 30:14). Israel was to learn and obey the will of God.

The term *mathētēs* (disciple or learner) is found 264 times in the Gospels and Acts and is the most frequently used term to identify followers of Jesus. The term indicated a close and total attachment of a disciple to the master. The purpose of the relationship was to learn the will of God in Jesus (Mt. 9:13; 11:29), not the Law, which motivated a relationship between a disciple and a rabbi. The disciple's context for learning was his relationship with the master. The content of learning was the master's will.

This understanding of a disciple's approach to learning may sound familiar but actually it was radically new. Müller identifies a number of unique characteristics of discipleship that grow out of the new type of relationship between Jesus and his disciples. These help us better understand discipleship and discipling.

First, even though Jesus presented himself as a rabbi, was called a rabbi (Mk. 9:5), taught like a rabbi (Mk. 12:18), and gathered a circle of disciples around him, the disciple-master relationship was new and different from the traditional pattern as we noticed earlier in the lesson.

Second, the disciples of Jesus entered a relationship involving their total lives (Mt. 10:37) and for the remainder of their lives (Jn. 11:16). They did not enter a learning relationship from which they could eventually become a master.

Third, Jesus broke through social and religious barriers that had been established by the rabbis. He called persons outside of the worshiping community to become his disciples such as a tax-collector, a zealot or zealots, and sinners. This action reveals the true nature of discipleship.

Fourth, Jesus combined the call to discipleship with the call to service. They were to become fishers of men (Mk. 1:17). They were to learn and to serve and to learn by serving.

Fifth, the service would expose the disciples to the same dangers as those faced by their master (Mk. 10:32). Service could lead to persecution.

Sixth, the reward of discipleship was fellowship with God, a share in the authority of Jesus, and a new and future life (Mt. 16:25; Jn. 14:6), not personal merit.

A unique and absolute requirement for discipleship was faith in Jesus (Lk. 12:8; Jn. 2:11; 6:69). A living faith relationship was necessary before true learning could take place.

The Gospel of John indicates the transition from disciples of the earthly Jesus to disciples of the exalted Jesus. John uses *mathētēs* as the term for "Christians" (8:31; 13:35; 15:8). *Mathētal* stands for the gathered community of those who follow

Jesus and continue to learn from him through his Spirit.
Müller concludes his discussion in the following way:

> The disciples are now no longer bound to the presence of the earthly Jesus.
> Instead, their dwelling 'in the Word' (8:31) and 'in the Spirit' (14:15-17;
> 15:26f.) means that they, his disciples, remain in full fellowship with him.
> This fellowship finds its visible expression in the world in the manner of
> their service. Everyone is to be able to recognize a disciple of Jesus by his
> practical love (Jn. 13:34f.).... The essence of discipleship lies in the disciple's fulfillment of his duty to be a witness to his Lord in his entire
> life....[1]

Anabaptist Writings

For the Anabaptists a disciple of Christ was both a follower
and a learner. However, they believed that there was a definite tie
between following and learning. A true knowledge of Christ, they
maintained, was only possible for those who followed. Learning of
Christ required putting his teachings and examples into practice.
The revelation of divine truth did not come through a collection
of theological ideas but primarily in the life and words of Christ
and the apostles. Since truth came through life, truth could only
be understood in life. These words of Hans Denck express
precisely this concept.

> But the medium is Christ whom no one can truly know unless he
> follow him in his life, and no one may follow him unless he has first known
> him. Whoever does not know him does not have him and without him he
> cannot come to the Father. But whoever knows him and does not witness to
> him by his life will be judged by him.... Woe to him who looks elsewhere
> than to this goal. For whoever thinks he belongs to Christ must walk the
> way that Christ walked.[2]

What lay behind the concern to keep knowing and following
Christ together? Many understood Luther to say that salvation
only involved having "faith in the merits of Christ, that this was
the only response God required of man, and that it was the only
one God accepted. This view appeared to the Anabaptists to be an
intellectual matter, for they could see in it no visible expression."[3]
The Anabaptists believed that true faith was clearly expressed in

attitudes and deeds which were Christlike. They did not reject salvation through faith, but rather they rejected an abstract interpretation of faith. Faith needed to result in more than a change of status with God. The following quote from Walter Klaassen provides a fitting conclusion to this discussion.

> The core of the matter, as has already been pointed out, was the fusion of theology and ethics. Truth was found in living, not in abstract reasoning. An example of their concern for the relationship between theology and life can be seen by comparing their view of the Lord's Supper with the two Protestant views. Luther took Jesus' word "This is my body" literally as meaning actually the body of Jesus. Then he resorted to the concept of the ubiquity of the body of Christ, (that is, that the body of Christ is everywhere), a totally abstract notion, to justify his literalism. Therefore when the individual eats the bread he receives the body of Christ and so is comforted and strengthened. Calvinism took a symbolic view of the statement of Jesus insisting that the "is" means "signifies". The Supper was a memorial act, remembering the death of Christ for man. In Anabaptism the memorial aspect was not absent but the centre of gravity was shifted from the individualist approach to the corporate. The Supper signified the oneness and unity of the church, and participation in it was a pledge of peace with one's neighbor and a commitment to each other. It was thus very intimately related to the life of the community. Hence also the insistence that the Supper should not be used without Christ's rule of binding and loosing.[4]

Contemporary Writings

Various Christian leaders today recognize the close relationship between following Christ and knowing Christ. They recognize that many "Christians" fail to truly know Christ because they fail to follow him. They differ in their specific call to the twentieth-century church but they have a similar concern and a similar goal. Elton Trueblood sees response to Christ's call as the key to knowing Christ or having "the mind of Christ."

> The profundity of Christ's recorded thought has led to the use of the expression "the mind of Christ." Certainly we do not know all that was, or is, in His mind, and there is no reason to suppose that the recorded utterances of the four Gospels give more than a mere fraction of what He said; but we know something. The crucial passage is stated in characteristic paradox when Paul quotes Isaiah 40:13, "For who has known the mind of the Lord so as to instruct him?" and then adds "But we have the mind of Christ" (I Cor. 2:16).

The Christian who uses the phrase "the mind of Christ" is not using language in the same way as if he were to speak of the mind of Plato or Marx. We know something of the minds of these men because we can read what they wrote, but we mean something different in reference to Christ. We mean that Christ can be in *us*, that His very mentality comes to dominate ours. "Do you not realize," asks Paul, "that Jesus Christ is in you?" (II Cor. 13:5). Shocking as it sounds, it is really possible for a finite man, as he responds to Christ's call to have a measure of the spirit of Christ. The central purpose of the gospel is that Christ may be formed in *us* (Gal. 4:19) and that He may dwell in our hearts (Eph. 3:17).[5]

Jim Wallis of the Sojourners community is challenging the Christian church to rediscover Jesus through ministries of compassionate service and life in Christian community. He believes these steps represent the call of Christ for our day.

In his recent book, *The Call to Conversion,* he describes what conversion meant to early Christians and what it should mean for us today. Concerning the early believers, he wrote:

First it is highly significant that they were called the people of *the Way.* Christians at the beginning were associated with a particular pattern of life. Their faith produced a discernible lifestyle, a way of life, a process of growth visible to all. This different style of living and relating both grew out of their faith and gave testimony to that faith. To all who saw, Christian belief became identified with a certain kind of behavior. Unlike our modern experience, there was an unmistakable Christian lifestyle recognized by believers and nonbelievers alike. That style of life followed the main lines of Jesus' Sermon on the Mount and his other teaching. To believe meant to follow Jesus. There was little doubt in anyone's mind: Christian discipleship revolved around the hub of the kingdom. The faith of these first Christians had clear social results. They became well known as a caring, sharing, and open community that was especially sensitive to the poor and the outcast. Their love for God, for one another, and for the oppressed was central to their reputation. Their refusal to kill, to recognize racial distinctions, or to bow down before the imperial deities was a matter of public knowledge.[6]

Reflecting on the present needs in our society, Wallis states:

The Christian answer to human hurt is not fixed doctrine; we do not solve problems with speculative theology; the Christian response to oppression is not moral philosophy. Our God does not render a detached pronouncement on our situation. Rather, God comes to join us, to enter into our circumstances, to feel what we feel, and to walk with us. The name Emmanuel means "God with us." Jesus gave up his divine prerogatives, becoming one of us in order to show us the way. The Philippians passage is known as the *kenosis*, the self-emptying of Jesus. God became a servant among men and women. The love that established the pattern of servanthood in Jesus Christ would forever be the heartbeat of Christian faith.[7]

Trueblood and Wallis speak a message similar to the Anabaptists. Knowing Christ in the New Testament sense requires much more than orthodox belief or a change of status with God (justification by faith). We know Christ through becoming a learner and we become a learner as we follow his call to faith and life.

Journaling Focus

Day One: Read the Scriptures referred to in the biblical teachings and identify new understandings of discipleship and discipling.

Day Two: Reflecting on the insight of Hans Denck, what have you learned about Christ through the experience of following him?

Spiritual Exercise: Spiritual Autobiography

As you continue reflecting on your own encounters with God, you may begin to see your spiritual autobiography as your own "personal salvation history." The history of the people of God is the history of special encounters between God and his people. You and I are members of this body of persons and our personal histories can be thought of as miniature "salvation histories." Paul Roy, S.J., raises a number of intriguing questions persons can ask themselves as they reflect on their past and present walk with God.

> How has God entered into their lives, acted in them, been present to them worked through them? What events in their lives might be called "God mo ments"? What people, places, things in their lives have spoken to them c

God? What is the good news of their lives? How is the Contemporary Testament being written in them?

The tendency, when such questions are asked, is to begin looking for what might be called "peak experiences" of one's life. (Have I ever been knocked off my horse, like St. Paul? Have I had a conversion experience analogous to St. Peter's? Has my Lord ever spoken to me through a burning bush?)

This is not the point of the Faith Experience. It is perhaps not even the way God generally reveals himself to his people. Rather, we look back at, reflect upon, remember the day-to-day experiences, the glimpses of God's presence in our lives. We seek in the small, the ordinary, the terribly human, a spark of hope which brings meaning to life, which allows the divine to manifest itself in and through the human.[8]

Day Three: On *Day Two* you journaled some of the things you have learned about Christ as you have followed him. The reading from Paul Roy suggests that God generally reveals himself to his people in the ordinary things of life. What have you learned about Christ through the small things of life in the past weeks? This will be your general journaling for this week.

Day Four: Examine the quotations from the contemporary writers. Identify the basic ideas with which you agree and those with which you disagree. Give reasons for your stance.

Day Five: Read the discussion related to Discipling Session. Reflect on the personal dialogue God has initiated with you. What have you learned through this dialogue? You may want to add this reflection to your spiritual autobiography.

Discipling Session

Sharing our spiritual autobiographies can be encouraging to some persons and discouraging to others, depending on the "size" of their God encounters. It is helpful to all persons in your group to remember that God is concerned about all persons and he speaks to them in differing ways.

In the Roman Catholic tradition, spiritual directors help persons understand the call of God in their lives and on their lives. They approach their task assuming God is speaking in his own way to each person. Damien Isabell, O.F.M., describes their assumption in the following way:

> God has initiated a personal dialogue with each individual and each will be as unique as that person is unique. The spiritual director is at the service of the individual's dialogue with God; the director does not determine what that dialogue will be, but he is able to be like the friend of the bridegroom who rejoices in his friend's possession. On the other hand, the director's expertise in theology and his own faith life will steer the directee away from those paths where God cannot be found, in sin, in romanticism, in destroying human nature, and will keep him rooted in the reality of love.[9]

As you become aware of God's dialogue with you and as you learn how to identify that dialogue in the lives of others, you are developing an important discipling skill.

1. Share with your discipling partner your responses to the journaling exercises on *Day One, Day Two,* and *Day Four.* You may choose to raise with the larger group questions you could not answer.

2. Have one or two persons share their spiritual autobiographies. Listen for evidence of God's personal dialogue and for its uniqueness. Keep in mind the value of their "personal salvation history" for later discussions of their vocational direction.

3. Desired Discipling Skills: ability to identify God's dialogue with persons. Listen especially for this dialogue as autobiographies are shared.

Lesson 5

Walking in the Resurrection

Discipleship Theme: Repentance and Regeneration

The terms "repentance" and "regeneration" are biblical words and concepts which reflect twin, foundational aspects of the Christian life. Repentance describes the response of persons to God's call through the good news of the gospel. Regeneration describes God's activity in the lives of those who repent making them new persons in Christ.

Biblical Teachings

Jesus began his ministry, according to Mark's Gospel, with a call to repent. "The time is fulfilled, and the kingdom of God is at hand; repent, and believe in the gospel" (Mk. 1:15).

But what is the meaning of repentance? John C. Wenger has identified three key aspects of repentance as being intellectual, emotional, and volitional.[1] The intellectual aspect of repentance is a personal awareness of one's sinfulness, a personal "knowledge of sin" (Rom. 3:20). It is seeing yourself in the light of God's holy law and being convicted of your sinful condition.

The emotional aspect of repentance is godly sorrow or godly grief which comes as the Holy Spirit causes us to ponder our sinful condition. The apostle Paul wrote to the church at Corinth, "I rejoice, not because you are grieved, but because you were grieved into repenting; for you felt a godly grief, so that you suffered no loss through us. For godly grief produces a repentance that leads to salvation and brings no regret, but worldly grief produces death" (2 Cor. 7:9-10).

The emotional aspect of repentance motivates the volitional dimension, namely, turning to Christ and his salvation. Repentance is only complete when there is an inward turning to Christ in faith. This was the call of Peter on the day of Pentecost (Acts 2).

These aspects of repentance are illustrated in Acts 2:36-42. The audience faced their sin of crucifying Jesus (v. 36, intellectual); they experienced deep sorrow or grief (v. 37, emotional); and they were pointed to the forgiveness offered by Jesus Christ (v. 38). Their response (volitional) made possible God's activity of regeneration. Their lives were radically changed and they became followers of Jesus (v. 42). They then walked in the resurrection (note Acts 4:2, 10, 30, 33). (The sequence in repentance may vary but the three aspects are usually present.)

Regeneration or the new birth "is the gracious act of God in which He implants spiritual life in the Christian convert and makes his governing disposition holy."[2] The Scriptures describe this experience with many different phrases. They refer to it as a "new birth" (Jn. 3:3), circumcision "of the heart" (Rom. 2:29), putting on "the new nature" (Eph. 4:24; Col. 3:10), "having the eyes of your hearts enlightened" (Eph. 1:18), "the washing of regeneration" (Titus 3:5), becoming "a new creation" (2 Cor. 5:17; Gal. 6:15), being raised with Christ (Col. 2:12; 3:1), being enabled to "walk in newness of life" (Rom. 6:4), and so on.

John C. Wenger summarizes the change regeneration brings in a person's life.

> The regenerated person has a new awareness of his own need of divine grace, he is now fitted with love for God, he now has Christian love for his fellow believers on Christ, he now lives for the glory of God rather than for selfish pleasure and for self-interest, he is now united with Christ in a union of love, devotion, and obedience; in short, he is God's new creation.[3]

Anabaptist Writings

In his excellent article "Walking in the Resurrection,"

Harold S. Bender points out that the notion of living a new life or a resurrection life was central to the Anabaptist view of the Christian life. He suggests that the often-quoted Scripture, "to walk in newness of life" (Rom. 6:4), might represent the Anabaptist motto. The fact that they lived on this side of the cross and resurrection was extremely significant to them. Bender states that their "theology and ethics were resurrection theology and ethics. The new life wrought by God's regenerated grace was essential to them; men must die with Christ to sin and be risen with Him to new life."[4] The concept of walking in newness of life was referred to by most of the Anabaptist writers, and the first article of *The Schleitheim Confession,* adopted in 1527, states that baptism shall be given to those who repent and "desire to walk in the resurrection of Jesus Christ." (See Appendix 1, page 237.)

The importance of resurrection living at the time of the Reformation was stated by Anabaptist leader Hans Hotz, who spoke in the colloquy at Berne with leaders of the Reformed Church in 1538.

> As said before, we do not deny that you of the preachers made a beginning and were the origin. But by God's providence it happened that the books were put into German. To the extent that you contributed to it, God thank you, although much was pointed out to us by the books of Luther, Zwingli, and others, so that we soon understood regarding the mass and other papist ceremonies that they are of no benefit. Nevertheless, I saw great lack in that they do not lead to Christian living, repentance, or conduct, on which I for my part set my mind and directed my thought and spirit toward a Christian life. So I put it off a year or two and waited, while there was preaching everywhere. The priest said much about reform, sharing, loving one another, desisting from evil, and forming community. I always felt that there was a lack in that we did not follow or establish what we were taught and the Word of God can accomplish. There was no initiation of godly conduct, for not all were so minded. And although the mass and images were abolished, there was still no penitence or mercy, and everything remained in evil living, gluttony, drunkenness, envy, hatred, etc., that should not have been in all the people. Because of this I found a reason for inquiring further in this matter. Then God sent his messengers, Conrad Grebel and others, with whom I conferred on the basis of the apostles as to how one should live and also with whom. I started and established a church as those who had yielded themselves in true repentance according to the teaching of Christ concerning hearts, who by abstaining

from wrongdoing, prove that they are in Christ, buried in baptism, and risen in newness of life.[5]

The first booklet written by Menno Simons (1536) after his break with the Roman Catholic Church was entitled "The Spiritual Resurrection." This he defined as "a spiritual resurrection from sin and death to a new life and a change of heart."[6]

In the years that followed, Menno continued to describe the lives of those who had been regenerated. In "The New Birth" written in 1537 he wrote as follows:

> The regenerate, therefore, lead a penitent and new life, for they are renewed in Christ and have received a new heart and spirit. Once they were earthly-minded, now heavenly; once they were carnal, now spiritual; once they were unrighteous, now righteous; once they were evil, now good, and they live no longer after the old corrupted nature of the first earthly Adam, but after the new upright nature of the new and heavenly Adam, Christ Jesus, even as Paul says: Nevertheless, I live; yet not I, but Christ liveth in me. Their poor, weak life they daily renew more and more, and that after the image of Him who created them. Their minds are like the mind of Christ, they gladly walk as He walked; they crucify and tame their flesh with all its evil lusts.
>
> In baptism they bury their sins in the Lord's death and rise with Him to a new life. They circumcise their hearts with the Word of the Lord; they are baptized with the Holy Ghost into the spotless, holy body of Christ, as obedient members of His church, according to the true ordinance and Word of the Lord. They put on Christ and manifest His spirit, nature, and power in all their conduct. They fear God with all the heart and seek in all their thoughts, words, and works, nothing but the praise of God and the salvation of their beloved brethren.
>
> Hatred and vengeance they do not know, for they love those who hate them; they do good to those who despitefully use them and pray for those who persecute them. Avarice, pride, unchastity, and pomp they hate and oppose; all drunkenness, fornication, adultery, hatred, envy, backbiting, lying, cheating, fighting, quarreling, robbing and plunder, blood, and idolatry, in short, all impure, carnal works, and they resist the world with all its lusts. They meditate upon the law of the Lord by day and by night; they rejoice at good and are grieved at evil. Evil they do not repay with evil, but with good. They do not seek merely their own good but that which is good for their neighbors both as to body and soul. They feed the hungry, give drink to the thirsty. They entertain the needy, release prisoners, visit the sick, comfort the fainthearted, admonish the erring, are ready after their Master's example to give their lives for their brethren.[7]

(See Appendix 4 for Menno's complete statement.)

Again Menno wrote:

> By this counsel we are all taught that we must hear Christ, believe in Christ, follow His footsteps, repent, be born from above; become as little children, not in understanding, but in malice; be of the same mind as Christ, walk as He did, deny ourselves, take up His cross and follow Him; and that if we love father, mother, children, or life more than Him, we are not worthy of Him, nor are we His disciples.[8]

In a later statement from Menno written in 1539, he declared:

> They verily are not the true congregation of Christ who merely boast of His name. But they are the true congregation of Christ who are truly converted, who are born from above of God, who are of a regenerate mind by the operation of the Holy Spirit through the hearing of the divine Word, and have become the children of God, have entered into obedience to Him, and live unblamably in His holy commandments, and according to His holy will all their days, or from the moment of their call.[9]

Contemporary Writings

Repentance and regeneration or the new birth are familiar themes today. Many preachers in churches and in the mass media are calling people to "get right with God" or to "be born again." However, the meaning of their call is often unclear. The call to walk in newness of life is often omitted.

An exception would be the writing and speaking of Jim Wallis referred to in Lesson 4. In describing the call of Jesus, Wallis notes that "Jesus inaugurated a new age, heralded a new order, and called the people to conversion. 'Repent!' he said. Why? Because the new order of the kingdom is breaking in upon you and, if you want to be a part of it, you will need to undergo a fundamental transformation. . . . God's new order is so radically different from everything we are accustomed to that we must be spiritually remade before we are ready and equipped to participate in it."[10]

Throughout his long and fruitful ministry, John R. W. Stott has called persons in many parts of the world to a new life in Christ. In his book *Basic Christianity*, he relates the call to follow

Jesus to the call of repentance, and to the call of lordship or a new life.

At its simplest Christ's call was, 'Follow me.' He asked men and women for their personal allegiance. He invited them to learn from Him, to obey His words and to identify themselves with His cause.

Now there can be no following without a previous forsaking. To follow Christ is to renounce all lesser loyalties. In the days when He lived among men on earth, this meant a literal abandonment of home and work. Simon and Andrew 'left their nets and followed him'. James and John 'left their father Zebedee in the boat with the hired servants, and followed him'. Matthew, who heard Christ's call while he was 'sitting at the tax office . . . left everything, and rose and followed him' (Mk. 1:16-20; Lk. 5:27, 28).

Today, in principle, the call of the Lord Jesus has not changed. He still says, 'Follow me', and adds, 'whoever of you does not renounce all that he has cannot be my disciple' (Lk. 14:33). For the majority of Christians, in practice, however, this does not mean a physical departure from their home or their job. Yet it includes an inner surrender of both, and a refusal to allow either family affection or wordly ambition to occupy the first place in our hearts.

Let me be more explicit about the forsaking which cannot be separated from the following of Jesus Christ.

First, there must be *a renunciation of sin*. This, in a word, is repentance. It is the first part of Christian conversion. It can in no circumstances be bypassed. Repentance and faith belong together. We cannot follow Christ without forsaking sin. Moreover, repentance is a definite turn from every thought, word, deed and habit which is known to be wrong. It is not sufficient to feel pangs of remorse or to make some kind of apology to God. Fundamentally, repentance is a matter neither of emotion nor of speech. It is an inward change of mind and attitude towards sin which leads to a change of behaviour. There can be no compromise here. There may be sins in our lives which we do not think we ever could renounce; but we must be *willing* to let them go as we cry to God for deliverance from them. . . .

Secondly, there must be *a renunciation of self*. In order to follow Christ we must not only forsake isolated sins, but renounce the very principle of self-will which lies at the root of all acts of sin. To follow Christ is to surrender to Him the rights over our own lives. It is to abdicate the throne of our heart and, putting our sceptre in His hand and our crown on His head, to do homage to Him as our King. . . .

Thus, in order to follow Christ, we have to deny ourselves, to crucify ourselves, to lose ourselves. The full, inexorable demand of Jesus Christ is now laid bare. He does not call us to a sloppy halfheartedness, but to a vigorous, absolute commitment. He invites us to make Him our Lord. The astonishing idea is current in some circles today that we can enjoy the benefits of Christ's salvation without accepting the challenge of His sovereign lordship. Such an unbalanced notion is not to be found in the New Testament. 'Jesus is Lord' is the earliest known formulation of the creed of Christians. In days when imperial Rome was pressing its citizens to say 'Caesar is Lord', these words had a dangerous flavour. But Christians did not flinch. They could not give Caesar their first allegiance, since they served the Emperor Jesus. God had exalted His Son Jesus far above all principality and power and invested Him with a rank far superior to every rank, that before Him 'every knee should bow . . . and every tongue confess that Jesus Christ is Lord' (Phil. 2:10, 11).[11]

The words of Wallis and Stott call for a newness of life, the kind of newness that only God can bring. They may r ʿound radically new but they deserve careful thought and reflection.

Journaling Focus

Day One: Reflect on the biblical teachings section, including the Scriptures. Describe the aspects of repentance, identified by John C. Wenger, that you experienced.

Day Two: Journal your response to the Anabaptist and contemporary writings. Identify both new insights and new questions.

Day Three: The New Testament and the Anabaptist writings suggest a progression in the Christian life: repentance, conversion, and walking in the resurrection. Describe what walking in the resurrection means for you.

Day Four: In your general journaling today, you may wish to reflect on areas of your life where conversion is not evident.

Spiritual Exercise: Spiritual Autobiography

Spiritual autobiographies are like a cube. They can be examined from many sides or perspectives. Another perspective is to reflect on the stage of the persons in their pursuit of Christlikeness. The Anabaptists did not adopt the "ladder" concept which was familiar in Roman Catholic spirituality;[12] however, they did speak of various stages or levels of spirituality. The terminology varied but there were at least three general stages. [13]

The first stage was being taught the Scriptures for the purpose of calling forth repentance. Genuine sorrow for sin was the beginning point in the Christian life.

Stage two was repentance, which resulted in regeneration evidenced by surrender to God. Some Anabaptists saw in surrender the ingredients of service to God, submission to the brotherhood, and the acceptance of suffering. We will notice later that the baptismal vow symbolized these areas of commitment.

The third stage was a combination of perseverance and progress in Christlikeness. There was concern that members under persecution continue in their baptismal commitments. But there was also concern that members continue personal growth or sanctification. There were several types of spiritual exercises intended to assist the growth process. These will be identified in a later lesson.

As you reflect on your spiritual autobiography or the autobiography of another person, listen for the stage of spirituality. This must be handled with sensitivity. The purpose is not to judge or condemn but rather to help others see their spiritual lives in a new light.

Day Five: As you read these stages of spirituality, did they describe your own pilgrimage? Describe the stages of your own faith and add this description to your autobiography.

Discipling Session

Discipling skills are similar to the skills needed for effective counseling. This is because the discipler is a part of the discipling process just as the counselor is a part of the counseling process. Empathic listening is a basic relational skill.

To listen with empathy is to listen "with" another person, not merely "to" another person. It is to live the experience of another. It is to hear the unspoken words and to feel the unspoken emotions. It means being deeply present to another person. [14]

In *Peer Counseling in the Church,* Paul M. Miller provides some helpful advice for counselors that is equally helpful for disciplers.

> Don't strain or agonize to achieve empathy, or the over-effort may block it. Don't play any little games of deceit. Just be loving in the counselee's presence, with all your antennae out, as caringly sensitive as you can honestly be. Do not feel above your counselees, looking down upon them, but as an equal with them, meet them on the level, seeking to appreciate them as persons of great worth.[15]

1. Share with your discipling partner your response to the journaling exercises for *Day One, Day Two* and *Day Three.*

2. Have one or two persons share their spiritual autobiographies. As you listen, reflect on their stage of spirituality. Also, listen as empathetically as possible. After reflecting on an autobiography, the person who shared may want to indicate the level of empathy experienced while sharing.

3. Desired Discipling Skill: empathic listening in the discipling relationship. Remember that this involves both an attitude of caring and the skill of listening.

Lesson 6

The Obedience of Faith

Discipleship Theme: Faith and Obedience

In Lesson 5 we noted the relationship between repentance and regeneration and their importance for a life of discipleship. In this lesson, we will examine the relationship between faith and obedience and explore their importance for discipleship living. We will also see the enablement of grace for obedience.

Biblical Teachings
What is the meaning of Christian faith and how is it related to obedience? John C. Wenger, an Anabaptist-Mennonite theologian and historian, has observed four elements of faith.[1] First, Christian faith involves an attitude of trust in God and his promises. This attitude is expressed by many Bible characters and certainly by the psalmist. Paul states this truth in his familiar words: "So faith comes from what is heard, and what is heard comes by the preaching of Christ" (Rom. 10:17).

Second, Christian faith involves a continuing self-surrender to God. Faith is not only needed for salvation, it is also needed for sanctification. In Romans 5:1, Paul declares the fact and promise of being "justified by faith." In chapter 6, he appeals to his readers to "yield yourselves to God as men who have been brought from death to life, and your members to God as instruments of righteousness" (Rom. 6:13). Self-surrender to God is a continuing and lifelong experience.

Third, true Christian faith desires to please God. It is not selfishly concerned only about peace for one's self. It involves the reorientation of one's life from self to God and the pleasing of God. Paul expressed this attitude in his defense before Felix. "So I always take pains to have a clear conscience toward God and toward men" (Acts 24:16).

Fourth, Christian faith obediently follows the command of Christ even when there are costly consequences. The person with true faith "serves God out of sheer love for Him, asking only for grace to perform whatever God asks."[2] In the words of Paul before King Agrippa, he "was not disobedient to the heavenly vision" (Acts 26:19; read also James 2:18-26).

This element of faith relates faith, obedience, and grace.[3] Obedience is initiated by faith and is undergirded by grace. True faith calls the believer to a life of obedience which is empowered by God's all-sufficient grace.[4]

Anabaptist Writings

The Anabaptists recognized the close association of faith and obedience by using the phrase "the obedience of faith." An early use of this phrase is found in *The Schleitheim Confession* of 1527. In Article IV it states that "all who have not entered into the obedience of faith and have not united themselves with God so that they will to do His will, are a great abomination before God...."[5]

There were also other terms used to convey the concept of faith expressed in obedience. Conrad Grebel wrote to Thomas Müntzer in 1524 regarding the Anabaptist view of baptism. He states that people will be saved if they live their faith by inner baptism (see Appendix I, Page 236).

Pilgrim Marpeck, the South German Anabaptist leader, wrote about the need for active faith. He said:

> We recognize as true Christian faith only such a faith through which the Holy Spirit and the love of God came into the heart, and which is active, powerful, and operative in all outward obedience and commanded works.[6]

Menno Simons stated the need to walk as Christ walked:

> I confess my Saviour openly; I confess him and dissemble not. If you repent not, and are not born of God, and become not one with Christ in Spirit, faith, life, and worship, then is the sentence of your condemnation on your poor souls already finished and prepared.
>
> All who teach you otherwise than we have here taught and confessed from the Scriptures deceive you. This is the narrow way through which we all must walk and must enter the strait gate, if we would be saved. Neither emperor nor king, duke nor count, knight nor nobleman, doctor nor licentiate, rich nor poor, man nor woman, is excepted. Whosoever boasts that he is a Christian, the same must walk as Christ walked. If any man have not the Spirit of Christ, he is none of his. Whosoever transgresseth and abideth not in the doctrine of Christ, hath not God.[7]

A classic statement of dynamic obedience is found in the tract by Michael Sattler, "On Two Kinds of Obedience." Servile obedience flows from command and is done for reward or self. Filial obedience flows from love of the Father without regard for reward. Filial obedience has its source in active faith. The tract reads, in part, as follows:

> There are two kinds of obedience; servile and filial. The filial springs forth from the love of the Father even if no other reward should follow; yea, even if the Father should wish to damn the child. The servile springs out of love of reward or of self. The filial ever does as much as it can, apart from any command. The servile does as little as it can; yea, does nothing unless it be commanded. The filial can never do enough for Him; the servile thinks it is always doing too much. The filial rejoices in the Father's chastisement even if it has transgressed in nothing. The servile wants never to be chastised by the Lord even though it does nothing right. The filial has its treasure and its righteousness in the Father whom it obeys solely in order to manifest His righteousness. The treasure and the righteousness of the servile are the works that it does to acquire righteousness. The filial remains in the house and inherits all that the Father has; the servile is driven out and receives its justly prescribed reward. The servile looks to the outward and prescribed command of his Lord; the filial is attentive to the inner witness and the Spirit. The servile is imperfect and therefore his Lord has no pleasure in him; the filial strives thereafter and becomes perfect, and therefore the Father cannot reject him.
>
> The filial is not contrary to the servile, as it might appear, but better and higher. Therefore let him who is in the servile, seek after a better [obedience] which is the filial, which needs the servile not at all.

The servile is Moses and brings forth Pharisees and scribes. The filial is Christ and makes children of God. The servile busies himself either with the ceremonies which Moses commanded or with those which men themselves have invented. The filial is busy with the love of God and the neighbor; yet he will also sometimes subject himself to the ceremonies for the sake of the serfs in order better to instruct them and bring them to sonship. The servile makes self-willed and vengeful people; the filial makes tolerant and mild. The servile is heavyspirited, would wish to come soon to the end of the work; the filial is light, takes no account of duration. The servile is malevolent; wishes good to no one but himself. The filial wishes that all men could be as he. The servile is the old covenant, and has the promise of temporal blessedness, i.e., the creature. The filial is the new covenant which has the promise of eternal blessedness, of the Creator Himself. The servile is a beginning and a preparation for blessedness; the filial is the end and completeness itself. The servile endured for a time; the filial shall stand eternally. The servile was a figure and a shadow; the filial is body and truth.[8]

Harold S. Bender describes the Anabaptist view of faith as follows:

... The Anabaptists understood faith as a dynamic response to God's approach; this response opened the life to the transforming grace of God, which resulted in obedience and discipleship; faith and obedience were as inseparable as regeneration and discipleship. Faith of this sort inevitably produces fruit. Anabaptist faith involved commitment to Christ to follow Him in all things, as Lord, as example, as forerunner. It meant not simply resting in grace, it meant "walking in the resurrection."[9]

It should be pointed out that Anabaptism at its best was joyful obedience to Christ enabled by grace, not legalism. Salvation was a gift of God's grace, not an achievement of personal merit. And salvation grace also enabled the believer to serve or obey. An *Ausbund* hymn writer wrote: "He who is not willing to serve me gets no grace from me."

Dirk Philips, an associate of Menno Simons, said:

But although we ... desire to be diligent to do God's will by His grace, yet let no one think or imagine nor say of us that we seek our salvation in any other way than in the grace of God and in the merits of Christ alone. For we firmly believe and openly confess that we are saved by the grace of our Lord Jesus Christ.[10]

Menno adds his own testimony to the centrality of grace:

> For all the truly regenerated and spiritually minded conform in all
> things to the Word and ordinances of the Lord. Not because they think to
> merit the atonement of their sins and eternal life. By no means. In this mat-
> ter they depend upon nothing except the true promise of the merciful
> Father, given in grace to all believers through the blood and merits of
> Christ, which blood is and ever will be the only eternal medium of our rec-
> onciliation; and not works, baptism, or the Lord's Supper.... For if our
> reconciliation depended on works and ceremonies, then grace would be a
> thing of the past, and the merits and fruits of the blood of Christ would end.
> Oh no, it is grace, and will be grace to all eternity....[11]

The Anabaptists believed that God's grace came to and
through the obedient life of the people of God. God's grace met
them at the point of their deepest need. Their most deeply felt
need was strength and courage to obey the will of God, namely,
faithfulness to the teachings and examples of Jesus. It was in their
life together as the people of God that their faith was evidenced,
their obedience was focused, and God's grace was manifested.

Contemporary Writer

Dietrich Bonhoeffer saw quite clearly the relationship
between faith and obedience. He believed that following Jesus involved certain definite steps, the first of which is to break away
from the past. This creates a situation where faith is possible. Bonhoeffer then wrote:

> This situation may be described by two propositions, both of which are
> equally true. Only he who believes is obedient, and only he who is obedient
> believes.
>   It is quite unbiblical to hold the first proposition without the second.
> We think we understand when we hear that obedience is possible only
> where there is faith. Does not obedience follow faith as good fruit grows on
> a good tree? First, faith, then obedience. If by that we mean that it is faith
> which justifies, and not the act of obedience, all well and good, for that is
> the essential and unexceptionable presupposition of all that follows. If
> however we make a chronological distinction between faith and obedience,
> and make obedience subsequent to faith, we are divorcing the one from the
> other—and then we get the practical question, when must obedience
> begin? From the point of view of justification it is necessary thus to separate

them, but we must never lose sight of their essential unity. For faith is only real when there is obedience, never without it, and faith only becomes faith in the act of obedience.

Since, then, we cannot adequately speak of obedience as the consequence of faith, and since we must never forget the indissoluble unity of the two, we must place the second proposition alongside of the first. Not only do those who believe obey, but only those who obey believe. In the one case faith is the condition of obedience, and in the other obedience the condition of faith.

If we are to believe, we must obey a concrete command. Without this preliminary step of obedience, our faith will only be pious humbug, and lead us to the grace which is not costly. Everything depends on the first step. It has a unique quality of its own. The first step of obedience makes Peter leave his nets, and later get out of the ship; it calls upon the young man to leave his riches. Only this new existence, created through obedience, can make faith possible.[12]

Journaling Focus

Day One: Four elements of faith are identified at the beginning of this lesson. Reflect on your own experience with each of these aspects of faith.

Day Two: The Anabaptists and Bonhoeffer related faith, obedience, and grace. What is your response to these readings? How have you found them related in your own experience? Please explain.

Day Three: When in your life have you experienced most deeply the grace of God?

Day Four: In your general journaling today, you may want to reflect on any changes in your life as a result of this discipling program.

Spiritual Exercise: Spiritual Autobiography

As you reflect on the last autobiography or autobiographies shared in your group, listen for examples of the relatedness of faith, obedience, and grace. That is to say, listen for examples of where faith called forth a step of obedience which was then supported and empowered by enabling grace. (We too, like Paul, can experience the grace and strength of God being perfected in our weakness.)

In the last lesson, reference was made to the several stages of spirituality identified by the Anabaptists. Also reference was made to the fact that there were various types of spiritual exercises intended to assist the growth process.

One exercise was self-examination and confession which was expected of all persons who participated in the Lord's Supper.

Another exercise was daily devotions "including prayer, contemplation, adoration, and praise, and fasting."[13] Both private and congregational prayer received strong emphasis. Hubmaier appears to have promoted devotional exercises similar to those practiced by the Tertiaries. He stated that he had "admonished the people to pray faithfully and without ceasing. Also in all my preaching I recited with the people loudly and kneeling a public confession, the Lord's Prayer, and a psalm."[14] Menno said that he prayed daily, "Holy Father, Thy will be done."[15]

Finally, there were the acts of brotherly love and charity toward neighbors and those of the household of faith.

Davis notes that these spiritual exercises had a close affinity with the penitential exercises practiced in the Christian ascetic tradition.[16] In this area, also, the Anabaptists appear to have borrowed and creatively adapted contemporary religious practices.

As you listen to the autobiographies, be alert to the role which such exercises may have had in spiritual growth.

Day Five: What spiritual exercises are most helpful in nurturing your faith and obedience?

Discipling Session

In the last lesson, the skill of empathic listening was identified. Another discipling skill which relates to counseling and spiritual direction is humble openness.

To relate to others with humble openness in a discipling relationship is to relate as equals in Christ rather than as a spiritual superior. It is being open to share one's own areas of need and search. It involves creating an atmosphere where sin and failure can be acknowledged and life reordered.

Tilden Edwards has interviewed a number of spiritual leaders to discover the most important qualifications for a spiritual companion. He found agreement around the qualities of spiritual commitment, experience, knowledge, and humility. The leaders also stressed the capacities to be caring, sensitive, open, and flexible.[17] These same qualities and capacities are necessary for effective discipling.

1. Share with your discipling partner your responses to the journaling exercise on *Day One, Day Two,* and *Day Three.*

2. Have one or two persons share their spiritual autobiographies. Listen for the interaction of faith, obedience, and grace. Also, listen for the role of spiritual exercises in spiritual growth.

3. During the sharing and interaction, attempt to maintain a spirit of humble openness. Help create an atmosphere where it is safe to face failures and where there is support for new beginnings.

4. Desired Discipling Skill: humble openness in the discipling relationship. Humble openness requires a spirit of humility and an attitude of openness but also the skill of allowing these qualities to be present in a relationship.

Lesson 7

Separated unto God

Discipleship Theme: Holy Living

Biblical Teachings

The history of the people of God in both the Old and New Testaments is the history of a separate or "called out" people. This theme begins with the call of Abraham (Gen. 12:1-2), is developed through the establishment of the old covenant (Ex. 20-24), and is expanded through the moral and ceremonial laws found in Leviticus. The message of the prophets was for Israel to return to the covenant, not merely by keeping ceremonies but by loving God with the whole heart and practicing holiness of life. The desire of God for Israel is stated in Leviticus 11:44-45.

> For I am the Lord your God; consecrate yourselves therefore, and be holy, for I am holy. You shall not defile yourselves with any swarming thing that crawls upon the earth. For I am the Lord who brought you up out of the land of Egypt, to be your God; you shall therefore be holy, for I am holy.

The New Testament continues God's call for a separate and holy people. We noticed in Lesson 5 that Jesus began his ministry with a call to repentance and the introduction of the kingdom of God (Mk. 1:15). In the Sermon on the Mount, Jesus set forth the conditions for membership in his kingdom (Mt. 5-7). The central condition is separation unto God and following his will and his ways.

The call for a special people continues through the New

Testament epistles. The people of the new covenant have been delivered from the dominion of darkness and transferred to the kingdom of his beloved Son (Col. 1:13). Of these people Peter says:

> But you are a chosen race, a royal priesthood, a holy nation, God's own people, that you may declare the wonderful deeds of him who called you out of darkness into his marvelous light. Once you were no people but now you are God's people; once you had not received mercy but now you have received mercy (1 Pet. 2:9-10).

Peter further appeals to his readers:

> As obedient children, do not be conformed to the passions of your former ignorance, but as he who called you is holy, be holy yourselves in all your conduct; since it is written, "You shall be holy, for I am holy" (1 Pet. 1:14-16).

Paul's words to Titus identify both the grace activity of God for persons and the consequent call that those responding to grace become God's own people.

> For the grace of God has appeared for the salvation of all men, training us to renounce irreligion and worldly passions, and to live sober, upright, and godly lives in this world, awaiting our blessed hope, the appearing of the glory of our great God and Savior Jesus Christ, who gave himself for us to redeem us from all iniquity and to purify for himself a people of his own who are zealous for good deeds (Tit. 2:11-14).

John C. Wenger, in *Separated unto God*, notes that the concept of separation in both Testaments is spiritual in nature. It is the life and presence of God that makes possible separation and holiness. Wenger concludes:

> We find therefore that the great spiritual principles of separation between the children of God and those who are of the world are found alike in the Old Testament and the New. This separation is a spiritual separation which works itself out in all of life. The main differences between the Old Covenant and the New on the matter of separation and nonconformity are that the ceremonial regulations of Mosaism are now done away in Christ, and that the revelation of the will of God is much clearer in Christ than it had been in Moses. This is true because of the fact that the Word became flesh and dwelt among us, revealing more perfectly to men the character and glory of God.[1]

Anabaptist Writings

From the beginning of the Anabaptist movement, there was a strong appeal for a Christian life chracterized by holiness, righteousness, and separation from sin and evil. In 1524 Conrad Grebel wrote concerning his desire to see a church radically different from the state churches of his day. He wanted a church that would display "true faith and divine practice" (see Appendix 1, page 242).

Article IV of *The Schleitheim Confession* focused on separation from evil (Appendix 1, pages 243-244). In this article, "Sattler first of all established the metaphysical basis for separation from the world. He held that the human family existed in two antagonistic groups, namely, those who have faith in God and those who have refused to unite themselves with God and are therefore an abomination in His sight."[2] The writer seems to be appealing to 2 Corinthians 6:17 which calls for separation unto God from an unclean world. By speaking of the two world systems as "Babylon" and "Egypt," Sattler shows that the Anabaptists, like many early Christians, anticipated the imminent judgment of God on the wicked.

Article VII of *The Schleithem Confession* dealt with a related theme, namely, the oath. It reads, in part, as follows:

> We have been united as follows concerning the oath. The oath is a confirmation among those who are quarreling or making promises. In the law it is commanded that it should be done only in the name of God, truthfully and not falsely. Christ, who teaches the perfection of the law, forbids His [followers] all swearing, whether true or false; neither by heaven nor by earth, neither by Jerusalem nor by our head; and that for the reason which He goes on to give: "For you cannot make one hair white or black." You see, thereby all swearing is forbidden. We cannot perform what is promised in swearing, for we are not able to change the smallest part of ourselves.
>
> Christ taught us similarly when He says: Your speech shall be yea, yea; and nay, nay; for what is more than that comes of evil. He says, your speech or your word shall be yes and no, so that no one might understand that He had permitted it. Christ is simply yea and nay, and all those who seek Him simply will understand His Word. Amen.[3]

By rejecting the use of the oath, the Anabaptists were not rejecting the state. Rather, they were rejecting the notions that the state had absolute authority and that honesty was not always the practice of the true follower of Christ. If your word was always "Yes" or "No" (Mt. 5:37), the oath was unnecessary.

Many Anabaptist leaders wrote about their desire for a church characterized by holiness of life. Pilgrim Marpeck saw the true church as *"the community of Christian believers"* who have denied and disowned the devil and the world (Appendix 1, page 238).

Menno Simons wrote frequently on the theme of separation and holiness. The church was to be the bride of Christ without "spot or wrinkle." She was to be "holy and without blemish" (Eph. 5:27; 2 Pet. 3:14).

In his "Reply to Gellius Faber," Menno wrote:

> The entire evangelical Scriptures teach us that the church of Christ was and is, in doctrine, life, and worship, a people separated from the world.... And since the church always was and must be a people, a separate people,... and since it is as clear as the noonday sun that for many centuries no difference has been visible between the church and the world, but that they have without differentiation run together in baptism, Supper, life, and worship, ... therefore we are constrained by the Spirit and Word of God ... to gather together ... not unto ourselves but unto the Lord, a pious and penitent congregation or church....[4]

Menno wrote in "Foundation of Christian Doctrine":

> In short, this matter we teach from the Word of God as much as in us is, in order to restrain those carnal lusts which war against the soul. We are to crucify the flesh with the affections and lusts, not to conform to this world, to put off the works of darkness and put on the armor of light; not to love the world, neither the things that are in the world. We must put off the old man with his deeds, and put on the new man, which after God is created in righteousness and true holiness, whose fruits are faith, love, hope, righteousness, peace, and joy in the Holy Ghost. We must be patient in suffering, merciful, compassionate, chaste, sincerely hating and rebuking all sin, having a sincere love and zeal for God and His Word.[5]

Again Menno wrote:

> Elect, faithful children, you who with me are called to a like grace, inheritance, portion, and kingdom, and are named after the Lord's name,

oh, hear the voice of Christ, our King; hear the voice of your Bridegroom, O thou bride of God, thou friend of the Lord. Arise and adorn thyself to honor thy King and Bridegroom. Although thou art pure, make thyself purer still; although thou art holy, make thyself holier still; although thou art righteous, make thyself more righteous still. Adorn thyself with the white silken robe of righteousness; hang about thy neck the golden chain of every piety; gird thyself with the fair girdle of brotherly love; put on the wedding ring of a true faith; cover thyself with the precious fair gold of the divine Word; beautify thyself with the pearls of many virtues; wash thyself with the clear waters of grace and anoint thyself with the oil of the Holy Ghost; wash thy feet in the clear, sparkling flood of Almighty God. Let your whole body be pure and immaculate, for thy lover hates all wrinkles and spots. So will he desire thy beauty and will praise thee and say: How fair is thy love, my sister, my spouse! how much better is thy love than wine! and the smell of thine ointments than all spices! Thy lips, O my spouse, drop as the honeycomb; honey and milk are under thy tongue. S. of Sol. 4:10, 11.[6]

In Appendix 1, pages 242-245, there is a further discussion of the theme of separation and holiness as well as an indication that the Anabaptists did achieve a significant level of holy living. On what did their success rest? Harold S. Bender identifies six reasons.

(1) They insisted upon personal conviction, conversion, and commitment as adults, based upon prior teaching. (2) They made the above a requirement for admission to church membership. (3) They worshiped mostly in small groups with intimacy of personal acquaintance, testimony, observation, and admonition. (4) They practiced church discipline. (5) They had high standards for the Christian life, which were so much higher than the average of the society of the time that only really committed persons would accept them and seek to fulfill them. (6) They practiced separation from the world and so were delivered from the constant influence of the low-living multitude.[7]

An emphasis on holiness can lead to judging and rejecting. This happened among the Dutch Anabaptists (see Appendix 1, pages 273-276).

Contemporary Writings

In his discussion on "Being a Christian," John R. W. Stott states that the crisis of justification must lead to the process of sanctification or growth in holiness. He writes:

There are two main spheres in which the Christian is meant to grow. The first is in understanding and the second in holiness. When he begins the Christian life, he probably understands very little and he has only just come to know God. Now he must increase in the knowledge of God and of his Lord and Saviour, Jesus Christ (Col. 1:10; 2 Pet. 3:18). This knowledge is partly intellectual and partly personal. In connection with the former, I would urge you not only to study the Bible but to read good Christian books. To neglect to grow in your understanding is to court disaster. The Christian way is strewn with such casualties.

We must also grow in holiness of life. The New Testament writers speak of the development of our faith in God, our love for our fellow men and our likeness to Christ. Every son of God longs to become more and more conformed in his character and behaviour to the Son of God Himself. The Christian life is a life of righteousness. We must seek to obey God's commandments and do God's will. The Holy Spirit has been given us for this purpose. He has made our bodies His temple. He dwells within us. And as we allow Him continuously to fill us with His power, He will subdue our evil desires and cause His fruit to appear, which is 'love, joy, peace, patience, kindness, goodness, faithfulness, gentleness, self-control' (Gal. 5: 16, 22, 23).[8]

Dietrich Bonhoeffer adds a helpful perspective in his discussion of "The Hidden Righteousness." He writes that "the hallmark of Christianty is our separation from the world, our transcendence of its standards, and our performance of something out of the ordinary."[9] Bonhoeffer then identifies the paradox of the visible and invisible righteousness.

The disciples are told that they can possess the "extraordinary" only so long as they are reflective: they must beware how they use it, and never fulfil it simply for its own sake, or for the sake of ostentation. The better righteousness of the disciples must have a motive which lies beyond itself. Of course it has to be visible, but they must take care that it does not become visible simply for the sake of becoming visible. There are of course proper grounds for insisting on the visible nature of Christian discipleship, but the visibility is never an end in itself; and if it becomes so we have lost sight of our primary aim, which is to follow Jesus. And, having once done that, we should never be able to carry on again where we had left off; we should have to begin all over again at the beginning. And that would bring it home to us that we were no true disciples. We are therefore confronted with a paradox. Our activity must be visible, but never be done for the sake of making it visible. "Let your light so shine before men" (v 16) and yet: Take care that you hide it! There is a pointed contrast between chapters 5 and 6. That which is visible must also be hidden. The reflection on which

Jesus insists is intended to prevent us from reflecting on our extraordinary position. We have to take heed that we do not take heed of our own righteousness. Otherwise the "extraordinary" which we achieve will not be that which comes from following Christ, but that which springs from our own will and desire.[10]

The paradox is resolved as Bonhoeffer explains that we are to hide our righteousness from ourselves, that is, keep our eyes on Jesus and not on ourselves and what we are doing. If we gaze on the extraordinary quality of our own lives, then we have taken our focus off our Lord and we are no longer following Christ.

Journaling Focus

Day One: As you read the biblical teachings, what was your inner reaction? Did you feel that your own life of separation and holiness was being described or did you feel otherwise? Explain your answer.

Day Two: The Anabaptists placed major emphasis on separation from the world, partly because they were a minority group wanting to be different from their society. Describe your reaction to the Anabaptist writings. What is your understanding and application of this theme?

Day Three: Reflect on the statements by Stott and Bonhoeffer. What new insights and applications do you find?

Spiritual Exercise: Bible Reading

Anabaptist spirituality viewed the Bible as the guide and norm for daily life. Members were to "exercise themselves in the teachings of Christ and his apostles." Their approach to truth was biblicism, not mysticism. Menno Simons wrote, "O dear Lord, I did not know myself until I viewed myself in Thy Word."[11]

The Bible will speak to us as it did to the Anabaptists as we follow an effective method of Bible reading and read with a proper attitude. One effective method is to read reflectively. This means "to read with your mind alert and your eyes open to some new discovery. It is to approach the Bible with a hunger to be fed and an anticipation of finding some fresh truth. It is to read with the prayer of Samuel, 'Speak, Lord, for your servant is listening' " (1 Sam. 3:9).[12]

The prayer of Samuel suggests reading with the attitude of practicing obedience. Jesus told his listeners, "If you continue in my word, you are truly my disciples, and you will know the truth, and the truth will make you free" (Jn. 8:31-32). Peter spoke similarly when he wrote, "Having purified your souls by your obedience to the truth for a sincere love of the brethren, love one another earnestly from the heart" (1 Pet. 1:22).

Normally, Christ does not open to us new truth until we begin living the truth we already know. Peter Marshall probably spoke for many of us when he said that the passages of Scripture that cause us the most problems are not those we cannot understand. Rather, they are the passages we understand well but do not want to follow. (For an enlarged discussion of Bible reading, see *Keys to Successful Bible Study* [Herald Press, 1981] by John R. Martin.)[13]

Day Four: Read reflectively 1 Peter 1 and 2 several times looking and listening for the message, especially regarding holy living. Write down your findings.

Day Five: For your general journaling, focus on your most pressing life issue.

Discipling Session

The ability to exercise constructive accountability is the skill of helping persons to be honest with themselves, with others, and with God. It is calling forth accountability in a way that communicates hope and not intimidation. It is confronting in a caring, redemptive manner.

In the group session, there will be opportunity to discuss accountability and to discover whether it is done constructively.

1. Share with your discipling partner your responses to the

journaling exercise on *Day One* and *Day Four*

2. As a total group, discuss your level of faithfulness to the group commitment associated with Lesson 1. After discussing the accountability issues, indicate whether the approach was constructive or intimidating. This should help you become aware of whether you have developed this discipling skill. As time permits, share insights from *Day Two* and *Day Three*.

3. Desired Discipling Skill: ability to exercise constructive accountability. It is difficult for most of us to confront or "carefront." However, it may be necessary in the discipling relationship. A good place to begin this practice is talking with a person about commitments they have made. In a constructive manner, help the person to be honest with himself or herself, with others, and with God.

Lesson 8

Progressing Toward Perfection

Discipleship Theme: Faithfulness, Growth, and Perfection

In Lesson 5, reference was made to three stages of spirituality identified by the Anabaptists. These were (1) being taught the Scriptures with a call to repentance, (2) regeneration evidenced by a life of surrender to God, and (3) perseverance in the faith and progression in Christlikeness. Lesson 8 is, in a sense, an enlargement of stage three.

The New Testament writers and the Anabaptists called on believers to progress in faith and knowledge. This call was expressed in three concepts: faithfulness—maintaining one's commitment to the Lord, growth—moving to more advanced levels of Christian living, and perfection—the level of life taught and practiced by Jesus Christ. (They did not teach perfectionism.)

These concepts probably cannot be separated in life because they are interrelated, yet they can represent the approach persons have in their Christian lives.

Biblical Teachings

Jesus was calling for faithfulness when he said, "No one who puts his hand to the plow and looks back is fit for the kingdom of God" (Lk. 9:62). Barnabas exhorted new believers "to remain faithful to the Lord with steadfast purpose" (Acts 11:23). Toward the end of his life, Paul could say with satisfaction, "I have fought the good fight, I have finished the race, I have kept the faith" (2

Tim. 4:7). The writer of Hebrews has a severe warning for those who become unfaithful (Heb. 6:4-6). A crown of life is promised those who are faithful unto death (Rev. 2:10).

A second level of biblical teaching focuses on growth. Not only are followers to be faithful to their commitment, they are to grow. Paul informs the believers at Ephesus that they are to "grow into a holy temple in the Lord" (Eph. 2:21). He further calls on them "to grow up in every way into him who is the head, into Christ" (Eph. 4:15). Peter speaks a similar message. New believers are to "long for the pure spiritual milk, that by it you may grow up to salvation" (1 Pet. 2:2). His further appeal is to "grow in the grace and knowledge of our Lord and Savior Jesus Christ" (2 Pet. 3:18).

The third level of biblical teaching goes beyond the concept of growth to the concept of perfection. Here the New Testament seems to speak a mixed message. It calls for perfection but also denies the possibility of perfection. Jesus said, "You, therefore, must be perfect, as your heavenly Father is perfect" (Mt. 5:48). Paul wrote to the church at Corinth: "Since we have these promises, beloved, let us cleanse ourselves from every defilement of body and spirit, and make holiness perfect in the fear of God" (2 Cor. 7:1). However, after Paul had listed his religious achievements and his life's goal of knowing Christ, he stated: "Not that I have already obtained this or am already perfect; but I press on to make it my own, because Christ Jesus has made me his own" (Phil. 3:12).

How is this seeming contradiction resolved? A part of the answer is that perfection, while not attainable by any finite being, does call us beyond our present level toward endless growth. However, on a deeper level, any achievement of perfection is the enabling of God, not the effort of humans. In the Old Testament, the perfect person was one whose heart was wholly devoted to God. On the human side is a devoted heart. God's part is sharing his own life with humankind. The Christian can only move toward perfection by looking to the One who is able to "make you perfect in every good work to do his will, working in you that which is wellpleasing in his sight, through Jesus Christ" (Heb. 13:21, KJV).

The Christian life can be lived only on the level of faithfulness (holding on), or it can be lived on the level of growth (moving forward), or it can be lived on the level of movement toward perfection (aiming toward God's goal). In the final analysis, successful living at any level always involves the joint participation of humans and their Master.

Anabaptist Writings

As we noticed in Lesson 7, the Anabaptists stressed a Christian life of holiness, righteousness, and separation from sin and evil. In addition, there was also a strong emphasis on faithfulness or "remaining constant," growth in biblical knowledge and obedience, and the perfect example of Christ. This type of life was not viewed as personal achievement or attainable alone. It could only be the result of a depth relationship with Christ and his body.

One of the early Anabaptist documents, circulated with *The Schleitheim Confession,* concerned congregational order (see Appendix 1, page 257). It is clear that they met together "to exhort one another to remain faithful to the Lord as they had pledged." Also they met to grow through Bible study, brotherly admonition, and observance of the Lord's Supper.

Pilgrim Marpeck called for instruction after baptism to assure faithfulness and assist growth. He wrote:

> After baptism, a different kind of teaching follows, a teaching which is directed to the regenerate and baptized children of God; they are taught to observe all that Christ has commanded, as is fitting for obedient children, and at all times to seek to do the will of their Father. These same baptized people are now given a command which Peter, in his second epistle, the second chapter, refers to as the holy commandment (2 Pet. 2:21). And they are instructed to accomplish the will of God and to complete their life in the way of righteousness as exemplified by Jesus Christ. For them never to have known the way of righteousness would be preferable than for them to fall back and return to their old way of life, which, after all, they abjured and

put away in their baptism. Through baptism, they fled from the sins of the world and turned away from the life of the world.[1]

In a letter to Swiss and Alsatian believers, Marpeck referred to the difficult times in which they lived and to his desire to visit them to discuss the will, mind, and Spirit of Christ. He believed this would help them in their faithfulness to Christ (see Appendix 1, page 268).

Menno Simons envisioned a church which would experience constant growth toward the standard of perfection called for by Christ. You will recall his appeal quoted in the last lesson for increased purity, holiness, and righteousness.

This vision gave great urgency to the task of congregational leaders. He spoke eloquently concerning the calling of those charged with teaching the Word of the Lord (see Appendix 1, p. 263). He also encouraged parents to be diligent in teaching their children and wrote prayers for use at mealtime (see Appendix 1, page 265).

For the Anabaptists, the Christian life involved total commitment. It became their vocation. Faithfulness was expected, growth was encouraged, and perfection was the ideal toward which they were to move.

The testimony of Marpeck helps clarify the conditions under which the Anabaptists lived and the level of life they desired to achieve. In the introduction to "The Admonition of 1542," Marpeck referred to the "terrible errors" of some groups and the "terrible enemy, Satan," with whom they contended. He encouraged the weary and weak to "raise their head together with us" because he is committed to fight the spiritual battle with the "sword of the Holy Spirit." He then described how he fights the battle so that he will be faithful to his calling and commitment, and will finally achieve the ultimate victory by the grace of God.

> This we do in humility, meekness, and patience, with tribulation, distress, and anxiety, with blows, prison, work, and watching, with fasting and praying, with purity, knowledge, and nobility, with friendliness, with the Holy Spirit and the Word of truth, and with the power of God through

the weapons of righteousness to the right and to the left, which take into captivity all reason under the obedience of faith in Christ (2 Cor. 10:1-6). Through praise and blame, through bad report and good report, we are like those who mislead and who yet are truthful, as the unknown and yet known; we are like the dying and yet we live, like those severely beaten but not killed, like the sorrowing and yet at all times joyful; we are like the poor and yet we are they who make many rich, like those who have nothing and yet possess everything (2 Cor. 6:3-13). Even though we walk in the flesh, yet we do not fight with physical means, for the weapons of our battle are not of the flesh, but rather are mighty in the presence of God. This we do to disrupt the fortress, and so destroy all attacks and all heights which raise themselves against the knowledge of God. Thus, we take captive all reason under obedience to Christ (2 Cor. 10:1-6). Our victory is not won with our own power and might, nor is it done with earthly or physical power and sword, but rather with the power and might of our Lord Jesus Christ. He, through patience, conquered it all, just as we also overcome, even in death, through Christ our Lord, if we are truly related to Him in the covenant by His grace, and we persevere until the end. For to this battle we have been called even from the beginning of our covenant in Christ Jesus, and our covenant witness referred to earlier, and it exists by the grace of God, which has always been and is now evident. This continues to be our hope through the grace of God, to which we will testify without wavering unto the end.[2]

Contemporary Writings

Donald G. Bloesch is a contemporary writer who combines a commitment to the best in Reformed theology, and a concern for vital spirituality and discipleship. Writing in *The Crisis of Piety*, Bloesch stresses the need for faithfulness and growth.

> Indeed, salvation cannot be said to have occurred apart from the obedience of faith. Our viewpoint approaches that of modern secular theology which places the accent upon the decision and commitment of the believer. But whereas secular theologians speak of the arena of salvation as the present struggle for social justice, we envisage it as the daily crisis of repentance and faith, one that is grounded in and indeed rises out of the crisis of the death and resurrection of Jesus Christ. In our view the conversion of the individual is prerequisite for the reformation of society. But this conversion refers not simply to a first decision for Christ but rather to the lifelong struggle to remain true to the faith into which we were baptized.[3]

Bloesch is also concerned about both the perfection to which Christ calls us and the danger of perfectionism. He writes as follows:

Closely related to Pharisaism is perfectionism. This might be defined as the belief that everything that Christ demands of us can be and sometimes is attained in this life. Spiritual disciplines become tools by which we supposedly enter into Christian perfection. Christian perfection is indeed the ultimate goal of the Christian, and yet it is not fully attainable in this life. It is well to bear in mind that Christ calls us to absolute perfection, and this means a state of perfect love comparable to that which characterizes God Himself (Mt. 5:48). We can attain a measure of perfection but not perfection itself. We can keep the law through the grace of God, but we cannot fulfil the law. We can have freedom from every particular sin; yet we cannot be totally free from the presence of sin. Spiritual disciplines are necessary to keep us on the path to Christian perfection, but they cannot procure this perfection. Wesley rightly maintained that final holiness is a gift of God just as is justification itself. It is tempting for a consecrated Christian to believe that he has arrived at the perfection Christ demands, that he is now in a state of entire sanctification or sinless perfection. But the Scripture tells us that no man is without sin (Ps. 14:3; 53:3; Rom. 3:10-12, 23; 1 Jn. 1:8). Indeed, even our most lofty desires and virtues are tainted by sinful pretension. This is why we must repent of our virtues as well as of our vices. We must repent of our imperfect self-discipline as well as our sins.[4]

Journaling Focus

Day One: This lesson touches on faithfulness, growth, and perfection. Which of these terms best describes your approach to the Christian life? Or do you view the Christian life in some other way? Explain your answer.

Day Two: Read the *Anabaptist Writings* section, including the sections in Appendix I. What difference do you sense between the Anabaptist emphasis and the emphasis in your congregation?

Day Three: David Bloesch suggests that one way to guard against perfectionism is to "repent of our virtues as well as of our vices." How do you respond to his suggestion?

Spiritual Exercise: Bible Study

The Anabaptists were called biblicists because of their deep commitment to discovering and following the will of God as revealed in the Bible. Robert Friedmann says that "they read assiduously from cover to cover, including the Apocrypha. To them it was an open book, and they claimed to have experienced a spirit akin to it. They read it as people seeking divine guidance."[5] They recognized the activity of the Holy Spirit in making the Scriptures alive and understandable. God needed to ignite the Word before it would become alive. Today we call this process illumination.

G. W. Bromiley has also expressed the need for illumination in Bible study. He writes: "Without the Holy Ghost it [the Bible] can be read only on the level of the human letter. What is given by the Spirit must be read in the Spirit."[6]

The first section of this lesson discusses the concepts of faithfulness, growth, and perfection. A number of Scriptures are identified with each concept. The spiritual exercise for this lesson is to study these passages. Read them reflectively and prayerfully asking the Holy Spirit to "ignite" them in your heart and mind.

Day Four: Study the Scriptures mentioned in the biblical teachings section. Note the motivation for faithfulness, the areas for growth, and the area of life in which we are to be perfect.

Day Five: In your general journaling, you may want to reflect on the areas of your life which are below the biblical standard.

Discipling Session

We have noticed that the Christian life is nurtured through various disciplines—including Bible study. However, Bible study has various levels and patterns. A method that has meaning at one period in life may not meet one's needs at a later period. A discipler needs to be aware of various methods and to be able to help persons discover those that are best suited for them.

In the group session there will be opportunity to discuss Bible study methods and to explore those that would be most meaningful.

1. Share with your discipling partner your responses to the journaling exercises on *Day Two, Day Three,* and *Day Four.*

2. Share with the total group your journaling for *Day One*. Then describe the Bible study method you find most valuable. As the persons report, identify their view of the Christian life and their preferred Bible study method. See if a pattern emerges. If some persons are not satisfied with their Bible study method, have the group suggest methods they would recommend in light of where those persons are in their Christian lives.

3. Desired Discipling Skill: ability to relate appropriate Bible study method to personal need.

Lesson 9

The Community of God's People

Discipleship Theme: The Church, A Community of Believers

Biblical Teachings

With this lesson, we begin an examination of corporate expressions of discipleship. In both the Old and New Testaments, the followers of God have been more than individual persons; they have been a people—believers in community with other believers. We noted in Lesson 7 that Israel became a covenant people. This meant that they not only had a special relationship to God, they also had a special relationship to each other. They were people of the covenant and a covenant people.

After Pentecost, there was a new Israel composed of both Jews and Gentiles. Paul called the Galatians "the Israel of God" (Gal. 6:16). He told the Ephesians that "he chose us in him before the foundation of the world. . . . He destined us in love to be his sons through Jesus Christ" (Eph. 1:4-5). Paul also said to them, "You are no longer strangers and sojourners, but you are fellow citizens with the saints and members of the household of God . . . a holy temple in the Lord; in whom you also are built into it for a dwelling place of God in the Spirit" (Eph. 2:19-22).

These new people of God gave themselves the name *ecclesia* (an assembly of God's people) or church. They saw themselves as the covenant people of God. Peter described them as "a chosen race, a royal priesthood, a holy nation, God's own people" (1 Pet. 2:9).

Harold S. Bender has explored the theological meaning of understanding the church as the people of God. Writing in *These Are My People,* he notes a number of theological implications. First, the church is a visible company of concrete living persons. It is not an invisible, mystical phenomenon.

Second, the church exists because of God's purpose and action. He calls it into being. The birth and survival of the church are the results of his faithful action.

Third, the boundaries of membership are determined by God. He crosses racial and cultural lines in his desire that all persons hear the good news.

Fourth, the church is composed of people who respond to God. God in his grace takes the initiative to call persons but they must respond in order to be a part of his special people. The people of God are persons who have responded to God. This response establishes a relationship between the persons and God. But those who have responded must continue a life of response in order to maintain the relationship.

Fifth, those who respond to God internally must confess God externally with their mouths and with their lives. This results in the visibility of the church. As persons confess together, they become the people of God. As they share life together, they become a community of believers. They experience the reality of *koinonia* or fellowship.

While many of these understandings about the church may seem to be familiar, they were not accepted by all religious groups at the time of the Reformation; neither are they accepted by all religious groups today. The Anabaptists declared this vision in the sixteenth century. A number of leaders are declaring this vision in our own day.

Anabaptist Writings

One of the earliest calls during the Reformation for a New Testament type of church appeared in the letter Conrad Grebel wrote to Thomas Müntzer in 1524. Grebel urged him to "go forward with the Word and establish a Christian church with the help of Christ and his rule, as we find it instituted in Matt. 18:15-18 and applied in the Epistles."[1]

This call was a rejection of the state church concept and practice. The call was finally initiated by a small group of Anabaptist leaders in 1525. Grebel was one of this group.

Bernhard Rothmann, who had been a Protestant cleric before becoming an Anabaptist leader, wrote the following concerning his view of the true Christian congregation:

> The true Christian congregation is a gathering large or small that is founded on Christ in the true confession of Christ. That means '¹ -ᵗ iᵗ holds only to his words and seeks to fulfil his whole will and his comᵢ. .ᵢments. A gathering thus constituted is truly a congregation of Christ. But if this is missing a gathering cannot in truth be called a congregation of Christ even if it has the name a hundred times. That this is true and that the proper knowledge of Christ is that he is the true Lord and only Saviour and Redeemer and that this is the basis of the Christian gathering, the Scriptures confirm in abundance.... It is necessary to remain on this foundation. That we adhere solely to the words of Christ and do his will, to this he himself witnesses when he said to his disciples: If you keep my words you are truly my disciples, and again: You are my friends if you do what I command you. But whoever concerns himself with other teachings and commandments cannot be a disciple or friend of Christ, nor do they belong in the church of Christ. To it belong only the disciples and friends of Christ who keep his teaching and commandments. When Christ sent out his apostles to gather his church he spoke to them and gave them this commandment: Go and teach all nations, baptize them in the name of the Father, the Son, and the Holy Ghost, and teach them to observe everything that I have commanded you. The first teaching is that they present to them the basics of God's will in Christ. If then they accept the teaching and wish to become disciples of Christ they shall baptize them so that they may put on Christ and be incorporated in his holy church. Finally, in order that they may remain friends of Christ, the ones baptized should be taught everything that Christ commanded. All this can be clearly seen in the apostolic writings. Behold, this is the true church of Christ from the beginning and still is. For although many others claim to be the church of Christ, as for example the anti-Christian papal crowd do, it is a vain claim. Not all that glistens is gold.[2]

A crucial issue in the Reformation was whether the church was visible or invisible. Luther, with his emphasis on justification by faith, held that the true church was invisible. Dirk Philips explained why he, and other Anabaptists, held that the true church was visible even though in a sense it was invisible because it exists in spirit and in truth.

> The church of the Lord, although existing in spirit and in truth, is nevertheless also visible, as I explained in my book on The Sending of Preachers, and still declare. The reasons are as follows: 1. The name church or congregation indicates that it is not only invisible, but also visible, for the term used is ecclesia, that is, a gathering or congregating together, and he who addresses the congregation is Ecclesiastes. Hence Solomon is called Ecclesiastes, because he spoke to the congregation or church of Israel. Now, it is certain and incontrovertible that as Solomon was, as a preacher, visible, so the church also was visible to whom he addressed his words. 2. Christ Jesus himself chose his apostles (Jn. 15:16), and gathered them together as a church, and was not always invisible in Jerusalem and Judea. 3. The apostles, according to the command of the Lord, through the preaching of the gospel, in faith and truth, and by proper Christian baptism, and the power and unity of the Holy Spirit, gathered a church (Mt. 28; Mk. 16). This was not an invisible body, for they did not write nor send their epistles in a general or indiscriminate way to all people, but specifically denominating the believer and God-fearing people, designating the places and calling many persons by name. How is it possible for all this to be invisible?[3]

Another issue in the Reformation concerned the marks of the true church. Luther's two marks of the true church were "the preaching of the gospel" and "the right administration of the sacraments." This definition says very little about the nature of church membership and does not assume an important role for the laity. The Anabaptist concept of the church as a community of believers stood in sharp contrast to the Lutheran view. This is why Anabaptist writers frequently addressed the issue.

In his "Reply to Gellius Faber," Menno Simons stated in summary form his understanding of the church and signs of the true church.

> *Question. What is the church of Christ?*
> *Answer.* A community of saints.
>
> *Q. With whom did she originate?*
> A. With Adam and Eve.
>
> *Q. Of whom is she?*
> A. Of God through Christ.

Q. Of what kind of servants is she begotten?
A. Of those who are irreproachable in doctrine and life.

Q. Whereby do they beget her?
A. By the Spirit and Word of God.

Q. To what purpose do they beget her?
A. That she may serve, thank, and praise God.

Q. Of what mind is she?
A. In her weakness, of Christ's mind.

Q. What kind of fruits does she bring forth?
A. Fruits which are conformable to the Word of God.

The True Signs by Which the Church of Christ May Be Known.
   I. By an unadulterated, pure doctrine. Deut. 4:6; 5:12; Isa. 8:5; Matt. 28:20; Mark 16:15; John 8:52; Gal. 1.
  II. By a Scriptural use of the sacramental signs. Matt. 28:19; Mark 16; Rom. 6:4; Col. 2:12; I Cor. 12:13; Mark 14:22; Luke 22:19; I Cor. 11:22, 23.
 III. By obedience to the Word. Matt. 7; Luke 11:28; John 7:18; 15:10; Jas. 1:22.
  IV. By unfeigned, brotherly love. John 13:34; Rom. 13:8; I Cor. 13:1; I John 3:18; 4:7, 8.
   V. By a bold confession of God and Christ. Matt. 10:32: Mark 8:29; Rom. 10:9; I Tim. 6:13.
  VI. By oppression and tribulation for the sake of the Lord's Word. Matt. 5:10; 10:39; 16:24; 24:9; Luke 6:28; John 15:20; II Tim. 2:9; 3:12; I Pet. 1:6; 3:14; 4:13; 5:10; I John 3:13.[4]

Contemporary Writings

Today an increasing number of church leaders are presenting a community view of the church and are calling church members to make this view a reality. Jim Wallis sees community as the New Testament plan.

Community is the great assumption of the New Testament. From the calling of the disciples to the inauguration of the church at Pentecost, the gospel of the kingdom drives the believers to community. The new order becomes real in the context of a shared life. Throughout the book of Acts and in the epistles, the church is presented as a community. The community life of the first Christians attracted many to their fellowship.

The preaching of the gospel is intended to create a new family in which those alienated from one another are now made brothers and sisters in Jesus Christ. "There is neither Jew nor Greek, there is neither slave nor free, there is neither male nor female; for you are all one in Jesus Christ" (Gal. 3:28). The existence of the church itself, that inclusive community which knows no human boundaries, becomes a part of the good news.

When we understand that community is the form of the church's life in the New Testament, the letters of Paul take on a clearer meaning than ever before. Reading them in the context of Christian community illuminates their message. [5]

David Watson also sees community as the concept of the church envisioned by Christ and Watson is calling for a return to that pattern.

We live in an age of personal insignificance, and great loneliness. More than ever the church needs to recapture the priority of community in Christian discipleship. In his three years of intimate relationship with his disciples, Jesus gave us the model for the church. He loved his disciples, cared for their needs, taught them, corrected them, stimulated their faith, instructed them concerning the kingdom of God, sent them out in his name, encouraged them, listened to them, watched them, guided them; and he told them to do the same for each other. The church which rediscovers something of the God-given quality of such a sharing community will speak with great relevance, credibility, and spiritual power to the world of today. The church, wrote Paul, is "built upon the foundation of the apostles and prophets, Christ Jesus himself being the chief cornerstone." Although Jesus taught his disciples many truths concerning the kingdom of God, he wanted them most of all to know him. This is the meaning of eternal life. In their corporate life together they came to know him who is the life, and only with that background were they able to share that life— his life—with others. The word "know" that is used for phrases like "knowing God" or "knowing Jesus Christ" is the same word that is used for a man knowing his wife. It speaks of the intimacy of a deep, personal union. For them to achieve such intimate knowledge, Jesus called his disciples into a living, loving community. He saw this as a top priority as he began building his church. [6]

Howard Snyder adds his voice to those calling for the church to return to the reality of community. Commenting on this theme, he wrote:

Unfortunately, we don't have an adequate English equivalent of New Testament *koinonia*. "Fellowship" doesn't do it; "community" is subject to misunderstanding; "communion" is a possibility, but most people associate that with the Lord's Supper. I use community to mean the church as the body of Christ, the family of God. It means building up the church so that the figures, "the body of Christ," "the family of God," "the household of faith," become sociologically real. We actually do become that kind of fellowship in the way we relate together in the church. *Koinonia* means "shared life," not only in our spiritual lives, but also in our social and economic relationships. How this works out will vary from church to church.[7]

Journaling Focus

Day One: Read the *Biblical Teachings* section and Ephesians 2:1-22. How do you respond to the five points by Harold Bender? Would you add points to the list?

Day Two: What expressions of community have you experienced in your congregation? What expressions have you desired that were not present?

Day Three: As you reflect on the Anabaptist and contemporary writings, do you find yourself in agreement? Please explain.

Spiritual Exercise: Meditation

In recent years, meditation (holding in one's mind a biblical teaching or image) has become an acceptable and desirable religious exercise. Practices associated with Eastern religions such as yoga and transcendental meditation have received broad promotion. Many Christian leaders warn against such practices because of questionable religious assumptions and failure to build community. Instead, they are attempting to revive the biblical practice of meditation on the Scriptures. What is behind the renewed interest in meditation? The answer likely includes our fast pace of living, our rational approach to religious faith, and our shallow spiritual level.

In Bible reading, we focus on an extended passage, perhaps several chapters. In meditation, we focus on a much smaller portion of Scripture, perhaps several verses or even one word. The purpose of meditation is to absorb truth into our minds and hearts. It is to both grasp and appropriate spiritual food. Andrew Murray described meditation as follows:

It is in meditation that the heart holds and appropriates the Word. Just as in reflection the understanding grasps all the meaning of a truth, so in meditation the heart assimilates it and makes it a part of its own life. We need continual reminding that the heart means the will and the affection. The meditation of the heart implies desires, acceptance, surrender, love. What the heart truly believes, that it receives with love and joy, and allows to master and rule the life. The intellect gathers and prepares the food upon which we are to feed. In meditation the heart takes it in and feeds on it.[8]

Dietrich Bonhoeffer offers the following helpful insight.

It is not necessary that we should discover new ideas in our meditation. Often this only diverts us and feeds our vanity. It is sufficient if the Word, as we read and understand it, penetrates and dwells within us. As Mary "pondered in her heart" the things that were told by the shepherds, as what we have casually overheard follows us for a long time, sticks in our mind, occupies, disturbs, or delights us, without our ability to do anything about it, so in meditation God's Word seeks to enter in and remain with us. It strives to stir us, to work and operate in us, so that we shall not get away from it the whole day long. Then it will do its work in us, often without our being conscious of it.[9]

Day Four: Identify new insights concerning meditation. Then spend ten to fifteen minutes meditating on 1 Peter 2:9-10. Find a quiet place and read these verses slowly, reflectively, repeatedly, and prayerfully. Allow the truths to speak to your own life. Listen to God's message to you. Then journal that message.

Day Five: In your general journaling, you may want to reflect on your most deeply felt need and whether it would be met if the church were truly a community of believers.

Discipling Session

Many Christians express interest in meditation, but few have developed the ability to meditate meaningfully. Also there are various approaches to meditation and some will be more meaningful to you than others. Approaches that are not useful to you may be helpful to others. It is therefore important that a discipler be aware of various methods and be able to explain them to others.[10]

In the group session, there will be opportunity to discuss the methods and meaning of meditation.

1. Share with your discipling partner your responses to the journaling exercises on *Day One* and *Day Two*.

2. As a total group, share your responses to *Day Three*. Then describe your experience in meditation. How did you go about doing it? What benefits did you receive? What difficulties did you encounter? Help each other with the difficulties encountered by suggesting some other approach or identifing the reason for the difficulty.

3. Desired Discipling Skill: ability to understand and practice meditation. Hearing the meditation experiences of others will enlarge your understanding and challenge your own practice.

Lesson 10

Christ Among His People

Discipleship Theme: The Church, the Body of Christ

The nature of the church parallels the nature of Christ. Christ was both God and man, human and divine. The church also is both human and divine.

In the last lesson, we focused on the human side of the church, a people living together in community. In this lesson, we will focus on the divine side of the church, "the body of Christ" (1 Cor. 12:27). Actually there are many additional terms which describe the nature of the church. Paul S. Minear has identified over eighty images and analogies to the church recorded in the New Testament.[1] However, the concepts of community and body are two of the most central.

Biblical Teachings

The term "body" is used exclusively by Paul. In addition, he uses two additional figures related to the body, namely, the head of the body and members of the body. These phrases identify and relate both the human and the divine aspects of the larger body concept.

Harold S. Bender has observed that the phrase "body of Christ" speaks to the centrality of Christ in and to the life of the church.[2] It was the Christ event that initiated the church, but the church continues to be wholly dependent on Christ as its source of life. It is for this reason that Paul warns against those "not holding fast to the Head, from whom the whole body, nourished and knit together through its joints and ligaments, grows with a growth that is from God" (Col. 2:19).

The close and intimate relationship between Christ and the church is further expressed in the Pauline terms "in Christ" and "Christ in us." God acted to create a people and Christ dwells in them making them members of his body. It thus becomes clear that "being a Christian means being in Christ; there is no Christian outside of Christ; there is no church outside of Christ."[3] No doubt Paul had in mind the centrality of Christ in the church and for the church when he wrote, "For no other foundation can any one lay than that which is laid, which is Jesus Christ" (1 Cor. 3:11).

The atoning act of Christ and our response of faith unites us to Christ, producing the body of Christ, the church. As members of his body, we are related to him and interwoven with other body members.

> Our solidarity with Christ in His body is not basically one of intellect or of feeling, but of will. His will becomes ours. As He always did the will of the Father, so our will becomes to do the will of the Father. This means that the relationship we here speak of is not so much a passive one of status as an active one of function. It produces a mood of joy, but it is the joy not only of reception but also of participation, joy not just of the peace which flows from forgiveness, but also of partnership in a cause. Thus, the entire church as His body becomes the instrument of His operation in the world, the channel of His grace and saving work. The awareness of this calling, and the experience of God's working in us produces ineffable joy.[4]

The concept of the body of Christ helps us to understand the promise of Jesus when he said, "Again I say to you, if two of you agree on earth about anything they ask, it will be done for them by my Father in heaven. For where two or three are gathered in my name, there am I in the midst of them" (Mt. 18:19-20). It is impossible to have the body of Christ apart from the presence of Christ. And the presence of Christ is found in his body, the church. When believers meet in Jesus' name, he is there in his presence and in his position as Head of the church.

Anabaptist Writings

Matthew 18:15-20 was a central passage for the Anabaptists. It reflected their view of the church and of life in the church. Christ was present among his people making them his body. They were to be his body, not only in name, but also in quality of life.

Pilgram Marpeck and Caspar Schwenckfeld held different points of view on the presence of Christ in the world. Schwenckfeld taught about Christ's spiritual presence; Marpeck emphasized Christ's presence in the church. Marpeck received correspondence from a follower of Schwenckfeld which reflected his spiritualist views. In his reply, Marpeck wrote the following:

> You further write that you know of no gathered congregation, or church of Christ, which assembles outwardly in the name of the Lord, in His divine strength and Spirit. You should also say that, while you believe in a holy Christian church, and you truly know it is also on earth, it is dispersed in distress. We agree with you, but add that the church of Christ does not come, nor should it be expected to come, with regard to numbers or persons, as you believe, nor with regard to any place or any time. Christ will be with His own until the end of the world, and will not leave them orphans. And where, on this basis, two or three are gathered in His name, there He is in the midst of them. And whatever they will agree to ask of the heavenly Father in His name and according to His will, that He will do or give.[5]

In correspondence with the Swiss Brethren, Marpeck wrote:

> The true saints of God and children of Christ are those whose ruler is the Holy Spirit in the Word of truth. Where two or three are gathered in His name, He is among them. He alone rules in faith through patience and love in His own. I pray God my heavenly Father that He will not allow me to be separated from such a gathering and fellowship of the Holy Spirit, it makes no difference who they are or where they gather in the whole world. I hope to be in their fellowship and to submit myself to the rule of the Holy Spirit of Christ in the obedience of faith.[6]

Menno Simons also taught the view that Christ was present in the church. True believers were members of his body and Christ dwelt among them. In his booklet "The New Birth," he wrote:

All those who are thus born of God with Christ, who thus conform their weak life to the Gospel, thus convert themselves to follow the example of Christ, hear and believe His holy Word, follow His commandments which He in plain words commanded us in the holy Scriptures, these are the holy Christian Church which has the promise; the true children of God, brothers and sisters of Christ. For they are born with Him of one Father, they are the new Eve, the pure chaste bride. They are flesh of Christ's flesh and bone of His bone, the spiritual house of Israel, the spiritual city Jerusalem, the spiritual temple and Mount Zion, the spiritual ark of the Lord in which is hidden the true bread of heaven, Christ Jesus and His blessed Word, the green, blossoming rod of faith, and the spiritual tables of stone with the commandments of the Lord written on them. They are the spiritual seed of Abraham, children of the promise, in covenant with God and partakers of the heavenly blessing.[7]

Contemporary Writings

We noted in the last lesson the renewed interest in the church as community. There is also renewed interest in the church as the body of Christ. Karl Barth has said: "The church does not exist in councils and presbyteries, and certainly not in bishops, but is present and only present where two or three are gathered together in my name and thereby in the visible—visible to itself and to others—community."

Donald R. Jacobs, a Mennonite mission leader, said: "My theology of missions is based on the words of Jesus that wherever in the world 'two or three are gathered in my name,' I am present. There the body of Christ can be experienced."

In *The Community of the King,* Howard Snyder stated his understanding of the church as the body of Christ.

The Bible says the Church is nothing less than the body of Christ. It is the bride of Christ (Rev. 21:9), the flock of God (1 Pet. 5:2), the living temple of the Holy Spirit (Eph. 2:21-22). Virtually all biblical figures for the Church emphasize an essential, living, love relationship between Christ and the Church. This underscores the key role of the Church in God's plan and reminds us that "Christ loved the church and gave himself up for her" (Eph. 5:25). If the Church is the *body* of Christ—the means of the head's action in the world—then the Church is an indispensable part of the gospel, and ecclesiology is inseparable from soteriology. Therefore, to adopt what might be called an "anti-church stance" would be to dilute the very gospel itself and at the same time to demonstrate a misunderstanding of what the Bible means by "the church."[8]

Dietrich Bonhoeffer added to our understanding by bringing together the themes of community and the presence of Jesus.

> Christianity means community through Jesus Christ and in Jesus Christ. No Christian community is more or less than this. Whether it be a brief, single encounter or the daily fellowship of years, Christian community is only this. We belong to one another only through and in Jesus Christ.
>
> What does this mean? It means, first, that a Christian needs others because of Jesus Christ. It means, second, that a Christian comes to others only through Jesus Christ. It means, third, that in Jesus Christ we have been chosen from eternity, accepted in time, and united for eternity.[9]

Bonhoeffer wrote further on the meaning of these themes for brotherhood.

> In this wise does one, whom God has placed in common life with other Christians, learn what it means to have brothers. "Brethren in the Lord," Paul calls his congregation (Phil. 1:14). One is a brother to another only through Jesus Christ. I am a brother to another person through what Jesus Christ did for me and to me; the other person has become a brother to me through what Jesus Christ did for him. This fact that we are brethren only through Jesus Christ is of immeasurable significance. Not only the other person who is earnest and devout, who comes to me seeking brotherhood, must I deal with in fellowship. My brother is rather that other person who has been redeemed by Christ, delivered from his sin, and called to faith and eternal life. Not what a man is in himself as a Christian, his spirituality and piety, constitutes the basis of our community. What determines our brotherhood is what that man is by reason of Christ. Our community with one another consists solely in what Christ has done to both of us. This is true not merely at the beginning, as though in the course of time something else were to be added to our community; it remains so for all the future and to all eternity. I have community with others and I shall continue to have it only through Jesus Christ. The more genuine and the deeper our community becomes, the more will everything else between us recede, the more clearly and purely will Jesus Christ and his work become the one and only thing that is vital between us. We have one another only through Christ, but through Christ we do have one another, wholly, and for all eternity.[10]

Journaling Focus

Day One: Reflect on the *Biblical Teachings* section, including the Scriptures. Which truths are the most significant to you?

Day Two: In what ways do you experience the presence of

Christ within the body of Christ that you do not experience as an individual Christian?

Day Three: Identify any new insights from the Anabaptist and contemporary writings. How do you respond to the statement by Bonhoeffer, "I have community with others and I shall continue to have it only through Jesus Christ"?

Spiritual Exercise: Meditation

Lesson 9 introduced the concept and practice of meditation. In this lesson, we want to go a step further in understanding and practice.

In his book *Celebration of Discipline,* Richard J. Foster identifies various forms of meditation. Basic to meditation is the ability to "center down." By this is meant becoming still, entering into silence, or allowing our minds to move from fragmentation to focus. The first form is an exercise to aid in "centering down" and is called "palms down, palms up."

> Begin by placing your palms down as a symbolic indication of your desire to turn over any concerns you may have to God. Inwardly you may pray "Lord, I give to You my anger toward John. I release my fear of my dentist appointment this morning. I surrender my anxiety over not having enough money to pay the bills this month. I release my frustration over trying to find a babysitter for tonight." Whatever it is that weighs on your mind or is a concern to you, just say, "palms down." Release it. You may even feel a certain sense of release in your hands. After several moments of surrender, turn your palms up as a symbol of your desire to receive from the Lord. Perhaps you will pray silently: "Lord, I would like to receive Your divine Love for John, Your peace about the dentist appointment, Your patience, Your joy." Whatever you need, you say, "palms up." Having centered down, spend the remaining moments in complete silence. Do not ask for anything. Allow the Lord to commune with your spirit, to love you. If impressions or directions come, fine; if not, fine. [11]

Practice this exercise several times or until you are able to "center down." (Repeat "palms down, palms up" only if it is helpful.)

The history of Christian meditation takes one very quickly to the Roman Catholic Church. Meditation or contemplation has been a significant part of Roman Catholic spirituality since the time of the Desert Fathers.

Since the time of the Reformation, Roman Catholic spirituality and Anabaptist spirituality have differed significantly due to different understandings of the body of Christ. Roman Catholics view Jesus as being uniquely present in the mass. The central focus of their spirituality is the Eucharist, where Christ is concretely present. Damien Isabell points out that "private spiritual activity is considered a preparation for liturgical celebration, and private spiritual activity is seen as a vital assimilation of the liturgy."[12]

There is something powerful in this concept. It provides a focus and a significant interrelationship between private and corporate spiritual activities.

If one believes, as did the Anabaptists, that Christ was concretely present in the congregation when they met in his name, what does this say about the focus of one's spirituality? Is it possible to discover a significant relationship between your private and corporate spiritual activities if you believe that believers compose the body of Christ? I believe this is an urgent and unique challenge. Gathering in Jesus' name should become the central religious event around which other religious activities cluster. This calls for the discipling skill of relating spiritual exercises, including meditation, to congregational life.

Day Four: Ponder the question of how you can relate meditation and congregation. Then try the meditation exercise recommended by Foster giving it congregational focus by picturing Christ uniquely present in his body, the church, rather than sitting on a throne in heaven or only present in you through the Holy Spirit. Journal your experience.

Day Five: Do general journaling on whatever issue you are facing. Perhaps there is an important decision you need to make.

Discipling Session

1. Share with your discipling partner your responses to the

journaling exercises on *Day One*, *Day Two*, and *Day Three*.

2. Discuss as a total group the concept of relating private spiritual exercises and corporate spiritual life. Share your experience with the exercise on *Day Four*. Then reflect on your experience of meditation. Were you able to "center down"? What benefits did you receive? What difficulties did you experience?

3. Desired Discipling Skill: ability to relate private meditation to Christ's presence within the congregation. To achieve this skill, you need to understand the concept, experience its reality, and then help others understand and experience the concept.

Lesson 11

Believer's Baptism

Discipleship Theme: Baptism as Commitment

Biblical Teachings

During the New Testament period, the practice of baptism was clearly evident. John the Baptist began his ministry with the baptism of repentance (Mt. 3:5). Jesus, at the beginning of his ministry, was baptized by John (Mt. 3:13-15). The disciples of Jesus baptized new followers during Jesus' ministry (Jn. 4:1-2). At the close of Jesus' ministry, he commanded his disciples to make, baptize, and teach disciples in all nations (Mt. 28:18-20). The book of Acts provides abundant evidence that the command was obeyed.

The practice of baptism was evident, but what did baptism symbolize? At least four meanings can be identified.

First, baptism was a symbol of the cleansing received through the blood of Christ (Acts 22:16). The water of baptism symbolized spiritual washing. Peter spoke of baptism "as an appeal to God for a clear conscience" (1 Pet. 3:21). The spiritual washing touched not only outward sin but also the inner self, the conscience.

Second, baptism symbolized "death" to sin. In Romans 6, Paul faced the issue of the relationship of the Christian to sin. He argued that the believer who had died to sin would stop living in sin. Baptism symbolized one's identification with Christ in his death so that the believer could also be identified with Christ in

119

his resurrection. It symbolized dying to sin and walking in newness of life (Rom. 6:1-4; Col. 2:12).

Third, baptism with water symbolized baptism with the Holy Spirit. Jesus promised that his followers would receive baptism with the Holy Spirit (Acts 1:5). This promise found fulfillment among Jews (Acts 2:4), Samaritans (Acts 8:17), and Gentiles (Acts 10:44).

Finally, some have seen in 1 Peter 3:21 a reference to baptism as a covenant with God. It was an act sealing a commitment between a believer and the Master. It was a commitment of faith and obedience. This understanding was also suggested by Paul when he wrote about being "baptized into Christ" (Gal. 3:27). Baptism was also a commitment of believers to each other (Acts 2:41-47).

Anabaptist Writings

The discussion of Anabaptist writings concerning believer's baptism is brief due to the discussion in Appendix 1, pages 236-240. As you read those pages, notice the importance of baptism for the Anabaptists and the meanings they attached to it. They viewed baptism as the entrance to the church, the sign of the new covenant, the symbol of a holy, Christlike life, and the pledge of faithfulness until death. It resembled the monastic vow of poverty, chastity, and obedience.

There were two additional understandings that will be identified here and developed in later lessons. The first was their view of "three types of baptism." These included the Spirit given internally in response to faith, water given externally in response to one's confession of faith before the church, and blood in martyrdom. This third type of baptism was related to their theology of martyrdom, which will be discussed later.

An additional understanding of baptism was related to the rule of Christ (Mt. 18:15-18). Balthasar Hubmaier wrote:

> In receiving water baptism, the baptizand confesses publicly that he has yielded himself to live henceforth according to the rule of Christ. In the

power of his confession he has submitted himself to the sisters, the brethren, and the church, so that they now have the authority to admonish him if he errs, to discipline, to ban, and to readmit him. . . . Whence comes this authority if not from the baptismal vow?[1]

In a later lesson, this understanding will be examined.

Contemporary Writings

The nature and meaning of baptism has again become a major issue during the past several decades. Harold S. Bender has written:

> External water baptism is a declaration of the church, in agreement with the believer, that the experience described in Romans 6 has actually occurred. The candidate for baptism must therefore be capable of making the required commitment to Christ and must openly confess that this has happened. As a rite of initiation, baptism matches the union with Christ by incorporation into the visible fellowship of believers.
> On this understanding only adult baptism is possible. The application of this ordinance to any non-responsible person destroys the New Testament meaning of the symbol. The clear New Testament evidence of this is the reason why two eminent modern theologians, the Reformed Professor Karl Barth of Basel, and the Anglican Dom Gregory Dix, have both declared in recent years, the former in 1943 and the latter in 1946, that believers' baptism is the only valid New Testament baptism.[2]

Lutheran theologian David P. Scaer, writing in *Christianity Today*, has stated:

> The fundamental issue in the controversy over infant baptism is essentially the same as it has always been since the Reformation. It is the question of how faith relates to baptism. The baptism of New Testament times was obviously administered in faith. And even before Luther asserted that the sacraments were ineffectual for the individual without faith in Christ, the Roman church had at least recognized the importance of faith in baptism and had tried to sidestep the issue by substituting the faith of the church for the faith apparently lacking in the child. The Reformed theologians referred to the faith of the parents or to the child's future faith in their teaching on baptism.
> All these attempts only verify what the Anabaptists contended in the days of the Reformation and what many scholars assert today about the subject. Certainly the New Testament does not explicitly state that everyone baptized had faith. But there is not one shred of evidence of the baptism of a person without faith.[3]

Scaer concludes his article by appealing for a middle way between the two positions of the baptism of believers and the baptism of infants. The middle way is the doctrine of infant faith. This is the belief that infants in fact do have faith and therefore the baptism of infants is the baptism of believers.

It appears that the central issue concerning baptism during the Reformation and today is whether the nature of baptism is linked to the nature of the church and of church membership. Ultimately, the nature of the church and of church membership does seem to determine the nature of baptism. Does church membership involve congregational commitment or only faith in Christ? The Anabaptists viewed baptism as a commitment to God and to other believers.

Journaling Focus

Day One: Of the four meanings of baptism identified in the biblical teachings section, which had relevance for you when you were baptized? How have your understandings changed since baptism?

Day Two: As you reflected on the Anabaptist and contemporary discussions of baptism, what new insights did you receive?

Day Three: What are the key issues for you regarding believer's baptism versus infant baptism?

Day Four: Instead of doing general journaling today, review your general journaling in the past ten lessons. Look for insights that may help you decide the focus of future general journaling exercises.

Spiritual Exercise: Meditation

In the last lesson, reference was made to the various forms of meditation identified by Richard J. Foster and the importance of being able to "center down." The first form of meditation was described and experienced. With this lesson, the second form of meditation will be described. The purpose of this form is to further develop one's ability to center down.

Another meditation aimed at centering oneself begins by concentrating on breathing. Having seated yourself comfortably, slowly become conscious of your breathing. This will help you to get in touch with your body and indicate to you the level of tension within. Inhale deeply, slowly tilting your head back as far as it will go. Then exhale, allowing your head slowly to come forward until your chin nearly rests on your chest. Do this for several moments, praying inwardly something like this: "Lord, I exhale my fear over my geometry exam, I inhale Your peace. I exhale my spiritual apathy, I inhale Your light and life." Then, as before, become silent outwardly and inwardly. Be attentive to the inward living Christ. If your attention wanders to the letter that must be dictated, or the windows that need to be cleaned, "exhale" the matter into the arms of the Master and draw in His divine breath of peace. Then listen once again.

At the end of each meditation, close with a genuine expression of thanksgiving.[4]

After you are able to center down and become quiet inwardly and outwardly, then add a brief period of meditation on a scriptural passage or truth. At the beginning, five minutes may be long enough. As the practice of meditation becomes more familiar, the length of time will likely increase.

As you continue to practice meditation, it would be well to remember the warning of Dietrich Bonhoeffer. He wrote:

Above all, it is not necessary that we should have any unexpected, extraordinary experiences in meditation. This can happen, but if it does not, it is not a sign that the meditation period has been useless. Not only at the beginning, but repeatedly, there will be times when we feel a great spiritual dryness and apathy, an aversion, even an inability to meditate. We dare not be balked by such experiences. Above all, we must not allow them to keep us from adhering to our meditation period with great patience and fidelity.[5]

(For more information on meditation read the full discussion in *Celebration of Discipline* by Richard J. Foster.)

Day Five: For your meditation period, select some fresh insight related to baptism and focus on it quietly, reflectively, and prayerfully. Allow that truth to penetrate your being.

Discipling Skill: Teaching Meditation

Meaningful meditation may be easy to explain but difficult to practice. It involves quieting one's inner being and focusing one's attention on a Scripture or truth. Both of these requirements will be difficult to achieve if they are new for you.

We learn about meditation through personal experience and through learning from others. It is therefore helpful to talk with others who practice meditation and to learn from their insights. This experience will be a part of the group activity.

1. Share with your discipling partner your responses to the journaling exercise on *Day One* and *Day Two*.

2. The total group should reflect on baptism as commitment. Also, they may want to discuss *Day Three*. Then discuss their experiences of meditation. Have the group describe their efforts at centering by concentrating on breathing, their ability to achieve outward and inward silence, and their ability to focus on a biblical truth. Discuss the problems encountered and the benefits gained. As your own questions are answered and your difficulties overcome, you will be developing the discipling skill of teaching others to meditate.

3. The group leader may direct the group in a meditation experience as a part of the learning process.

4. Desired Discipling Skill: ability to teach meditation to others. Learning about meditation through our own experience and the experiences of others prepares us to lead others into the experience of meditation.

Lesson 12

Communion and Community

Discipleship Theme: The Lord's Supper

Baptism and communion are two major ordinances of the apostolic church. In Lesson 11 we noticed that baptism symbolizes at least four different truths. Also, we noticed various approaches to baptism such as believer's baptism and infant baptism. In this lesson, we will identify the symbolisms of the communion emblems and the central meanings of the communion service.

Biblical Writings

The two communion emblems each symbolize several truths. The bread represents Christ's broken body (Mt. 26:26), our participation in the body of Christ (1 Cor. 10:16), and the unity of the body (1 Cor. 10:17). The fruit of the vine symbolizes the blood of Christ "poured out for many for the forgiveness of sins" (Mt. 26:28) and the new covenant inaugurated by Christ's death (Mt. 26:28; 1 Cor. 11:25).

In that it is to be observed in remembrance of Christ's death, the Lord's Supper is a memorial occasion (1 Cor. 11:24-25). Just as the Passover meal reminded the Jews of their deliverance from bondage in Egypt, so also the Lord's Supper reminds Christians of their deliverance from the bondage of sin through the death of Christ.

Since it is to be observed "until he comes," the Lord's Supper is also a prophetic occasion (1 Cor. 11:26). This special "meal" finds its fulfillment in the marriage supper of the Lamb (Rev. 19:9). When Christ and his bride, the church, are united for eternity, the need for the Lord's Supper will have ceased.

In addition, the Lord's Supper is a celebration of the oneness and unity of brothers and sisters in Christ (1 Cor. 10:17). Many grains of wheat are brought together to become "one bread." The concepts of one bread and one body speak of the oneness and unity of Christ's followers.

Anabaptist Writings

The Anabaptists placed a major emphasis on baptism and the Lord's Supper, both of which were given a strong communal interpretation. Their concern was not proper liturgical form but actual heart and life experience.

Pages 257 and 258 of Appendix I should be read as a part of this discussion of the Anabaptist perspective on the Lord's Supper. The "Congregational Order" developed by Michael Sattler called for the Lord's Supper to be held as often as they were together. The purpose was to proclaim the Lord's death and to encourage members to give their lives for each other as Christ had given his life for them.

The Schleitheim Confession also assumed the frequent observance of the breaking of the bread and the unity of those who participated. It reads as follows:

III. Concerning the breaking of bread, we have become one and agree thus: all those who desire to break the one bread in remembrance of the broken body of Christ and all those who wish to drink of one drink in remembrance of the shed blood of Christ, they must beforehand be united in the one body of Christ, that is the congregation of God, whose head is Christ, and that by baptism. For as Paul indicates, we cannot be partakers at the same time of the table of the Lord and the table of devils. Nor can we at the same time partake and drink of the cup of the Lord and the cup of devils. That is: all those who have fellowship with the dead works of darkness have no part in the light. Thus all who follow the devil and the world, have no part with those who have been called out of the world unto God. All those who lie in evil have no part in the good.

So it shall and must be, that whoever does not share the calling of the one God to one faith, to one baptism, to one spirit, to one body together with all the children of God, may not be made one loaf together with them, as must be true if one wishes truly to break bread according to the command of Christ.[1]

Balthasar Hubmaier wrote extensively on the theme of the Lord's Supper. He viewed it as a testimony of love which one member had for another. Furthermore, he saw it as a public token that each would offer their body and blood for the other just as Christ offered his body and blood for them. Hubmaier wrote a liturgy entitled "The Congregation Celebrates the Lord's Supper." As you read the liturgy, notice that the central part relates to their corporate life. Communion helped build community.

(Confession)
Father, we have sinned against heaven and against you.
We are not worthy to be called your children.
But speak the consoling word and our souls shall be healed.
God be gracious to us sinners.

(Absolution)
May the almighty, eternal, and merciful God have compassion on all our sins and graciously forgive them.
Having pardoned us,
May He lead us without blemish or impurity into eternal life.
Through Jesus Christ our Lord and Savior, Amen.

(Pledge of love)
Brothers and sisters: Do you will, in the power of his holy and living Word, to love God in and above all things, to serve, honor, and worship Him alone, henceforth to hallow His name, to subject your carnal and sinful will to His divine will, which He has called forth within you through His living Word, in life and death? If so, let each say,
I WILL.

Do you will to love your neighbor, to accomplish toward him the works of brotherly love, to offer your flesh and shed your blood for him, to be obedient according to the will of God to father, mother and government, doing this in the power of our Lord Jesus Christ, who also offered His flesh and shed His blood for us? Let each say,
I WILL

Do you will to exercise fraternal admonition toward your brothers and sisters, foster peace and unity among them, reconcile yourself with all those whom you have offended, renounce all envy, hatred, and evil will toward anyone, cease every practice which may harm or offend, love even your enemies, and do them good? Let each say,
I WILL.

Do you desire, by eating and drinking the bread and wine of the Supper of Christ, to confirm and attest publicly before the church the pledge of love which you have just spoken, in the power of the living memory of the suffering and death of Jesus Christ our Lord? If so, let each say,
I SO DESIRE IN THE POWER OF GOD.

(Institution)
The Lord Jesus, on the night of His arrest, took bread.
After giving thanks to God, he broke it and said:
This is my body, which is for you.
Do this as a memorial of me.
In the same way, He took the cup after supper, and said:
This cup is the new covenant sealed by my blood.
Whenever you drink it,
Do this as a memorial of me.[2]

Pilgram Marpeck also viewed the commemoration of the Lord's body as the bond of love in which the Lord keeps his own children in the unity of faith.[3]

Menno Simons described his view of the true Supper of the Lord with its symbolism and mystery. He likewise emphasized the unity of the body or being one bread.

Similarly we believe and confess concerning the Lord's holy Supper that it is a holy sacramental sign, instituted of the Lord himself in bread and wine, and left to his disciples in remembrance of him. Mt. 26; Mk. 14; Lk. 22; 1 Cor. 11. It was also taught and administered as such by the apostles among the brethren, according to the commandment of the Lord, in which in the first place the Lord's death is proclaimed. 1 Cor. 11. And it also serves as a remembrance how he offered his holy flesh and shed his precious blood for the remission of our sins. Mt. 26:27; Mk. 14:24; Lk. 22:19.

Second, it is an emblem of Christian love, of unity, and of peace in the church of Christ. Paul says, For we, being many, are one bread and one body; for we are all partakers of that one bread. 1 Cor. 10:17. For as a loaf being composed of many grains is but one bread; so we also being composed of many members are but one body in Christ. And as the members of a natural body are not disharmonious, but are altogether united and at one among themselves; so it is with all those who are in Spirit and faith true members of the body of Christ. For this reason this same Supper was called by Tertullian a brotherly meal or love feast.

Third, it is a communion of the flesh and blood of Christ. As Paul says, The cup of blessing which we bless, is it not the communion of the blood of Christ? The bread which we break, is it not the communion of the body of Christ? I Cor. 10:16. This communion consists in the fact that Christ has accepted us in his great love, and we are become partakers of him. As Paul says, We are made partakers of Christ, if we hold the beginning of our confidence steadfast unto the end. Heb. 3:14.

Since it is a sign of such force which is left of Christ, that it is to represent and admonish us of his death, the love, peace, and unity of the brethren, and also the communion of his flesh and blood as was said, therefore none can rightly partake of this Supper except he be a disciple of Christ, flesh of his flesh, and bone of his bone, who seeks the forgiveness of sins in no other means than in the merits, sacrifice, death, and blood of Christ alone; who walks in unity, love, and peace with his brethren, and who leads a pious, unblamable life in Christ Jesus, according to the Scriptures.

Here you have the true Supper of our Lord Jesus Christ with its symbolism and mystery briefly stated, which the mouth of the Lord has left and taught you by his holy Word. If you would be a proper guest at the Lord's table and would rightly partake of his bread and wine, then you must also be his true disciple, that is, you must be an upright, pious, and godly Christian. Therefore prove yourself according to the doctrine of Paul before you eat of this bread and drink of this cup, for before God no feigning counts. He did not institute this ceremony as though mere bread, wine, and eating are pleasing to him. Oh, no. He has left this sacrament with you in order that you might by it faithfully observe and carefully conform yourself to the mystery represented by this sign or sacrament. For not the ceremony itself but the matter represented by it, if rightly understood and fulfilled in actions, constitutes a sincere Christian.[4]

For the Anabaptists the communion service became a powerful expression of their new identity as the body of Christ, the people of God in whom Christ was present. This realization called them to unity, love, sacrifice, and purity. It was a significant factor in nurturing their spirituality. Communion was a time to cultivate and nurture their sense of being the body of Christ, the community of God's people.

Contemporary Writings

Among renewal movements today, two developments are almost uniform. First, the Lord's Supper has taken on fresh meaning. Sometimes this means observing communion more frequently. It usually means seeing a clearer relationship between the communion service and their daily lives or ministry. Second, the Lord's Supper speaks to their common life together, not merely to their private Christian lives. Communion and community become closely related.

Dietrich Bonhoeffer saw the way in which preparation for communion served the Christian community. He wrote:

> Though it is true that confession is an act in the name of Christ that is complete in itself and is exercised in the fellowship as frequently as there is desire for it, it serves the Christian community especially as a preparation for the common reception of the holy Communion. Reconciled to God and men, Christians desire to receive the body and blood of Jesus Christ. It is the command of Jesus that none should come to the altar with a heart that is unreconciled to his brother. If this command of Jesus applies to every service of worship, indeed, to every prayer we utter, then it most certainly applies to reception of the Lord's Supper.[5]

Jim Wallis has described the central place now given to communion at the Sojourners community and what that religious service symbolizes for them. He writes:

> This need and desire to live as God's people has greatly affected the evolution of worship in Sojourners community. The celebration of the Lord's Supper has gradually moved to the center of our corporate life, despite the fact that many of us come from church backgrounds where communion was not often observed. Regardless of religious training, the experience of Christian community seems to create fellowships where the celebration of the eucharist is central. The eucharist graphically reminds us of what Christ has done for us. Communion roots us in the love of Christ. At the table, we are reminded of that love, which is the very basis of our life together. The eucharist is the drama of remembering who we are as God's people. Jesus says, "Do this in remembrance of me." Why are we told to eat this bread and drink this wine over and over again? Because we are so forgetful. We need to be reminded again and again.
> Christian community is the arena in which we learn the way of the cross, experience vulnerability, and see the path for the church's future. Our life together and the offering of it for the world will teach us, often painfully, the meaning of Jesus' way. The eucharist stands in the center of our community life to picture all that for us, to explain what we are experienc-

ing and why, to assure us that what we now experience is a part of God's plan, and to remind us that this is the way the world will be saved. The eucharist is for our sake, and we desperately need it. It becomes a place of anguish, where the pain of letting go is deeply felt; a place of great joy and thanksgiving as we recognize what God has done and is doing among us; a place that absorbs our hate and heals our fears; a place that sets us free to give our lives away boldly for the sake of the kingdom.[6]

Journaling Focus

Day One: Reflect on the biblical writings, including the Scriptures, and identify what is for you the most significant symbolism of the Lord's Supper. Explain your choice.

Day Two: From the Anabaptist and contemporary writings, what new insights did you receive concerning communion and community? What questions emerged?

Day Three: Bonhoeffer refers to confession as a preparation for communion. The Anabaptists stressed being one body before partaking in communion. What meaningful approaches to preparation for communion have you experienced?

Spiritual Exercise: Praying the Psalms

The spiritual exercises of the past several lessons have focused on meditation. Most of us find meditation moving us toward prayer. After meditation on the truths of Scripture, it is easy and natural for these truths to direct our prayers. Dietrich Bonhoeffer takes this reality one step further by recommending that we pray the Psalms.

In his excellent book, *Psalms: the Prayer Book of the Bible,* Bonhoeffer points out that Jesus Christ wants us to pray with him and he wants to pray with us. Praying in the name of Jesus means, among other things, that we pray the prayers of Jesus. How is this possible? "In the Psalms of David," says Bonhoeffer, "the promised Christ himself already speaks (Hebrews 2:12; 10:5) or, as may also be indicated, the Holy Spirit (Hebrews 3:7). These same words which David spoke, therefore, the future Messiah spoke through him. The prayers of David were prayed also by Christ. Or better, Christ himself prayed them through his forerunner David."[7]

When we pray the Psalms, we are therefore praying the prayers of Jesus or praying in Jesus' name. Furthermore, the prayers of Christ for his church are being prayed. As the church unites in praying the Psalms, the prayers of Christ for the church continue to be uttered by the body of Christ. The Psalms should therefore be viewed as prayers for individuals and for the whole church.

Bonhoeffer reveals the richness of the Psalms for prayer and learning prayer when he writes:

> If we want to read and to pray the prayers of the Bible and especially the Psalms, therefore, we must not ask first what they have to do with us, but what they have to do with Jesus Christ. We must ask how we can understand the Psalms as God's Word, and then we shall be able to pray them. It does not depend, therefore, on whether the Psalms express adequately that which we feel at a given moment in our heart. If we are to pray aright, perhaps it is quite necessary that we pray contrary to our own heart. Not what we want to pray is important, but what God wants us to pray. If we were dependent entirely on ourselves, we would probably pray only the fourth petition of the Lord's Prayer. But God wants it otherwise. The richness of the Word of God ought to determine our prayer, not the poverty of our heart.[8]

Day Four: Praying the Psalms is a refreshing spiritual exercise and all the Psalms can be prayed with profit. However, for this exercise, I would recommend that you pray Psalm 22. This psalm brings together the themes of the sufferings of Christ and worshiping with the great congregation. (Christ quoted from this psalm on the cross.) Pray this psalm reflectively. It will be good preparation for communion and community.

Day Five: Let your general journaling this week reflect what you discovered as you reviewed your journaling last week.

Discipling Session

The disciples asked Jesus to teach them to pray. Since that

day followers of Jesus are still asking to be taught how to pray. How can they be taught?

Bonhoeffer suggests that the Psalms are a great school of prayer. Why? Because they teach prayer based on the Word of God; they teach the scope of prayer; and they teach us to pray as a fellowship.[9]

As you learn about prayer by praying the Psalms and learn from others who also are praying the Psalms, you will be developing the skill of teaching others to pray.

1. Share with your discipling partner your responses to the journaling exercise on *Day One* and *Day Two*.

2. Discuss as a total group your response to *Day Three*. Then share your experience in praying the Psalms. What did you learn about prayer? What do you want to learn about prayer that you might be able to learn as you pray the Psalms? How do you see Christian community being nurtured through praying the Psalms?

3. Desired Discipling Skill: ability to teach others to pray the Psalms. Teaching others to pray the Psalms primarily involves experiencing the benefits of this practice and sharing your discoveries with others. It is teaching through testimony.

Lesson 13

Admonish One Another

Discipleship Theme: Fraternal Admonition

In Lesson 11, we examined the concept of baptism as a commitment and testimony to a renewed life in Christ. Baptism also involved a commitment to other members of the church. The new life in Christ would be lived within the body of Christ. Lesson 12 focused on one religious observance, the Lord's Supper, and its value in nurturing the body of Christ. Communion built community. Communion symbolized and nurtured growth in love and unity.

Biblical Teachings
A religious practice related to and growing out of both baptism and communion is the practice of encouraging one another to live daily one's commitment of baptism and one's witness of communion.

The New Testament conveys this concept with terms such as "encourage"[1] and "admonish."[2] The apostle Paul sent Tychicus to the churches at Ephesus and Colossae "that he may encourage your hearts" (Eph. 6:22; Col. 4:8). Paul told the church at Colossae that he was greatly striving for them "that their hearts may be encouraged" (Col. 2:2). To the believers at Thessalonica, Paul wrote: "Therefore encourage one another and build one another up, just as you are doing" (1 Thess. 5:11). He also told them to "encourage the fainthearted" (1 Thess. 5:14). The

135

ministry of encouragement was to be the ministry of all believers. This ministry is needed when one is tempted to "lose ground" or to shrink back from a commitment or standard.

Another type of ministry is identified by the term admonish. This suggests a ministry to move persons from where they presently are to new levels of understanding, commitment, and practice. The term suggests giving earnest advice. When Paul met for the last time with the elders of the church at Ephesus, he said: "Therefore be alert, remembering that for three years I did not cease night or day to admonish every one with tears" (Acts 20:31). Writing to the church at Corinth, Paul told them how he faced suffering and hardship. He reflected, "I do not write this to make you ashamed but to admonish you as my beloved children" (1 Cor. 4:14). Paul then admonished them in numerous areas of church life (1 Cor. 5—16). The church at Thessalonica was instructed "to respect those who labor among you and are over you in the Lord and admonish you" (1 Thess. 5:15).

According to Paul, the ministry of admonition was to be practiced by all believers. After instructing the Thessalonian believers to respect those who admonished them, he exhorted them to "admonish the idle" (1 Thess. 5:14). To the Colossian believers he wrote: "Let the word of Christ dwell in you richly, as you teach and admonish one another in all wisdom. . . ." (Col. 3:16).

Encouragement and admonition are expressions of the commitment made at baptism and the love for brothers and sisters symbolized by communion. The Scriptures indicate that these ministries are expected of all believers.

Anabaptist Writings

The concept and practice of fraternal admonition or brotherly admonition (fraternal and brotherly referred to both brothers and sisters) was very central for the Anabaptists. It grew out of their view of the Christian life and the nature of the church. Frequently in their writings, it was associated with the rule of Christ or binding and loosing (Mt. 18:15-18). (This use will be examined in the next lesson.) But the term also had a more general reference to the care and concern members would show for each other. This practice is one aspect of discipling.

Pages 263-265 of Appendix 1 discuss the importance the Anabaptists placed on individual members discipling each other. As you read this section, notice the statements by Michael Sattler, Pilgrim Marpeck, and Menno Simons. (They stressed admonition more than encouragement.)

Fraternal admonition was based on their understanding of the baptismal vow. Reference was made in Lesson 11 to the statement by Balthasar Hubmaier that the person receiving water baptism submits himself or herself to the sisters and brothers of the church so that they have the authority to admonish him or her if he or she errs. This view of baptism is described further in Appendix 1, pages 259-261. Notice in particular the baptismal pledge to live according to the divine Word, and that if one should fail, "he desires virtuously to receive . . . fraternal admonition."

Contemporary Writings

Few contemporary writers deal with the concept or practice of admonition. Some who focus on discipling come close to the subject. However, it is viewed as a special concern of the discipler in relation to the disciple, not the normal relationship between believers.

One writer who does speak helpfully to the subject is Dietrich Bonhoeffer. In his discussion of "The Ministry of Proclaiming," Bonhoeffer writes first concerning the spirit with which we admonish.

> What we are concerned with here is the free communication of the Word from person to person, not by the ordained ministry which is bound to a particular office, time, and place. We are thinking of that unique situation in which one person bears witness in human words to another person, bespeaking the whole consolation of God, the admonition, the kindness, and the severity of God. The speaking of that Word is beset with infinite perils. If it is not accompanied by worthy listening, how can it really be the

right word for the other person? If it is contradicted by one's own lack of active helpfulness, how can it be a convincing and sincere word? If it issues, not from a spirit of bearing and forbearing, but from impatience and the desire to force its acceptance, how can it be the liberating and healing word?[3]

Later in Bonhoeffer's discussion, he points out that the basis on which admonition takes place is Christian brotherhood which God has given the church.

The basis upon which Christians can speak to one another is that each knows the other as a sinner, who, with all his human dignity, is lonely and lost if he is not given help. This is not to make him contemptible nor to disparage him in any way. On the contrary, it is to accord him the one real dignity that man has, namely, that, though he is a sinner, he can share in God's grace and glory and be God's child. This recognition gives to our brotherly speech the freedom and candor that it needs. We speak to one another on the basis of the help we both need. We admonish one another to go the way that Christ bids us to go. We warn one another against the disobedience that is our common destruction. We are gentle and we are severe with one another, for we know both God's kindness and God's severity. Why should we be afraid of one another, since both of us have only God to fear? Why should we think that our brother would not understand us, when we understood very well what was meant when somebody spoke God's comfort or God's admonition to us, perhaps in words that were halting and unskilled? Or do we really think there is a single person in this world who does not need either encouragement or admonition? Why, then, has God bestowed Christian brotherhood upon us?[4]

The realities of Christian brotherhood, our sinfulness, and God's grace provide the basis for brotherly admonition.

Journaling Focus

Day One: Respond to the discussion of encouragement and admonition including Bonhoeffer's view of the basis of brotherly admonition. Reflect both your thoughts and feelings.

Day Two: For your general journaling you may want to reflect on your past experience with admonition, either admonishing another or being admonished. How was it approached and what was the outcome?

Spiritual Exercise: Admonition and Accountability

A spiritual exercise related to admonition is difficult to develop because there are few models to follow. In this section, I will develop a working concept and outline preparation exercises.

One approach to admonition is to begin with a comprehensive, predetermined standard or pattern of the Christian life. Persons who fall short of this pattern need admonition. Persons who practice this pattern do not need admonition. This approach also assumes that the church needs to clearly define faith and conduct, and that the church has the authority and duty to maintain its defined order. This order is maintained by preaching and direct admonition.

This approach can be maintained when members have a high commitment to community and the concept of uniformity. However, it encounters difficulty when members have a strong orientation to individualism, such as is evident in most churches today.

As was noted earlier, a discussion of admonition is strikingly absent in most contemporary writings. Furthermore, the practice of admonition is foreign to most church members. Is it possible to bring together the biblical teachings on admonition and the individualistic mood of our day?

I believe an effective model would be admonition based on accountability. This model assumes that: 1) biblical discipleship is a dynamic following of the risen Christ, not following a predefined order; 2) members of congregations are at various levels of spiritual maturity; and 3) most members live below the level of their spiritual understanding.

The model I am proposing would see the primary function of admonition as helping another Christian to clarify his or her spiritual understanding and to become accountable to live that level of knowledge through the grace and power of God. The primary task of the person doing the admonishing is to help the other person live the truth God has shown him or her, not to dictate the details of their life or to enforce a defined order.

The following exercises are intended to develop this approach to admonition.

Day Three: The concept of encouragement is more familiar than admonition so we will begin at that level. Read reflectively and prayerfully the Scriptures related to encouragement which are identified at the beginning of this lesson. Journal your response to these Scriptures. Then identify a person or persons you know who need encouragement. Pray for them and then speak or write an encouraging word.

Day Four: Identify an area in your own life where you know that your practice is below your spiritual understanding. Reflect on why this gap exists. What type of admonition would you respond to? What type of admonition would you give another person with a similar "life gap?" Journal your reactions to this reflective process.

Day Five: Read carefully and prayerfully the Scriptures related to admonition which are discussed at the beginning of this lesson. Journal your interaction with these Scriptures. Identify a person you know whom you believe needs to be admonished. Begin praying for that person.

Discipling Session

In this group session you will focus on your attitude toward giving and receiving admonition and will begin developing the skill of admonishing another person.

1. Share with the total group your feelings about the concepts of encouragement and admonition reflected in your journaling on *Day One* and the approach promoted in this lesson. Are your feelings negative or positive? Why?

2. Share with your discipling partner an area of your own life where there is a gap between your spiritual understanding and your level of living (*Day Four*). Invite the other person to "admonish" you and help you become accountable to God and another person in that area which needs growth.

3. Continue praying for the person identified on *Day Five* whom you believe God would have you to admonish. Pray for God's timing, wisdom, and guidance.

4. Desired Discipling Skill: ability to give constructive admonition. It is relatively easy to admonish but difficult to admonish constructively. Constructive admonition requires the proper spirit as mentioned by Bonhoeffer and experience.

Lesson 14

Moral Discernment

Discipleship Theme: Binding and Loosing

Lesson 13 discussed the concept of admonition and referred to its relationship to the rule of Christ or binding and loosing (Mt. 18:15-18). This lesson will examine the Matthew 18 passage and observe the way in which it moves beyond the level of admonition to moral discernment and either confession and forgiveness or discipline. The passage reads as follows:

Biblical Teaching

> If your brother sins against you, go and tell him his fault, between you and him alone. If he listens to you, you have gained your brother. But if he does not listen, take one or two others along with you, that every word may be confirmed by the evidence of two or three witnesses. If he refuses to listen to them, tell it to the church; and if he refuses to listen even to the church, let him be to you as a Gentile and a tax collector. Truly, I say to you, whatever you bind on earth shall be bound in heaven, and whatever you loose on earth shall be loosed in heaven. Matthew 18:15-18.

In the discussion of this passage, I am indebted to an article by John Howard Yoder entitled "Binding and Loosing."[1]

When Jesus used the terms "bind" and "loose," he assumed that his listeners knew the meaning of these terms. This was likely true in the first century but it is not true today.

There are two aspects to the meaning of these verbs. The first meaning relates to forgiveness. The term "bind" means to withhold fellowship. The term "loose" means to forgive. (See the parallel text in Luke 17:1-4.)

The second meaning concerns moral discernment. The term "bind" also means to forbid. The term "loose" also means to free or to permit.

These meanings reflect the use of the terms by the rabbis in Jesus' time. The rabbis decided problem cases brought to them which involved moral decisions. They had the authority to bind or loose based on their interpretation of the law. Jesus assigned this authority to his disciples (Mt. 16:19). However, in Matthew 18 the authority of moral decision-making is assigned to the entire church.

The two aspects of forgiveness and discernment flow together in practicing these instructions of Jesus. The act of forgiveness assumes that the one who sins and those who confront the one who has sinned share a common moral understanding. When there is forgiveness, the issue is not one's definition of sin but the fact of sin. The definition has already been discerned.

Furthermore, the process of reproving a brother or sister may result in a challenge to the group's understanding of morality or definition of sin. Through this process, moral understanding may be enlarged and the definition of sin clarified.

Finally, the primary reason to challenge the actions of another is concern for forgiveness and restored fellowship. When the actions of another person disrupt the fellowship between the two of you and by implication disrupt the person's fellowship with God, there is need for forgiveness. The desire for forgiveness becomes the motivation for approaching another person.

This motivation determines the method of working with the "brother." The first step of personal conversation guarantees confidentiality and stops the temptation to gossip. The second step involves a small-group effort at mediation. The values are continued confidentiality and moral testing or discernment. The final step involves the church. Here the sphere of moral discernment is enlarged. This discernment involves both moral discernment regarding the act and the spirit of the one accused. His attitude toward the discernment of the brotherhood is revealed. His desire or lack of desire for forgiveness becomes apparent. The desire for forgiveness motivates the church. The affirmation or rejection of forgiveness determines the outcome.

The response of the church to the reaction of the "brother" is to either bind or loose, and this action is recognized by God. "Whatever you bind on earth shall be bound in heaven, and whatever you loose on earth shall be loosed in heaven" (Mt. 18:18).

Anabaptist Writings

Every religious movement emphasizes certain biblical truths. Whereas Martin Luther emphasized justification by faith, the Anabaptists emphasized the Christian life as discipleship and the church as a committed body of true believers. In order to help the church be the body of Christ, they placed particular emphasis on the concept and practice of binding and loosing or moral discernment. For a brief discussion of this theme, read Appendix 1, pages 273-276. Note the unique approach to the ban by the Anabaptists as compared to the Catholics and Protestants. Note also the variation within the Anabaptist church concerning the application of Matthew 18. This variation will be expanded in the discussion which follows.

Hans Denck placed the primary value on love. Love would move one person to admonish another person if it was needed. If the admonition was rejected, that person would be avoided. This constituted the ban.

For the children of love may not for the sake of love act against love. Here all the wise need wisdom and all the friends of God need love so that they do not prefer the love of man to the love of God. For whoever loves someone, but not according to God's truth and love, hates him. But if someone hates another for the sake of divine love, he loves him more than the former. But for the sake of love one may not hate another beyond earnestly admonishing him, and if he will not hear, to avoid him with a sorrowing heart. This is also loving in truth. Herein consists the separation of the children of God from the children of the world, and also the ban or exclusion of false brethren. This too must happen only for the sake of true love, unless indeed one wishes to deny the basis of the covenant of the children of God.[2]

Pilgram Marpeck felt that when a church had regulations about trivial matters, it violated the Christian freedom of the members. Furthermore, he believed that the law of love prevented the church from dealing harshly and hastily with weak members. Marpeck emphasized admonition rather than the ban.

> Therefore, even if one is concerned about a lapse and sees the leaves and blossoms of evil appearance, one ought to warn and admonish, but not judge, before the time of the fruit.
> The Lord does not say: "By their blossoms or leaves," but rather, "by their fruits you shall know them." For love also covers a multitude of sins (1 Pet. 4[8]) and judges all things in the best light. Even though it is concerned about evil appearances and evil fruit, it nevertheless always hopes for the best.[3]
> Even the world does not judge anyone on the basis of hearsay, suspicion, or appearance, but only on the words of the accused and of reliable witnesses. Christ also commands his own that all testimony must be substantiated by two or three witnesses. Only when evidence has been presented before the church, and he will not hear, does the judgment begin with tribulation, anxiety, sorrow. The other members of the body of Christ experience great pain and suffering for at stake is a member of the body of Christ the Lord. They must lose a member in order that the other members, who are well, are not hurt and the whole body destroyed, be it eye, foot, or hand. It should be pulled out or cut off according to the commandment of Christ, our Head: "If your eye offends you, or your hand, or foot," etc. The other members of the body of Christ will not be able to do this without great pain and tribulation. If the member is honourable and useful to the body, the tribulation is so much greater. It cannot possibly happen easily or simply. The natural body cannot lose a member without pain. Nor does it immediately cut it off, even if it is failing and weak; rather it uses all kinds of medicines. As long as it is not dead and is only painful, the body bears it with patience and longsuffering, and delays the penalty to allow for improvement. If, however, it allows the body no rest, nor improves by any medicine from the Lord Jesus Christ, through suffering and pain, it must be cut off in order that the other members of the body of Christ remain healthy in the fear and love of God and the neighbor, to whom alone the judgment to retain and to forgive sin has been committed (Mt. 16[19]; 18[15-19]; 20[23]).[4]

The Swiss Brethren emphasized admonition but also gave strong emphasis to the ban. This is evident in Article II of *The*

Schleitheim Confession (see page 274 of Appendix 1). Notice also that the ban was used primarily with communion and secondarily with excommunication. It should also be noted that the practice of the ban among the Swiss Brethren was in the form of communal discipline. That is, it was a group process rather than merely the action of the leaders. (An example of fraternal admonition appears on pages 266 and 267 of Appendix 1.)

Menno Simons emphasized admonition and the ban or excommunication but also emphasized shunning or social avoiding. In contrast to the Swiss Brethren, the Dutch placed discipline primarily in the hands of the leaders. The practice of shunning was based on Scriptures such as 1 Cor. 5:9-13. (Contemporary Mennonite scholars do not support this interpretation.)

> Dear brethren, this is the true nature and mind of the children of God, who are by grace converted in their hearts and with Christ born of God the Father. Therefore I beseech you as my sincerely beloved brethren, by the grace of God—nay, I command you with holy Paul, by the Lord Jesus Christ, who at his coming will judge the living and the dead—diligently to observe each other unto salvation, in all becoming ways teaching, instructing, admonishing, reproving, warning, and consoling each other as occasion requires, not otherwise than in accordance with the Word of God and in unfeigned love, until we increase in God and become united in faith and in the knowledge of the Son of God, into one perfect man and according to the measure of the gift of Jesus Christ. Eph. 4:7.
>
> Therefore take heed. If you see your brother sin, then do not pass him by as one that does not value his soul; but if his fall be curable, from that moment endeavor to raise him up by gentle admonition and brotherly instruction, before you eat, drink, sleep, or do anything else, as one who ardently desires his salvation, lest your poor erring brother harden and be ruined in his fall, and perish in his sin.[5]
>
> Wherefore, brethren, understand correctly, no one is excommunicated or expelled by us from the communion of the brethren but those who have already separated and expelled themselves from Christ's communion either by false doctrine or by improper conduct. For we do not want to expel any, but rather to receive; not to amputate, but rather to heal; not to discard, but rather to win back; not to grieve, but rather to comfort; not to condemn, but rather to save. For this is the true nature of a Christian brother. Whoever turns from evil, whether it be false doctrine or vain life, and conforms to the Gospel of Jesus Christ, unto which he was baptized, such a one shall not and may not be expelled or excommunicated by the brethren forever.

But those whom we cannot raise up and repentingly revive by admonition, tears, warning, rebuke, or by any other Christian services and godly means, these we should put forth from us, not without great sadness and anguish of soul, sincerely lamenting the fall and condemnation of such a straying brother; lest we also be deceived and led astray by such false doctrine which eats as does a cancer (2 Tim. 2); and lest we corrupt our flesh which is inclined to evil by the contagion. Thus we must obey the Word of God which teaches and commands us so to do; and this in order that the excommunicated brother or sister whom we cannot convert by gentle services may by such means be shamed unto repentance and made to acknowledge to what he has come and from what he is fallen. In this way the ban is a great work of love, notwithstanding it is looked upon by the foolish as an act of hatred.[6]

Methinks, beloved brethren, the Holy Spirit of God has done well, and fully performed the duties of his office, and his faithful service of divine love toward his chosen people, by admonishing, warning, teaching, and commanding, in Moses and the prophets, in Christ and the apostles, in regard to the shunning of heretics and apostates. If we through obstinacy or disobedience still associate with the leprous against the faithful counsel, teaching, and admonition of God, and intermingle with them, then we may expect to be infected with the same disease. It is the recompense of those who know the nature of the disease, and yet neither fear nor avoid it.[7]

From reviewing these various approaches to church discipline and the considerations out of which the discipline emerged, it becomes clear that the Anabaptists understood and applied Matthew 18 in light of other primary considerations. It appears that Denck and Marpeck gave primary emphasis to love and therefore focused on admonition. The Swiss Brethren viewed the practice of church discipline as the mark of the true church due to the decadence of the state church. Consequently they focused on the ban. The Dutch Anabaptists were greatly concerned about the purity of the church and therefore freely practiced excommunication and shunning. While this analysis may be simplistic I believe that it is reasonably accurate.

Contemporary Writings

Few contemporary writers use the terms "binding and loosing" or "fraternal admonition." However, some do address the realities of correction or reproof, confession, and forgiveness.

In his discussion of the marks of a spiritual leader, David Watson states:

> When giving correction, concentrate on important issues, not on trivial matters that happen to irritate us. Always we need to be positive. Paul, in his letters, repeatedly encouraged his readers with the evidence of God's grace in their lives, even when he also had hard things to say. Our world is quick to condemn and slow to encourage; so it is especially important that we speak positively about what is good. Correction should be accompanied by teaching: what went wrong, and why? How can it be avoided the next time? Even if the lesson has been taught before, we must not fight shy of repetition.
>
> The leader needs also to give clear warnings—about false teaching and teachers, about temptations and trials, about the activities of the Evil One. "Warning every man and teaching every man" was Paul's constant concern. Prevention is better than correction. Good church leaders will not be ignorant of Satan's devices.
>
> The pattern of discipline in any church has been given clearly to us by Jesus in Matthew 18:15-17. Discipline within the leadership group will follow the same guidelines. . . .[8]

It is interesting to observe Watson's assumption that correction is the task of leaders. Also, Watson refers to Matthew 18:15-17 but does not elaborate on it.

Dietrich Bonhoeffer provides a helpful understanding of brotherly reproof.

> Reproof is unavoidable. God's Word demands it when a brother falls into open sin. The practice of discipline in the congregation begins in the smallest circles. Where defection from God's Word in doctrine or life imperils the family fellowship and with it the whole congregation, the word of admonition and rebuke must be ventured. Nothing can be more cruel than the tenderness that consigns another to his sin. Nothing can be more compassionate than the severe rebuke that calls a brother back from the path of sin. It is a ministry of mercy, an ultimate offer of genuine fellowship, when we allow nothing but God's Word to stand between us, judging and succoring. Then it is not we who are judging; God alone judges, and God's judgment is helpful and healing. Ultimately, we have no charge but to serve our brother, never to set ourselves above him, and we serve him even when we must speak the judging and dividing Word of God to him, even when, in obedience to God, we must break off fellowship with him. We must know that it is not our human love which makes us loyal to the other person, but God's love which breaks its way through to him only through judgment. Just because God's Word judges, it serves the person. He who accepts the ministry of God's judgment is helped. This is the point where the limita-

tions of all human action toward our brother become apparent: "None of them can by any means redeem his brother, nor give to God a ransom for him (for the redemption of their life is costly, and it faileth for ever)" (Ps. 49:7-8, A.R.V.).[9]

The intended results of reproof are confession and forgiveness. Richard J. Foster comments on both of these responses in his discussion of "The Discipline of Confession." He writes:

> Confession is so difficult a Discipline for us partly because we view the believing community as a fellowship of saints before we see it as a fellowship of sinners. We come to feel that everyone else has advanced so far into holiness that we are isolated and alone in our sin. We could not bear to reveal our failures and shortcomings to others. We imagine that we are the only ones who have not stepped onto the high road to heaven. Therefore we hide ourselves from one another and live in veiled lies and hypocrisy.
>
> But if we know that the people of God are first a fellowship of sinners we are freed to hear the unconditional call of God's love and to confess our need openly before our brothers and sisters. We know we are not alone in our sin. The fear and pride which cling to us like barnacles cling to others also. We are sinners together. In acts of mutual confession we release the power that heals. Our humanity is no longer denied but transformed.
>
> The followers of Jesus Christ have been given the authority to receive the confession of sin and to forgive it in His name. "If you forgive the sins of any, they are forgiven; if you retain the sins of any, they are retained" (Jn. 20:23). What a wonderful privilege! Why do we shy away from such a life-giving ministry? If we, not out of merit but sheer grace, have been given the authority to set others free, how dare we withhold this great gift? "Our brother . . . has been given to us to help us. He hears the confession of our sins in Christ's stead and he forgives our sins in Christ's name. He keeps the secret of our confession as God keeps it. When I go to my brother to confess, I am going to God."[10]

Journaling Focus

Day One: Reflect on the various understandings of the focus of Matthew 18:15-18. Which focus is nearest to your own understanding? Read all of Matthew 18, looking for the primary theme. Is it confession, forgiveness, excommunication, or some other theme? Journal your answer and its importance for applying verses 15-18.

Day Two: Reflect on your own experience with church discipline. Identify examples that you can recall. Based on what you have read and what you have experienced, what factors are necessary in order for church discipline to be a redemptive process?

Spiritual Exercise: Discernment, Confession, and Forgiveness

In this exercise, several of the key themes of this lesson will receive attention.

Day Three: In the discussion of Matthew 18, special attention was given to the dimension of moral discernment. Jesus gave to the church the authority and the enablement to make moral decisions, to bind and to loose (Mt. 18:15-20 and Jn. 20:22-23). The task of moral discernment and the authority to make moral decisions stands behind the authority to declare forgiveness. Journal your interaction with this task and this authority.

Day Four: One thread running throughout this lesson has been the importance of confession. If confession were not necessary, there would be no need for admonition (as used in this lesson), reproof, or correction. But not all confession leads to forgiveness. Foster describes this type of experience.

> The individual who has known through private confession the forgiveness and the release from persistent nagging habits of sin should rejoice greatly in this evidence of God's mercy. But there are others for whom that has not happened. Let me describe what it is like. We have prayed, even begged, for forgiveness, and though we hope we have been forgiven we have sensed no release. We have doubted our forgiveness and despaired at our confession. We have feared that perhaps we had made confession only to ourselves and not to God. The haunting sorrows and hurts of the past have not been healed. We had tried to convince ourselves that God only forgives the sin, He does not heal the memory, but deep within we know there must be something more. People have told us to take our forgiveness by faith and not to call God a liar. Not wanting to call God a liar, we do our best to take it by faith. But because misery and bitterness remain in our life we again despair. Eventually we begin to believe either that forgiveness is only a ticket to heaven and not meant to affect our lives now, or that we are not worthy of the forgiving grace of God.[11]

In your journaling, identify significant experiences of confession. What were the necessary ingredients to secure release and peace? How would you respond to a person who has confessed sin but has no sense of forgiveness?

Day Five: For your general journaling, focus on whatever is most important in your life today.

Discipling Session

This group session will focus on moral discernemnt and declaring forgiveness. Attention will be given to the skills necessary for these activities.

1. Share with your discipling partner your feelings about the general theme of church discipline reflected in your journaling on *Day One* and *Day Two*. Do you view it as outdated or relevant? Why? Also, you may want to share your journaling from *Day Five*.

2. The first part of the lesson discussed the process of moral discernment (*Day Three*). Share with the group your experiences and insights concerning this activity. What attitudes, approaches, and procedures are necessary in order for the process to be effective?

3. The goals of moral discernment are confession and forgiveness. Most congregations in the free church tradition do not have a formalized confessional. How then is forgiveness declared either to individuals or to the congregation? If we are moral communities, we must also be forgiving communities. *The Mennonite Hymnal* contains a "Statement of Restoration," No. 731, for use after there has been public confession by a member. This statement does declare forgiveness. Share with the group your experience and insights regarding the declaration of forgiveness for private and public confession. Scriptures such as John 20:21-23 and 1 John 1:9 may be helpful. Declaring forgiveness is an important aspect of discipling.

4. Desired Discipling Skill: ability to engage in moral discernment and to declare forgiveness.

Lesson 15

Brotherhood and Material Sharing

Discipleship Theme: Mutual Aid

Lessons 9 to 14 dealt with themes related to the corporate life of the people of God. These past themes, as well as the next two lessons, are included in this study because discipleship clearly involves one's life in the larger body of Christ, not only one's individual life.

In this study, the church has been described as a brotherhood community, or as a group of believers who share life on many levels and in many areas. They worship together, admonish one another, meet each other's spiritual needs, and make moral decisions. They have a commitment to one another and attempt to be the people of God.

The New Testament describes and teaches an additional level of brotherhood, namely, meeting one another's material needs. This sharing grows out of the nature of the church, not Jesus' warnings against wealth or his instructions to care for the poor. While these latter considerations are important in understanding the life of the disciple, they are not the primary considerations for understanding sharing within the brotherhood.

Biblical Teachings

Two key New Testament terms which describe the quality of life among the people of God and relate to material sharing are "koinonia" (fellowship) and "brotherhood." Two uses of koinonia

153

in the New Testament are Acts 2:42 and Galatians 2:9. It describes an important life reality among those who had repented and received the Holy Spirit. They were drawn together into a close-knit body where they experienced a oneness and fellowship beyond their experience with other people. The new spiritual reality which tied them together was so strong that they shared material goods (Acts 2:44; 4:32-35).

These people of God participated in the important areas of life including the spiritual and the material. All believers shared in the spiritual possession of the total community. Harold S. Bender vividly described the reality of koinonia when he wrote that "the apostles' teachings belonged to all; the message of Christ belonged to all; the material needs of each were the concern and responsibility of all. This was Christian love, God's love at work in the community."[1]

The New Testament also uses the term "brotherhood" for the church and "brethren" for members of the church, both male and female. If believers are children of God, they are members of the same family possessing the same Father. This makes them brothers and sisters. It is significant that the term "brethren" is used more frequently in the New Testament to designate Christians than any other term.

According to Bender, "Brotherhood means mutual love and responsibility, full participation of all in the family of God, full sharing in the ordering of the life of the church, in exactly the same sense as fellowship does. It means a love because of which all the members minister to each other in all their needs, both temporal and spiritual."[2]

In light of this view of the church it is easy to understand why Paul urged the Gentile believers to contribute to the material needs of their Jewish brothers and sisters in Jerusalem (Rom. 15:26-27; 2 Cor. 8—9). Paul's appeal for an offering for the saints is based on the relationship between spiritual unity and economic equality. It is also easy to understand the appeal of the apostle John to share with brothers in need (1 Jn. 3:16-18). True love cannot do otherwise.

Anabaptist Writings

J. Winfield Fretz has observed three distinct Anabaptists approaches to private possessions.[3] One type was the revolutionary Münsterites who practiced enforced communism and wanted to change the social order by means of violence. Another type was that of Christian communism practiced by the Hutterian Brethren which was purely voluntary. The third type found among the Swiss Brethren and followers of Menno Simons is identified by Fretz as the brotherhood type. These Anabaptists did not practice common ownership of goods or live together in simple households, but they did share temporal possessions as there was need among them.

The general position of the Swiss Brethren was that private property was acceptable, provided the owner saw himself as a steward and shared with the needy. Further discussion of this issue is found in Appendix 1, pages 241-242. Note especially the practice of linking baptism to the willingness to devote all possessions to the service of the brotherhood and to help any member in need.

Not only was brotherhood sharing based on the baptismal vow, it was also nurtured by the communion service. Note the liturgy for the Lord's Supper written by Balthasar Hubmaier which appeared in Lesson 12. The pledge of love asked, "Do you will to love your neighbor, to accomplish toward him the works of brotherly love, to offer your flesh and shed your blood for him . . . ?"

Pilgram Marpeck held a view similar to the Swiss Brethren. Describing his understanding of the Acts 4 account, he said:

> No coercion or commandment, however, made them share all things communally. Rather, the sharing was done simply out of a free love which caused the community to be of one heart and soul. Furthermore, nobody laid claim to his own goods, even though each individual could have kept them for himself, nor would he have been excluded from the church of Christ for doing so. As Peter says to Ananias: "Could you not have retained that which was yours?" (Acts 5:4). Among the believers, there is only a free giving of love, and no coercion. Each individual may give or retain. Such a practice is unlike the practice of some who, desiring to have common

property more out of greed than of love, coerce others into giving, even though common property is best when it comes from the freedom of love. But it is only a freedom of love. The Corinthians, Macedonians, and Romans did not share their possessions, as Paul clearly shows in 1 Corinthians 16. Concerning the alms-gathering, Paul says: "Now, concerning the contribution for the saints: As I directed the churches of Galatia, so you are also to do. On the first day of every week, each of you is to put something aside and store it up, as he may prosper, and collect what he has to give at the time" (1 Cor. 16:1-2).

Here, it can be clearly seen that community of possession was not practiced in all churches. But, even though they control their possessions, such true believers do not say in their hearts that these are theirs; rather, their possessions belong to God and the needy. For this reason, among true Christians who display the freedom of love, all things are communal and are as if they had been offered, since they have been offered by the heart.[4]

Menno Simons wrote a classic description of true evangelical faith (see Appendix 1, page 241). The movement in the description is from personal faith, to sharing with the needy, to loving enemies, to seeking the lost.

During Menno's ministry, the Dutch Anabaptists were charged with having property in common. Menno answered:

This charge is false and without truth. We do not teach and practice community of goods. But we teach and maintain by the Word of the Lord that all truly believing Christians are members of one body and are baptized by one Spirit into one body (1 Cor. 12:13); they are partakers of one bread (1 Cor. 10:17); they have one Lord and one God (Eph. 4:5, 6).

Inasmuch as then they are one, therefore it is Christian and reasonable that they piously love one another, and that the one member be solicitous for the welfare of the other, for this both the Scripture and nature teach. The whole Scripture speaks of mercifulness and love, and it is the only sign whereby a true Christian may be known. As the Lord says, By this shall all men know that ye are my disciples (that is, that ye are Christians), if ye love one another. John 13:35.

Beloved reader, it is not customary that an intelligent person clothes and cares for one part of his body and leaves the rest destitute and naked. Oh, no. The intelligent person is solicitous for all his members. Thus it should be with those who are the Lord's church and body. All those who are born of God, who are gifted with the Spirit of the Lord, who are, according to the Scriptures, called into one body and love in Christ Jesus, are prepared by such love to serve their neighbors, not only with money and goods, but also after the example of their Lord and Head, Jesus Christ, in an evangelical manner, with life and blood. They show mercy and love, as much as they can. No one among them is allowed to beg. They take to heart the need of the saints. They entertain those in distress. They take the stranger into their houses. They comfort the afflicted; assist the needy; clothe the naked; feed the hungry; do not turn their face from the poor; do not despise their own flesh. Isa. 58:7, 8.[5]

Contemporary Writings

On March 17-21, 1980, the International Consultation on Simple Lifestyle was held at Hoddesdon, England. The consultation wrote and endorsed a statement entitled "An Evangelical Commitment to Simple Lifestyle." The section on "The New Community" reads in part as follows:

> We rejoice that the church is the new community of the new age, whose members enjoy a new life and a new lifestyle. The earliest Christian church, constituted in Jerusalem on the Day of Pentecost, was characterized by a quality of fellowship unknown before. Those Spirit-filled believers loved one another to such an extent that they sold and shared their possessions. Although their selling and giving were voluntary, and some private property was retained (Acts 5:4), it was made subservient to the needs of the community, "None of them said that anything he had was his own" (Acts 4:32). That is, they were free from the selfish assertion of proprietary rights. And as a result of their transformed economic relationships, "there was not a needy person among them" (Acts 4:34).
>
> This principle of generous and sacrificial sharing, expressed in holding ourselves and our goods available for people in need, is an indispensable characteristic of every Spirit-filled church. So those of us who are affluent in any part of the world, are determined to do more to relieve the needs of less privileged believers. Otherwise, we shall be like those rich Christians in Corinth who ate and drank too much while their poor brothers and sisters were left hungry, and we shall deserve the stinging rebuke Paul gave them for despising God's church and desecrating Christ's body (1 Cor. 11:20-24). Instead, we determine to resemble them at a later stage when Paul urged them out of their abundance to give to the impoverished Christians of Judea "that there may be equality" (2 Cor. 8:10-15). It was a beautiful demonstration of caring love and of Gentile-Jewish solidarity in Christ.[6]

Jim Wallis and the Sojourners community in Washington, D.C., have adopted brotherhood sharing as a part of their life and witness. Commenting on the various efforts to avoid dealing with Acts 2 and 4 Wallis has written:

Despite all the attempts to rationalize the meaning of the verses quoted here, what they mean is not that complicated: they are simply descriptions of what happened when the Holy Spirit invaded the lives of the early Christians. The coming of the Spirit among them shattered the old and normal economic assumptions and created an entirely different economic order. The Spirit established a new way of thinking and a new way of living that affected their relationships to money and goods. It created a new economy among the Christians, a common life in which economics was no longer a private matter; economics was a matter of fellowship, in fact, a central matter of fellowship. The early Christians could not have conceived of a way to share their lives spiritually without sharing their lives economically. The sharing recorded in Acts 2 and 4 was the attempt by the early Christians to make practical their understanding of the mind of Christ on economic matters.

The relationship between the coming of the Spirit and the creation of the new economy is key. The Christians were making the teachings of Jesus real, and their decisions were empowered by the coming of the Spirit.

Later, Paul was taking a collection for the Jerusalem church, which was suffering from famine. In 2 Corinthians 8, he makes a vital connection between spiritual unity and economic equality. We are called to share, not just to be ready to share. Accumulating wealth while brothers and sisters are in poverty is evidence of sin in the church's life. Why should Christian congregations live such different economic lives in different places? Why should some Christians be poor while others have more than they need? Are we not family? Paul uses the word *equality* (verse 14). He wanted the Corinthians to understand that the unity of heart and mind God wanted them to have with their brothers and sisters in Jerusalem had to do with, among other things, economic equality between them. What does that say to us, rich Christians in a rich land, about a world of poverty in which many Christians and their churches are poor?[7]

Journaling Focus

Day One: Respond to the readings concerning brotherhood and sharing. What term best describes your feelings? If the congregation to which you now belong would have required the level of material sharing demanded by the Anabaptists as described on page 242 of Appendix 1, would you have become a member? Explain your answer.

Day Two: Reflect on your own experience of brotherhood sharing. Identify significant occasions of receiving and of giving. If you were to follow the principles outlined in "An Evangelical

Commitment to Simple Lifestyle," what changes would be required?

Spiritual Exercise: Living into the Scriptures

One relevant way of studying the Scriptures is to put oneself into a biblical story or event by personally identifying with each person or group. This method is especially useful when studying the stories in the Gospels. It is also effective when studying the instructions in the Epistles.

Reference has been made to the teachings of Paul in 2 Corinthians 8 and 9, and Romans 15:26-27 regarding an offering for the poor saints in Jerusalem. In these passages, there is reference to three churches: the Jerusalem, Macedonian, and Corinthian churches. For this spiritual exercise, identify with each of these churches for one day. Assume you are a member of those churches experiencing what they experienced and listening to Paul's message to you.

Day Three: Today you are a member of the church in Jerusalem. Read the passages in Romans 15 and 2 Corinthians 8 and 9 to learn about yourself. As you read, note the important things about your circumstances. Take on this identity. Live with it for one day. Then journal your experience of "being" a poor saint in Jerusalem.

Day Four: Today you are a member of the church in Macedonia. From the passages in Romans and 2 Corinthians, listen to what Paul is saying about you and to you. Now take on this identity for one day. Then journal your experience of identifying with this church.

Day Five: For today you are a member of the church at Corinth or Achaia. Again from the passages, identify what Paul is saying about you and to you. In your own mind, become a member of this church for a day. Then journal what you have experienced.

Day Six: General journaling is optional this week.

Discipling Session

This group session will focus on accountability in brotherhood sharing. It is concerned with developing appropriate attitudes and skills necessary to work with this sensitive area.

1. Share with the total group your experience of identifying with the three New Testament churches. How did you respond to this method of Bible study? What unique learnings did you gain?

2. Share with your discipling partner a term which best describes your relationship to your possessions. In light of the various readings, what relationship would you like to have? What steps are you willing to take toward that goal? The freedom to discuss these issues in a sensitive way is important for discipling.

3. Desired Discipling Skill: ability to aid accountability in brotherhood sharing. Development of this skill requires the spirit of humility, the attitude of openness, and the willingness to risk conversation.

Lesson 16

Gift Discernment

Discipleship Theme: The Discovery and Exercise of Gifts

Lesson 15 focused on sharing material possessions or the place of material gifts in the life of the body of Christ, the church. Lesson 16 will focus on the discernment of spiritual "gifts" and their importance for the life of the church.

Biblical Teachings

The primary New Testament passages dealing with spiritual gifts are found in 1 Corinthians 12, Romans 12, Ephesians 4, and 1 Peter 4. First Corinthians 12 is the most detailed passage in the Scriptures on this theme. David Watson has identified four key words found in verses 4-7 of this chapter which help us understand spiritual gifts. [1]

First, Paul speaks about "varieties of gifts." Bible students identify from sixteen to twenty basic gifts. Some see these as an exhaustive list of God's gifts to the church; others, including Watson, see the list as examples of spiritual gifts. Furthermore, while some make a sharp distinction between spiritual gifts and natural talents (see Body Life by Ray C. Stedman), others, including Watson, believe the New Testament does not make a sharp distinction between "natural" and "supernatural" gifts. God is the source of all good gifts.

It is important that we see gifts as belonging to God rather than ourselves. They are "his" gifts, not "ours." This perspective will make the difference between using gifts for self-fulfillment and using gifts for the benefit of others. The very term "gift" refers to a capacity or function in relationship to body life and a gift must be given to others in order to truly be a gift.

The second word is "service," *diakonia*, which implies an eagerness to serve. It is important to notice that Paul links together his discussion of gifts of the Spirit and his discussion of the body of Christ (1 Cor. 12 and 14). It is in the body of Christ that gifts are discerned and that they find primary expression.

The third important word is "working." One of the ways God works in the church and in the world is through gifts that he has given believers. While it is true that God is not limited in his ways of working, he desires the freedom to work as he chooses through available and dedicated gifts.

The fourth term is "manifestation." Gifts of the Spirit manifest or make visible the giver of the gifts who is invisible. God is revealed as his gifts are used. His power becomes evident. His message and will are made known. His love and compassion are expressed. Paul reminds us that all gifts are given for "the common good," the good of the total body. To achieve this goal, the gifts not only need to be exercised, they need to be exercised in love (1 Cor. 13).

The other passages identified earlier also contribute to our understanding of spiritual gifts. Romans 12:4-8 tells us how gifts are to be used. Ephesians 4:11-16 identifies gifts as leadership persons who are to equip the members for their ministry. Through this process, the total body is matured in faith. First Peter 4:10-11 calls for our stewardship of God's gifts. We are poor stewards of God's gifts of grace if we fail to discern or use our God-given gifts.

Anabaptist Writings

Pilgram Marpeck, perhaps more than any other Anabaptist leader, wrote about the importance of spiritual gifts. He wanted the gifts of believers to be discerned, appreciated, and exercised for the enrichment of the body. (See Appendix 1, pages 271-272, for quotations from Marpeck.)

Several points of emphasis stand out in Marpeck's writings. First, all believers are gifted by God. There are "no unendowed members." Second, gifts reveal God, the Giver. Contemplating the gifts should lead to praising God. Third, all gifts are to be used. The gifts of every member must be "heard and seen." The use of gifts should "flow voluntarily" rather than be compelled. Fourth, the results of the full use of gifts are strong and trained members.

Menno Simons also referred to spiritual gifts in his writings. All who are born of God, said Menno, "are proper members of the body of Christ and labor according to the gift received."[2] Writing about his own ministry, Menno said, "I have served you all with this small talent as I have received it from my God. I could wish that I could at some time do it with greater and richer grace to the praise of the Lord."[3]

In his "Foundation of Christian Doctrine," Menno discussed the unity, love, and peace signified by the Lord's Supper. He concluded his discussion as follows:

> Likewise, even as in the natural body the more honorable members such as the eye, the ear, and the mouth do not reproach the less honorable members on account of their inferiority; and even as the inferior members do not envy the superior members for their nobility, but every member in its place is peaceable and serves the whole body, be its own functions high or low; so it is also in the church of the Lord. Paul says, Some he appointed apostles; some prophets; some evangelists; some pastors and teachers. Let everyone be mindful that he boast not of what he is, has, or possesses, for it is all the grace and gift of God. Let everyone attend to his duty, for the perfecting of the saints, for the work of the ministry, for the edifying of the body of Christ; till we all come in the unity of the faith, and of the knowledge of the Son of God, unto a perfect man, unto the measure of the stature of the fullness of Christ. This is also set forth in the Holy Supper, but how the world calling itself Christian lives up to this is shown by its fruits and action.[4]

Contemporary Writings

In contemporary writings about spiritual gifts, there are at least two prominent themes. First, all members are uniquely gifted and their gifts are needed for the wholeness of the body. There is a story about Michelangelo pushing a huge rock down a street. When asked why he worked so hard pushing an old piece of stone, Michelangelo reportedly said, "Because there is an angel in that rock that wants to come out."

This story reflects the vision that an increasing number of church leaders have of individual Christians and of congregations.

Howard A. Snyder writes:

> *·The Bible sees the Church in charismatic, rather than in institutional, terms.* While the Church is, in a broad sense, an institution, it is more fundamentally a charismatic community. That is, it exists by the grace (*charis*) of God and is built up by the gifts of grace (*charismata*) bestowed by the Spirit. As seen biblically, it is not structured the same way a business corporation or university is, but is structured like the human body—on the basis of life. At its most basic level it is a community, not a hierarchy; an organism, not an organization (1 Cor. 12; Rom. 12:5-8; Eph. 4:1-16; Mt. 18:20; 1 Pet. 4:10-11).[5]

The Church of the Saviour in Washington, D.C., has, for many years, recognized the importance of calling forth gifts and requires members to serve in a mission group where their gifts are used. Out of this experience, Pastor Gordon Cosby writes about his understanding of gifts:

> Christ makes each of us something unlike any other creation ever fashioned by God—something wonderful, exciting, unique; something specifically needed in the total Body of Christ. This uniqueness, this very self that is so hard to describe, this charismatic person, is the gift of the Holy Spirit. It is the primary gift that we bring to the Body, and without it the Body is immeasurably impoverished.[6]

Again Cosby writes:

> God has not created a single person whose essence and uniqueness are not eternally needed. He will keep longing for you and for me and keep reaching out for us; he will keep searching for that one lost sheep until we discover our charisma. The only way we can really take our hands off, when we love a person, is by committing him in a new way to God's care, to God's love. It is being willing to trust God for whatever strange new work may emerge in the person we release.[7]

A second prominent theme related to spiritual gifts involves the task of leadership. Increasingly, the task of church leaders is seen through the perspective of Ephesians 4. Leaders are to call forth gifts or equip the saints for their ministry. Gordon Cosby has this task in mind when he writes:

> Now, since the calling forth of uniqueness is God's mission, it seems self-evident that this is our primary calling as Christians. We are to call forth the gifts of other people, to set them free, to throw the lifeline to them and be the one who, under God, helps a person discover that for which he was created.
>
> The question is, how to call forth the gifts in others? It is amazing how long we can be with people and not call forth any gifts. In fact we often do just the opposite. But to love a person means to help them recognize their uniqueness and to discover their gifts.[8]

In an article which appeared in *Christianity Today,* Howard Snyder spoke specifically about the task of the pastor in relationship to gift discovery. Responding to a question regarding the difference between lay persons and the professional ministers, Snyder said:

> Since every believer is gifted, the question answers itself when we discover our gifts and allow the ministry of the church to be determined on the basis of those gifts, rather than trying to squeeze people into already-existing forms of ministry. The challenge for the pastor is to equip the saints for the work of the ministry. But if he has the gifts, he also teaches, preaches, counsels and so on. He must be very capable in the area of discipleship, because the gift of discipling is essential, and the pastoral function is a discipling function.
>
> The pastor's priority is to invest in a group of people to the point where they become colleagues in ministry. When their own gifts are discovered and developed they become the primary persons to equip the rest of the body.[9]

Elizabeth O'Connor who is on the staff of the Church of the Saviour in Washington, D.C., has written widely about gifts and creativity. She relates the gift discerning and developing process to both the church and the home. Both pastors and parents have a role to play.

A primary purpose of the Church is to help us discover our gifts and, in the face of our fears, to hold us accountable for them so that we can enter into the joy of creating. The major obligation of the Church to children is to enjoy them and to listen to them so that each can grow according to the design which is written into his being and emerges only under the care and warmth of another life. One of the reasons we experience so much difficulty with our gifts is that parents have thought their chief function in life to be feeding, clothing, and educating the young. However, their really important ministry is to listen to their children and enable them to uncover the special blueprint that is theirs. There is one line in Scripture that will instruct us in these matters: "But Mary treasured up all these things and pondered over them" (Luke 2:19, NEB).

Every child's life gives forth hints and signs of the way that he is to go. The parent that knows how to meditate stores these hints and signs away and ponders over them. We are to treasure the intimations of the future that the life of every child gives to us so that, instead of unconsciously putting blocks in his way, we help him to fulfill his destiny. This is not an easy way to follow. Instead of telling our children what they should do and become, we must be humble before their wisdom, believing that in them and not in us is the secret that they need to discover.[10]

Journaling Focus

Day One: Respond to what you have just read regarding the discovery and exercise of gifts. Do the readings leave you with excitement, confusion, or some other emotion? Describe your response and identify why you have responded in that way. Describe your own experience with gift discernment. This might be assistance you gave another person or assistance you received from someone else. What did you learn through this experience?

Spiritual Exercise: Discerning Gifts and Vocation

Gift discernment is one part of a larger discernment process. There are at least three aspects to our finding our place in the body of Christ. They are tied together like three links of a chain. These aspects are identified with three terms: call, gifts, and vocation.

In Lessons 3 to 6, we shared our spiritual autobiographies. Special attention was given to the God moments in our lives or God's dialogue with us. Through this process, we were exploring our call, our sense that God has laid his hand on our shoulder and told us he has a work for us to do.

Often our call is general and we need to discern our gifts in order to know what we are equipped by God to do. Gift discernment may seem difficult because different persons recommend different approaches. Some say that we should study ourselves. We should reflect on our dreams, our urges, our abilities. Our gifts, they say, are written into the fabric of our being. Others who see spiritual gifts as significantly different from natural gifts say we should reflect on what the Holy Spirit has uniquely gifted us to do. Still others stress the call of the congregation. The important consideration is what others see in us.

Which approach is best? Obviously, all three approaches have some validity to them and there is some overlap. The approach that I recommend and find helpful will relate to these three approaches.

Before this approach is outlined, mention should be made of the way in which our vocation flows out of our gifts. After gifts are discerned, they need to be developed and exercised. The use or exercise of our gifts flows into our vocation or vocations. Our vocation is the role or niche we fill in the life and ministry of the people of God. It is the concrete expression of our call and grows out of the use of our gifts.

Day Two: Make a list of the gifts mentioned in the following passages: Romans 12:4-8; 1 Corinthians 12:8-10, 28; Ephesians 4:11; 1 Peter 4:10-11. Identify the gifts in this list that you feel you have been given. List additional gifts you believe God has given you that can be used in the life and ministry of your congregation. Check the gifts in your total list that you are now using.

Day Three: Elizabeth O'Connor recommends the use of silent prayer as a method of discovering our gifts and possible vocation. She says that we can listen to ourselves as we practice the silence of listening. Find a quiet place for prayer. Prayerfully

ask the Holy Spirit to show you your gifts and role in life. Then do **the following:**

> Concentrate your attention deep within yourself. When you have reached a place of quiet, begin to think about your gifts. Pay attention to the images that pass across your mind. Write them down and ponder their meaning. Fantasy what you would do if you could do anything in the world you chose. Watch yourself doing what you would most love to do and name the talents essential for that fantasy to become real. Then see whether you can discover those talents in yourself. What we would most love to do is a strong indication of what we have the potential to achieve.
>
> When you have named your talents or gifts, list the risks that you will have to take in order to actualize them. What will you have to give up if you are to develop these gifts? What are the obstacles that you foresee?[11]

Day Four: This lesson plus the next three lessons will focus, in part, on discerning gifts and vocations. As a part of each lesson, you will attempt to discern the gifts and vocation of one or two members of your group. (The group order should be determined so all of the group will focus on the same member at the same time. This exercise could be done for the entire group in a retreat setting.)

The approach to this exercise will be the silence of listening. In silent prayer, you will "listen" to the life of another person.

Focus on a group member. In silent prayer reflect on that person's life. This should include the spiritual autobiography shared earlier. It should also include personal things the person has shared, your experience of relating to the person, and observations about the person's life. From these reflections, what gifts do you discern and what vocation do you see emerging? Write these reflections on a piece of paper and give it to the person.

Day Five: For today do general journaling or discern the gifts and vocation of a second group member.

Discipling Session

This group session will center around the gift discernment process.

It will focus on the discipling skill of listening to our own life and the life of another person. Also, it will focus on the skill of relating call, gifts, and vocation.

1. Share with your discipling partner your journaling for *Day One* and *Day Two*.

2. Have the group members share their discernment of the designated person's gifts and vocation. Then have the designated person share his or her own discernment of his or her gifts and emerging vocation. Process questions and issues that emerge. Attempt to reach a consensus concerning gifts and vocational direction.

3. Desired Discipling Skill: ability to listen to the life of another. This skill involves in-depth listening, both to other persons and to God. The process relates to persons across the age span.

Lesson 17

Christianity and Ethics

Discipleship Theme: Separation from Evil

This lesson functions as a link between earlier lessons on the nature of the Christian life and the remaining lessons which deal with the application of discipleship in society.

Lessons 5 through 8 touched on the renewed character of the regenerated, the centrality of obedience in true faith, the concern for holy living, and the importance of growth toward the goals of faith set forth by Jesus. These lessons relate to personal ethics (personal behavior such as honesty). Lessons 9 through 16 relate to the corporate life of disciples within the community of faith. The last group of lessons (17 through 23) focus on living the life of discipleship in society. Lesson 17 introduces the concept of social ethics (living one's faith in society). What principles of conduct or behavior guide the life of the believer in the world? What is the standard or norm for making moral decisions?

Biblical Teachings

Both the Old and New Testaments describe the people of God as a group of persons living in the world but separating themselves from the evils of the world. Furthermore, there are many teachings calling for this manner of life.

Jesus prayed in his high priestly prayer, "I do not pray that thou shouldst take them out of the world, but that thou shouldst keep them from the evil one" (Jn. 17:15).

Paul frequently touches the same theme. In Romans 12:2, he tells his readers not to "be conformed to this world." In 2 Corinthians 6:14—7:1, he goes further in his teaching when he instructs against being "mismated with unbelievers" and calls on believers to "be separate from them."

Peter declares that we should no longer live "by human passions but by the will of God." He also identifies both the expressions of human passions and the role of suffering in dealing with sin (1 Pet. 4:1-4).

James affirms a number of times that faith apart from works is dead (Jas. 2:14-26). The works of which James speaks refer to doing the will of God, which includes our relationships in society.

John warns against loving the world and following its patterns of evil (1 Jn. 2:15-17; 3:8-10). It thus becomes clear that moral behavior or ethics is an important consideration for the biblical writers. Stated negatively, they call for separation from evil. Stated positively, they call for participation in the life of Jesus.

In *The Politics of Jesus*, John Howard Yoder points out that Jesus' teaching and example provide guidance in social ethics.[1] Furthermore, the believer's attitude and behavior is to "partake of" the same nature as that of his lord. As the believer shares in the divine life of Jesus and lives life in society as he lived it, there will be a separation from evil and a practicing of social ethics.

Yoder identifies numerous Scriptures which indicate ways in which disciples participate in the life of Jesus. A few examples follow:

First, the disciple participates in the nature, forgiveness, and love of God (1 Jn. 3:1-3; Eph. 4:32; Mt. 5:43-48).

Second, the disciple participates in the life of Christ (1 Jn. 2:6; Rom. 6:6-11; 1 Jn. 3:11-16; Jn. 13:1-17).

Third, the disciple participates in the death of Christ (Phil. 3:10; Eph. 5:1, 2; Mk. 10:42-45).

The New Testament, then, calls on disciples to live life out of and in harmony with their new life in Christ. One expression of this new life will be separation from evil. The Christian life will have an ethical dimension.

Anabaptist Writings

With these words, J. Lawrence Burkholder begins his article on "Ethics" which appears in *The Mennonite Encyclopedia:*

> It is impossible to exaggerate the importance of ethics in the life and testimony of the Anabaptist-Mennonites. Throughout their history, Mennonites have sought above all to be holy, pure, and obedient to Christ. Consequently Mennonite preaching, writing, and piety have had a strong ethical emphasis. In fact, the ethical emphasis is so predominant in the writings of Menno Simons and others, that one is sometimes tempted to say that for Mennonites Christianity and ethics are one. At least it is fair to say that Mennonites have given ethics a position of centrality not generally found in Protestantism.[2]

Burkholder identifies a number of significant insights concerning the ethics of the Anabaptists:

First, the norms of ethics were the life and teachings of Jesus, or testimony to his life by an apostle. His earthly life was the pattern for their lives. This is the only criteria for ethics in *The Schleitheim Confession.*

Second, their participation in Christ and his living presence provided the context in which the Scriptures came alive spiritually. They had a sense of obedience to Christ, not merely obedience to a biblical command.

Third, Christian ethics were really church ethics. The Anabaptists made moral decisions in the context of the church and they only expected committed Christians to follow their ethical teachings.

Fourth, they held to a separation of church and world. They saw the world as the rule of evil and the church as a body of believers obedient to the principles of the kingdom of God. Ethical judgments needed to be made about cultural practices.

Fifth, the central concept of Christian ethics was love. Since Christ's life and death on the cross was the supreme expression of love, they thought in terms of sacrificial love. This understanding was expressed in the ethic of nonresistance and the ethic of brotherhood.

Sixth, the Anabaptists held to both personal morality and

social ethics. While they were not concerned with the larger issues of social justice, they were committed to living their faith in the church and in the world.

These ethical positions led to concrete expressions. They practiced believer's baptism even though there was an old Roman law which made rebaptism punishable by death.

They refused to take part in warfare or to carry a sword. They refused to swear oaths, partly because of their concern for truth and partly because an oath to the state involved a commitment to bear arms on behalf of the state.[3]

Their personal lives reflected a high level of personal morality and piety. Their corporate life involved sharing spiritually and materially. The result of their ethical expressions was suffering at the hands of those who also called themselves Christians.

In *The Anabaptist Vision,* Harold S. Bender compares the social ethics of four Christian groups of the Reformation period. It reads as follows:

> The Anabaptist vision may be further clarified by comparison of the social ethics of the four main Christian groups of the Reformation period, Catholic, Calvinist, Lutheran, and Anabaptist. Catholic and Calvinist alike were optimistic about the world, agreeing that the world can be redeemed; they held that the entire social order can be brought under the sovereignty of God and Christianized, although they used different means to attain this goal. Lutheran and Anabaptist were pessimistic about the world, denying the possibility of Christianizing the entire social order; but the consequent attitudes of these two groups toward the social order were diametrically opposed. Lutheranism said that since the Christian must live in a world order that remains sinful, he must make a compromise with it. As a citizen he cannot avoid participation in the evil of the world, for instance in making war, and for this his only recourse is to seek forgiveness by the grace of God; only within his personal private experience can the Christian truly Christianize his life. The Anabaptist rejected this view completely. Since for him no compromise dare be made with evil, the Christian may in no circumstance participate in any conduct in the existing social order which is contrary to the spirit and teaching of Christ and the apostolic practice. He must consequently withdraw from the worldly system and create a Christian social order within the fellowship of the church brotherhood. Extension of this Christian order by the conversion of individuals and their transfer out of the world into the church is the only way by which progress can be made in Christianizing the social order.[4]

Contemporary Writings

Contemporary response to the teachings and examples of Jesus varies greatly as it has in every age since the early church. There are some who "spiritualize" the commands of Jesus to such an extent that they lose their ethical edge. David Watson illustrates this approach. After commenting on the call of Jesus for total loyalty and allegiance, Watson warned:

> With such a call to a life of total and uncompromising obedience, we should not be surprised if we are strongly tempted to qualify Christ's call, to modify its stringent demands by taking a more "reasonable" line in the light of modern culture, which, we tell ourselves, is so different from that of the first century. With our intellectual and theological approach we may try to hold a "more balanced" view or reinterpret the teaching of Jesus in order to avoid its direct and disturbing challenge. It is important, we say, not to take things too literally. We must not become legalistic. We must not ignore the vital principles of hermeneutics. Jesus may have said, "Do not lay up for yourselves treasures on earth"; but what he *meant* was, "Enjoy the beautiful things in this world, but do not allow them to hold a central place in your hearts." Jesus may have said, "Love your enemies"; but what he *meant* was, "Do not take active revenge against someone who has wronged you." When Jesus said, "Seek first the kingdom of God," what he really *meant* was, "Although there will be many other things you must seek in order to exist and have a normal life, make sure that you do not leave God's kingdom out of your life altogether." In these ways we evade the clear call of Jesus to absolute obedience; in this our whole attitude to him is wrong. We do not believe that he loves us and plans only for what is best for us. And our unbelief and disobedience disqualify us as his disciples.[5]

Another response to the life of Jesus is to mimic certain aspects of his lifestyle and thus to miss the central thrust of true separation from evil. John Howard Yoder exposes the inadequacy of this approach when he writes:

> A long history of interpretation and application which we might designate as 'mendicant' has centered its attention upon the outward form of Jesus' life; his forsaking domicile and property, his celibacy or his barefoot itinerancy. Again, without disrespect for the nobility of the monastic tradition and its needed critique of comfortable religion, we must be aware that it centers the renunciation at another point than the New Testament. Both the few who seek thus to follow Jesus in a formal mimicking of his life style and the many who use this distortion to argue Jesus' irrelevance, have failed to note a striking gap in the New Testament material

we have read. As we noted before more briefly: there is no general concept of living like Jesus. According to universal tradition, Jesus was not married; yet when the Apostle Paul, advocate *par excellence* of the life "in Christ," argues at length for celibacy or for a widow's not remarrying (I Cor. 7), it never occurs to him to appeal to Jesus' example, even as one of many arguments. Jesus is thought in his earlier life to have worked as a carpenter; yet never, even when he explains at length why he earns his own way as an artisan (I Cor. 9), does it come to Paul's mind that he is imitating Jesus. Jesus' association with villagers, his drawing his illustrations from the life of the peasants and the fishermen, his leading his disciples to desert places and mountaintops, have often been appealed to as examples by the advocates of rural life and church camping; but not in the New Testament. His formation of a small circle of disciples whom he taught through months of close contact has been claimed as a model pastoral method; his teaching in parables has been made a model of graphic communication; there have been efforts to imitate his prayer life or his forty days in the desert: but not in the New Testament.

There is thus but one realm in which the concept of imitation holds— but there it holds in every strand of the New Testament literature and all the more strikingly by virtue of the absence of parallels in other realms: this is at the point of the concrete social meaning of the cross in its relation to enmity and power. Servanthood replaces dominion, forgiveness absorbs hostility. Thus—and only thus—are we bound by New Testament thought to "be like Jesus."[6]

The twin enemies of faithful ethical living and biblical separation from evil appear to be spiritualizing Jesus' teachings and legalizing Jesus' examples. It is the task of the church in every generation to find its way between these two extremes.

Journaling Focus

Day One: Reflect on the Anabaptist and contemporary writings. Separation from evil seems to be a negative approach to ethics. Participation in the life of Jesus sounds like a positive approach.

Which of these best describes your approach? What would change if you adopted both emphases? What new expressions of social ethics are you considering? What resources are you drawing on to discern the path of obedience?

Spiritual Exercise: Discernment
Through Presence

Earlier in this lesson, we noticed that the Anabaptists ap-proached ethical decisions with the awareness of Christ's living presence which caused the Scriptures to seem alive spiritually. As a result, they had a sense of being obedient to the person of Jesus, not merely obedient to a command. This distinction may not seem to be major but the contrast means the difference between dynamic Christian obedience and legalism. One approach leads to "life" and the other to "death."

Day Two: Read again the Scriptures identified at the begin-ning of this lesson which speak of separation from evil. Then identify some pattern of separation you presently follow but which you would like to ignore because it seems to be only obedience to a command or the mores of church or society.

In a spirit of quiet, reflective prayer, picture Jesus standing beside you. Discuss with him the pattern you are questioning and the Scriptures you have read. Does he seem to affirm your pattern of separation as an application of these commands? If he affirms your pattern, does this change your attitude toward the practice you are following? If he does not affirm your pattern, what is his word of direction to you? Journal your experience in this exercise. Be prepared to test your sense of direction with others during the discipling session.

Day Three: Read reflectively the Scriptures supporting a dis-ciple's participation in the life of Jesus. Then recall the new expression of social ethics you considered on *Day One.* Prayerfully picture Jesus beside you and reflect with him on the Scriptures and the step of obedience you are considering. What does Christ seem to be asking of you? Journal your experience and be pre-pared to share with others at the discipling session.

Day Four: The exercise associated with *Day Four* of the last lesson (16) focused on discerning the gifts and vocation of a group member. Reread that discussion and do the exercise for a designated group member(s).

Day Five: Do general journaling or discern the gifts and vocation of a second group member.

Discipling Session

The new activity of this group session relates to ethical discernment. The concern is to develop skill in helping others determine their ethical practices through the use of Scriptures, reflective conversation with Jesus, and discussion with other believers.

1. Share with your discipling partner your experience with the exercises on *Day Two* and *Day Three*. What difference did your awareness of the presence of Jesus bring to your reflections? Test with others new steps of faithfulness you feel called to take.

2. As a total group move through the gift discernment process as outlined in Lesson 16 with one or two persons. Have the designated person share perceptions of his or her own gifts after each group member shares his or her perceptions of the gifts and emerging vocation of that same person. Attempt to reach consensus on these issues.

3. Desired Discipling Skill: ability to assist others in ethical discernment. This skill grows out of personal experience in ethical discernment and the ability to enter into the discernment process with other persons.

Lesson 18

The Kingdom of God

Discipleship Theme: The Two Kingdoms

In the last lesson, reference was made to the evils of the world and the need for Christians to practice separation from evil in their ethical practices. Lesson 18 will reflect further on the spheres of righteousness and unrighteousness as it examines the realities of the kingdom of God and the kingdom of the world.

Biblical Teachings

The concept of the kingdom of God in the midst of the kingdom of the world was introduced in the Old Testament[1] and expanded in the New Testament.

Jesus began his ministry by announcing that "the kingdom of heaven is at hand" (Mt. 3:2; 4:17). With this announcement came a call to repentance. Furthermore, Jesus began teaching and "preaching the gospel of the kingdom and healing every disease" (Mt. 4:23). He told his disciples, "I must preach the good news of the kingdom of God to the other cities also; for I was sent for this purpose" (Lk. 4:43). During his ministry, Jesus told stories about the kingdom (Mt. 13), which revealed something about the nature of the kingdom and how it would come.

Later in Jesus' ministry, he referred to the kingdom of Satan and the kingdom of God as two separate but conflicting realities (Lk. 11:18-20). Jesus indicated to Pilate that his kingdom or kingship emerged from a source other than this world and his kingdom called him to a manner of life different from the pattern of this hostile world. He said, "My kingship is not of this world; if my kingship were of this world, my servants would fight, that I might not be handed over to the Jews" (Jn. 18:36). After his resurrection, Jesus appeared to his disciples over a period of forty days and spoke to them "of the kingdom of God" (Acts 1:3).

The Epistles continued the same theme. Paul, Peter, and John wrote about the two kingdoms in terms of light and darkness (2 Cor. 6:14; 1 Pet. 2:9; 1 Jn. 1:6-7). There was always the assumption that the Christian had moved from the kingdom of darkness to the kingdom of light. Paul wrote that God "has delivered us from the dominion of darkness and transferred us to the kingdom of his beloved Son" (Col. 1:13; Gal. 1:4).

In John's writings to believers, he warned them not to love "the world" because this kingdom "is not of the Father" and in fact is passing away (1 Jn. 2:15-17).

The New Testament then presents a dualism of two opposing kingdoms. One is ruled by Satan and the other is ruled by Christ. One is a kingdom of darkness and the other is a kingdom of light. The Christian has moved from the one to the other through the act of repentance and regeneration by the power of the Holy Spirit. However, the Christian lives in tension with the kingdom and power of darkness even though he or she lives in the kingdom and power of the light of Christ.

Anabaptist Writings

To understand the importance of the doctrine of the two kingdoms for the Anabaptists, we must first understand the change which took place in the fourth century. This change is traced by Harold S. Bender in his book *These Are My People*. After describing the duality of the church and world as pictured in the New Testament, Bender writes as follows:

> Behind this duality lies the concept of the two kingdoms. The one is "the dominion of darkness," the kingdom of this world; the other is "the kingdom of his beloved Son." To enter the church is to be delivered from the one and transferred into the other. Colossians 1:13. Thus the church is

distinct from the world, not of it. It is the realm of redemption, the realm in which the Holy Spirit operates and Christ is Lord. In the New Testament the line of distinction between the two kingdoms is sharply drawn, the church and its members are separate from the world, yet operating redemptively in it to bring men to faith in Christ that they may be redeemed and incorporated into the fellowship of the body of Christ.

The two-kingdom relationship as outlined above has been broken in two opposite directions in the history of the church. On the one hand, as a result of the Constantinian compromise in the fourth century the line between church and world disappeared, and the concept of Christendom as the *Corpus Christianum* replaced it. In effect the world as such disappeared, and the patterns of culture became the patterns of Christian living. This concept continued to dominate not only medieval Catholicism both East and West, but also the state churches which emerged from the Reformation. These latter carried no mission into the world to make disciples, bound as they were by the territorial concepts of magisterial Protestantism. In the opposite direction various groups of earnest Christians down through the ages, including the free churches emerging in the Reformation and in the century following it, as well as certain modern groups, have been inclined to draw the line of separation between church and world so sharply as to retreat from the world into a sectarian isolation. These groups have been "not of the world" indeed, but also, alas, often not "in the world." Their temptation has been to "pass by on the other side" like the priest and Levite in the story of the Good Samaritan, leaving the world to perish in its misery while drawing the cloaks of their righteousness about them. The Anabaptists of the Reformation time were an exception, with their strong urge to fulfill the Great Commission. And in modern times it is these free churches which have been the pioneers in missionary outreach. Isolationism developed in the intervening centuries.[2]

A major contribution of the Anabaptist movement was the rediscovery of the world as a result of rediscovering the church. They attempted to bring back into being in the sixteenth century the dualism which the New Testament taught and described in the first century (see Appendix 1, pages 274-275).

Robert Friedmann has identified the kingdom theology held by certain Christian groups throughout church history and which was accepted by the Anabaptists. This theology enabled the Anabaptists to embrace both New Testament dualism and discipleship. How was this possible? Friedmann gives the following explanation:

The answer comes very simply if we look closely at the two sides of this dualism. We see the tension between the kingdom of God (or kingdom of heaven) on the one hand and the kingdom of the prince of this world (or the kingdom of darkness) on the other. If the reborn believer decided for the former kingdom, his "theology" was clearly marked. It is generally known as *kingdom theology*. It is the hidden theology of Jesus Himself and His deepest message. "Be prepared," He says (Matthew 24; Mark 13; or Luke 21), "the kingdom is imminent. But only the pure will enter into it, while all the rest will perish." This is definitely an eschatological idea, and requires some effort to decide either for or against "the world." Yet it is a glorious idea and far superior to any worldly philosophy, a promise not of a "yonder" after death, but of a present possibility.

This kingdom theology fits almost perfectly to everything said above. It requires a close brotherhood of committed disciples as the citizens of the expected kingdom. It also implies discipleship as basic, and finally makes the believer aware of the eternal warfare between the "children of light against the children of darkness," roughly corresponding to the aforementioned "theology of martyrdom."[3]

In *The Schleithem Confession* of 1527, the concept of two kingdoms is clearly evident. Article III says:

All those who have fellowship with the dead works of darkness have no part in the light. Thus all who follow the devil and the world, have no part with those who have been called out of the world unto God. All those who lie in evil have no part in the good.[4]

Article IV reads:

Now there is nothing else in the world and all creation than good or evil, believing and unbelieving, darkness and light, the world and those who are [come] out of the world, God's temple and idols, Christ and Belial, and none will have part with the other.[5]

Menno Simons also spoke of two kingdoms which he described as opposing kingdoms.

The Scriptures teach that there are two opposing princes and two opposing kingdoms: the one is the Prince of peace; the other the prince of strife. Each of these princes has his particular kingdom and as the prince is so is also the kingdom. The Prince of peace is Christ Jesus; His kingdom is the kingdom of peace, which is His church; His messengers are the messengers of peace; His Word is the word of peace; His body is the body of peace; His children are the seed of peace; and His inheritance and reward are the inheritance and reward of peace. In short, with this King, and in His kingdom and reign, it is nothing but peace. Everything that is seen, heard, and done is peace.[6]

The Anabaptists viewed the church as functioning in the kingdom of God or the kingdom of peace. The magistrate or government functioned in the kingdom of Satan or the kingdom of strife, as did most of society. The function of the state was God-given and was twofold: to punish the evildoer and protect the good (Rom. 13). It controlled violence with violence. Members of the kingdom of peace could not participate in the violence of the old order or kingdom of strife. This led to a life of separation and doctrine of the two kingdoms.

Contemporary Writings
Today a fresh emphasis on the kingdom of God is found in the writings of scholars concerned about church renewal. The focus is not on the isolation of the church from society but rather the church living the radical demands of the kingdom within and speaking to society.

For many years, some religious leaders came close to equating America with the kingdom of God. As a result, the church made its peace with society by accepting and supporting many of society's values. This position is being challenged and rejected by twentieth-century prophets such as John Howard Yoder, Howard A. Snyder, Donald G. Bloesch, Waldron Scott, David Watson, Jim Wallis, and others.

How is the kingdom understood by these authors? Snyder defines the kingdom as "the dominion or reign of God and not primarily a place or realm."[7] Again he states, "It is Jesus Christ and, through the Church, the uniting of all things in him. For the present it is the growth in the world of the grace, joy, health, peace, and love seen in Jesus. The kingdom is both present and future, both earthly and heavenly, both hidden and becoming manifest."[8]

Prior to 1900, there was a kingdom-consciousness in America which envisioned God transforming the total of society. However, according to Snyder, "social gospelers secularized this kingdom vision and conservatives spiritualized it."[9] Today there is an attempt to revive a kingdom-consciousness which has a biblical balance of social and spiritual reality and optimism and pessimism.

One additional insight from Snyder is important. He sees the church not only as the messianic community but also as the agent of the kingdom of God. The church is more than a sign or symbol of the kingdom to come, it is the agent of God's redeeming work on earth.[10] However, the kingdom is always more comprehensive than the visible church. The kingdom of God implies that God is the sovereign Lord. His will and purposes are being, and will be, carried out on earth.

If the church is the agent of the kingdom, what is the role of the church in society? Waldron Scott sees the total Christ event as God's action in history "to reconcile and heal the human race."[11] Jesus is our norm and this calls us to oppose the values of all uncovered societies. All that opposes the purposes of the King in history is outside the purpose and will of God (Mt. 6:10).

Scott relates this concept to his view of evangelism and discipleship in the following statements:

> An evangelistic invitation oriented toward discipleship will include a call to join the living Lord in the work of his Kingdom. It will point to specific needs in the larger world beyond the individual's private concerns. It will direct attention to the aspirations of ordinary men and women in society, their dreams of justice, security, full stomachs, human dignity, and opportunities for their children. It will forthrightly name the "principalities and powers" opposed to the Kingdom, the demonic forces and institutions that thwart the aspirations of the vast majority of mankind's poor, and thereby defy and contradict the rule of God.[12]
>
> The evangelist oriented toward discipleship will speak of sin not only in traditional terms, that is, individual acts of lying, adultery, drunkenness, and so forth, but he or she will also specify the individual's social sins—sins of ommission as well as commission (Matthew 25:45). He or she will go even further and point out the individual's complicity in structural evil, institutionalized sin, and national unrighteousness. Then the evangelist will announce good news![13]

Another missions leader who promotes world evangelism with the kingdom of God orientation and values is Orlandos Costas. His summary of the goal of Third World missions is a fitting summary and conclusion of this discussion.

The ultimate goal of Third World missions should be the final revelation of the kingdom [of God], understood as the total transformation of history by Jesus Christ and the power of his Spirit. This will involve the redemption of creation, the definitive abrogation of evil, chaos and corruption and the birth of a world of love, peace, and justice. Third World missions, as any Christian mission, should see themselves, fundamentally, as witnesses to the coming Kingdom.

The kingdom of God, however, is not just a future, transcendent reality. It is also a present and eminent order of life, characterized by the forgiveness of sins, the formation of a new community, and commitment to a new ethic. This order of life is centered on the person and work of the Lord Jesus Christ. Hence to witness to the kingdom is to declare the name of Jesus Christ as the Lord and Saviour of humankind.

This in turn implies that the announcement of Jesus Christ in the world has personal, communal, and socio-political dimensions. Personal, in the sense that it is accompanied by the call to faith and repentance and the concomitant experience of forgiveness of sin. Communal, in that it implies incorporation into the church, understood as a community of faith and commitment. And socio-political, in the sense that it involves a new life-style based on love, whose practical expression is justice and ultimate hope is peace (or well-being) for all. . . .

This means that Third World missions, if they are to be faithful to God's Kingdom, will have a three-fold orientation: (1) the communication of the gospel, (2) the growth and development of the church, and (3) the advocacy of a fraternal life-style, social justice and world peace. This triple orientation will have its fulcrum on Jesus Christ.[14]

Journaling Focus

Day One: Reflect on what you have read regarding the two kingdoms. What new insights have you received? Where have you most graphically experienced the reality of the kingdom of God and the kingdom of Satan?

Spiritual Exercise: Discerning Kingdom Orientation

The New Testament is clear in identifying two kingdoms, one a kingdom of light and the other a kingdom of darkness. People give their loyalties to one kingdom or the other. Their lives reflect one kingdom orientation or the other.

186 Ventures in Discipleship

The Anabaptists tended to associate the kingdom of God with the true church and the kingdom of Satan with the world (everything outside of the church community). The result was a sharp distinction between church and world and the practice of physical separation. Reflecting their ascetic theology, they became monasteries without walls.

The contemporary writers tend to define the kingdom of God and Satan in terms of values, attitudes, and actions which express the will of God or which represent a rejection of God's reign in one's life. This would suggest that reflections of the kingdom of Satan may be found in the lives of believers and in the Christian church, and that reflections of the kingdom of God may be found outside of the church.

The Christian then is called to incarnate the ideals of the kingdom of God in all aspects of life and to discern and remove all expressions of the kingdom of Satan in his or her personal and corporate or community life. The following spiritual exercises relate to the discernment of one's kingdom orientation.

Day Two: Identify the five or six most important values or attitudes that influence and direct your life. Through a process of journaling, reflect on each value or attitude in terms of the kingdom from which it springs. Will faithfulness to Christ as king call for some change? If so, what change?

Day Three: The New Testament ties together commitment to Christ and commitment to the kingdom of God (Acts 28:30-31). This suggests that the life and power of Jesus are needed in order to live the new life of the kingdom of God. What does this say to you about the type of prophetic witness necessary to bring genuine change in society? You may wish to reflect further on the biblical teachings and the quotation by Orlando Costas before journaling your response.

Day Four: The exercise for today is the same as the *Day Four* exercises of the past two lessons, namely, discerning the gifts and vocation of a group member. Review those instructions if the assignment is unclear to you.

Day Five: Do general journaling or discern the gifts and vocation of a second group member.

Discipling Session

The group activity for this session in addition to gift discernment relates to discerning one's kingdom orientation and approach to prophetic witness. The concern is developing the skill of helping others relate the realities of the two kingdoms to their own lives.

1. Share with your discipling partner your journaling on *Day One* and *Day Two*. Be sensitive to what Christ might be asking of that person and help them respond to Christ's call.

2. The gift discernment process outlined in Lesson 16 should be followed with another group member. Have the designated person share his or her view of his or her own gifts, after the group members share their insights concerning that person's gifts and emerging vocational direction. If time permits, discuss your journaling for *Day Three*.

3. Desired Discipling Skill: ability to discern one's kingdom orientation. If the kingdom of God and of Satan are defined in terms of values, attitudes, and actions, then all Christians have the potential of expressing the kingdom of Satan in and through their lives.

Lesson 19

The Cost of Discipleship

Discipleship Theme: Bearing the Cross of Christ

This lesson is directly related to the study of the two kingdoms in that the cross symbolizes the response of the kingdom of Satan when encountered by the kingdom of God. The cross symbolizes the clash between the church and the world. The disciple, like the master, becomes involved in the struggle against evil and experiences the cross, a symbol of this struggle.

Biblical Teachings

The theme of the cross and suffering runs through the teachings of Jesus and the apostles. Jesus indicated that each follower would have "his cross" and it would in some way be related to the cross of Jesus. This is seen most clearly in Mark's Gospel. Jesus told the disciples about his own suffering, death, and resurrection. He then invited any who wished to follow him to take up his own cross and follow (Mk. 8:31-38). Matthew reports Jesus' words concerning the family divisions that will come because of the gospel. This is followed by the warning that the worthy follower is the one who takes his cross and follows (Mt. 10:34-39). Luke places the emphasis on Jesus' insistence on counting the cost before deciding to follow because to follow truly means bearing one's own cross (Lk. 14:25-33). It is significant to observe that in each of these passages, an individual's cross and following Jesus are brought together.

Paul continued the theme of the cross and suffering in his teaching and Epistles. When visiting the new churches at the end of his first missionary journey, he exhorted them to be faithful because they would enter the kingdom of God through many tribulations (Acts 14:22). To the Corinthians he linked his suffering for Christ and his authority as an apostle (2 Cor. 11:21-33). Furthermore, Paul saw his suffering for Christ as a way of sharing in Christ's suffering (Phil. 3:10) and in some sense completing the suffering of Christ (Col. 1:24).

Peter upheld the suffering of Christ as an example of the experience of Christ's followers. We are called to follow in his steps of suffering (1 Pet. 2:18-25).

In summary, Christ identified the cross as a central symbol for viewing his life of suffering as he encountered a world of unbelief and evil. This was what it cost to follow the will of the Father. This is also what it will cost for believers to follow the will of the Son.

Anabaptist Writings

In Appendix 1, pages 248-253, there is a discussion of the Anabaptists' call to bear the cross of Christ and to suffer willingly in the spirit of Christ. Because of the length of that discussion, additional reading sources do not need to be included in this lesson. As you read in Appendix 1, give particular attention to the following points:

First, from the very beginning of the movement the Anabaptists assumed that suffering would be the price of true discipleship.

Second, their own suffering was viewed as a continuation of Christ's suffering, which meant that suffering was normal and should be expected by Christians.

Third, their own cross was the consequence of their encounter with evil.

Fourth, the nature and depth of their suffering was almost beyond description.

Fifth, the theology of martydrom was central to their willingness to suffer and die for Christ.

Sixth, their theology was in sharp contrast to the theology of the cross and its emphasis on internal suffering.

Seventh, suffering was viewed as a means of sanctification and therefore beneficial for one's Christian life.

If you have access to *The Complete Writings of Menno Simons*, I would recommend that you read "The Cross of the Saints," pages 580-622. It is a deeply moving experience.

Contemporary Writings

The title of this lesson certainly brings to mind the very significant book by Dietrich Bonhoeffer, *The Cost of Discipleship*. In his reflection on Mark 8:31-38, Bonhoeffer notes Jesus' prediction that he "must" suffer and be rejected. He further points out that "the 'must' of suffering applies to his disciples no less than to Himself."[1] This conviction is at the center of Bonhoeffer's writings.

Howard A. Snyder writes with a similar conviction. He holds that the church in the present age is called to live by "crucifixion ethics not triumphal ethics."[2] "We are called to be cross-bearers more than cross wearers."[3] Christians today follow a king whose life led him to a cross. This life experience represents the demands of discipleship.

Some Christians today see in Christ's suffering primarily his role as our substitute, suffering in our place. Others see in his suffering the role of our example. He pioneered the path of victory through suffering and we follow that same path.

Snyder helpfully reflects on these points of view.

> Some say Christ suffered so we wouldn't have to. Jesus took our place on the cross and suffered there to save us. By his death we have life. Through his sorrow we have joy. By his self-emptying we are made rich.
>
> But others look differently at the suffering of Jesus. They say his suffering reveals the dimensions of Christian discipleship. Christ's death and resurrection show us what happens to every person who seeks first the Kingdom of God. The crucifixion is a demonstration to us of the meaning and cost of discipleship. The cross, therefore, is not our escape from suffer-

ing, but rather our guarantee of suffering. Jesus is more our model than he is our route of escape.

Which view is biblical?

Both are. Jesus did take our place on the cross; through that sacrifice we have life. We have been made rich. "For you know the grace of our Lord Jesus Christ, that though he was rich, yet for your sakes he became poor, so that you through his poverty might become rich" (2 Cor. 8:9).

But that's not the whole story, and it's not the definition of discipleship. For Paul says, "Your attitude should be the same as that of Christ Jesus: Who, being in very nature God, did not consider equality with God something to be grasped, but made himself nothing, taking the very nature of a servant, being made in human likeness. And being found in appearance as a man, he humbled himself and became obedient to death—even death on a cross!" (Phil. 2:5-8). And John says, "In this world we are like him" (1 Jn. 4:17). Jesus said, "If anyone would come after me, he must deny himself and take up his cross daily and follow me" (Lk. 9:23). "Whoever claims to live in him must walk as Jesus did" (1 Jn. 2:6). And the apostle Peter tells us, "To this you were called, because Christ suffered for you, leaving you an example, that you should follow in his steps" (1 Pet. 2:21).

When we speak about our redemption, our eternal salvation, then we can joyfully say that Christ has suffered so we might not have to suffer. He has taken upon himself the guilt and punishment of sin. But when we speak of our life in the world, of discipleship, we see another truth at work. Scripture is consistent in showing that the disciple must be like his master and that self-denial, self-emptying and crucifixion are universal marks of those who follow Jesus.[4]

David Watson believes that the gospel is calling believers to an alternative society with values that will challenge those of existing society. To adopt a lifestyle that challenges covetousness, oppression, or self-centeredness will likely result in strong opposition or persecution.[5]

The specific function of the Christian, according to Jacques Ellul, is defined by the Scriptures in three ways. We are to be the salt of the earth, the light of the world, and sheep in the midst of wolves.[6] In describing the "sheep" role of the Christian in society, Ellul states:

He is a 'sheep' not because his action or his sacrifice has a purifying effect on the world, but because he is the living and real 'sign,' constantly renewed in the midst of the world, of the sacrifice of the Lamb of God. In the world everyone wants to be a 'wolf,' and no one is called to play the part of a 'sheep.' Yet the world cannot *live* without this living witness of sacrifice. That is why it is essential that Christians should be very careful not to be 'wolves' in the spiritual sense—that is, people who try to dominate others. Christians must accept the domination of other people,[7] and offer the daily sacrifice of their lives, which is united with the sacrifice of Jesus Christ.[8]

Journaling Focus

Day One: As you ponder these readings regarding the cross of Christ, what message are you hearing? The message may seem old or new but listen to it carefully. Reflect on the message in your journaling.

Day Two: What has the cross of Christ meant in your own life? Identify in specific terms the experiential meaning of the cross to you. What price are you willing to pay if tests should come in areas such as economic hardship, social rejection, or physical violence?

Spiritual Exercise: Counting the Cost

One of the New Testament themes we observed in the teachings of Jesus was the need to consider the cost of being his follower before beginning to follow him.

One of the contemporary themes is the warning that discipleship may be costly. The future reality of the kingdom will be

One of the contemporary themes is the warning that discipleship may be costly. The future reality of the kingdom will be triumphant. The present reality of the kingdom may have the cost of suffering or death.

These various themes call us to count the cost, to consider the personal price we are willing to pay to follow King Jesus. The following exercises will help you ponder these issues.

Day Three: One response to this lesson might be guilt because you are not now suffering for Christ. If that is your feeling, explore your guilt in your journaling. Reflect on why you have this feeling. Is it related to some specific act of disobedience in discipleship or is it a vague accusation of Satan (Rev. 12:10). Did the feeling start recently or have you had it for some time? If you were attempting to help another person who had guilt feelings because he or she was not suffering for Christ, how would you proceed? (Remember, suffering can motivate self-righteousness.)

Day Four: Today you may conclude the exercise in discerning the gifts and vocation of a member of your group. Review the instructions found in previous lessons if you are unsure of the process.

Day Five: Do general journaling or discern the gifts and vocation of a second group member if necessary.

Discipling Session

Before completing the gift discernment process, attention will be given to the way we have experienced the cross of Christ and the discipleship cost we would be willing to pay. This session should help to develop skill in discipling persons regarding costly discipleship.

1. Share with your discipling partner your journaling on *Day One* and *Day Two.* Do not push the other person beyond his or her present commitment but do encourage him or her to identify that commitment. As time permits, discuss your response to the *Day Three* exercise either with your discipling partner or the total group.

2. The final member of the group should experience the discernment process. Have the person share his or her own discernment of personal gifts and vocational direction after each group member shares their perceptions.

3. Have the total group reflect on accountability and faithfulness in developing and using one's gifts. This may well be included in costly discipleship.

4. Desired Discipling Skill: ability to help persons face costly discipleship. Sharing with another person your commitment to costly discipleship will likely be a new experience but it can be very beneficial.

Lesson 20

Children of Peace

Discipleship Theme: Love and Nonresistance

In the last lesson, we studied the potential cost of being a disciple when evil is encountered. The cost for Christ was the cross or suffering and death. It can be the same for us, his followers. The theme of love and nonresistance defines how a child of peace responds in the face of hostility and violence.

Biblical Teachings

The Sermon on the Mount identifies Christ's pattern for kingdom living. Peace, love, and nonviolence are the norm. In the Beatitudes, a primary ethical calling is to be peacemakers (Mt. 5:9). This general calling is defined negatively in terms of not resisting evil (nonresistance) (Mt. 5:38-39). Positively, it is defined in terms of "going the second mile" and also loving one's enemies even to the point of doing them good and praying that God will bless them (Mt. 5:40-48).

As violence and evil increased toward the end of Christ's life, he repeatedly rejected the use of the sword. Peter was reprimanded for attempting to protect Christ with the sword (Mt. 26:52-54). Pilate was informed that even though swords are a part of his' earthly kingdom, they have no place in the kingdom of Christ (Jn. 18:36).

Christ modeled his own teachings when he faced the cross. Instead of encountering violence with violence, he absorbed and conquered evil through redemptive love.

Paul taught the same approach to evil when he instructed believers at Rome to do good to their enemies and leave vengeance to the wrath of God (Rom. 12:14-21).

Peter apparently profited from the instructions Jesus gave him when he used the sword in the garden. Years later, he instructed suffering believers to follow the example Christ gave us when he faced hostility and the cross (1 Pet. 2:21-25).

John relates the ethics of love to life among believers and in a world of hate. To truly love means that we love our brothers and sisters in the faith to the point of laying down our lives for them and not being surprised by the hatred of the world (1 Jn. 3:11-18).

Anabaptist Writings

For a discussion of the Anabaptist ethic of redemptive love, read Appendix 1, pages 245-248. Note in particular the following points:

First, from the very beginning of the movement, they rejected the use of the sword for purposes of war, personal protection, or church discipline. Furthermore, they were aware that taking this stance could mean persecution and death.

Second, the Anabaptists recognized the legitimacy of the sword for the state but that even this was outside the perfection of Christ.

Third, functionally their position was based on the teachings and examples of Christ in his earthly ministry. Theologically, it was based on their view of Christianity as a transformed life of love and obedience.

Fourth, the love of God was their source of divine strength enabling them to love the enemy or the one persecuting them.

Fifth, their pattern resembled in part the practice of ascetic separation from the world also found in monastic orders.

Michael Sattler viewed true New Testament love as the evidence of being a Christian congregation. Love needed to be lived in the church before it could be lived in the world. In his "Letter to the Church at Horb," he wrote the following instructions:

Further, dear fellow members in Christ, you should be admonished not to forget love, without which it is not possible that you be a Christian congregation. You know what love is through the testimony of Paul our fellow brother; he says: Love is patient and kind, not jealous, not puffed up, not ambitious, seeks not its own, thinks no evil, rejoices not in iniquity, rejoices in the truth, suffers everything, endures everything, believes everything, hopes everything. If you understand this text, you will find the love of God and of neighbor. If you love God you will rejoice in the truth and will believe, hope, and endure everything that comes from God. Thereby the shortcomings mentioned above can be removed and avoided. But if you love the neighbor, you will not scold or ban zealously, will not seek your own, will not remember evil, will not be ambitious or puffed up, but kind, righteous, generous in all gifts, humble and sympathetic with the weak and imperfect.

Some brothers, I know who they are, have fallen short of this love. They have not wanted to build up one another in love, but are puffed up and have become useless with vain speculation and understanding of those things which God wants to keep secret to Himself. I do not admonish or reject the grace and revelation of God, but the inflated use of this revelation. What is the use, says Paul, if one speaks with all sorts of tongues of men and angels? And knows all mysteries, wisdom, and has all faith, he says, what is all that worth if the one and only love is not exercised?[1]

Contemporary Writings

The central importance of love for the Christian is evident in current writings. However, the focus or application varies considerably. In this section, I will identify and briefly describe three areas of application. Each area is important and the Christian whose life is centered in love will apply the love of God in each of the areas.

The first and basic area in which love must be applied is in the human relationships of everyday life. In her helpful book *Adventures in Prayer*, Catherine Marshall tells about a friend whose life and home was filled with tension because a nagging aunt was constantly finding fault with the children. The friend had been praying that God would change the aunt's disposition but the aunt did not change. Catherine Marshall suggested that she try asking God to bless the aunt in anything and everything. This would be following the command of Jesus to love our enemies and bless those that curse us (Mt. 5:44).

Within a week, the atmosphere of the home had completely

changed. Reflecting on the incident Catherine Marshall observed, "As soon as we begin to obey Him, we find that blessing those with whom we are having difficulties and the *answer* to these difficulties, go hand in hand."[2]

Another area requiring the application of love is in the arena of social improvement. Prophets, in the name of love and compassion, can be quite unloving toward those persons or groups they wish to change. Elton Trueblood has an instructive word related to this area needing the application of love.

> In many ways the recognition that love is the final test of orthodoxy is shocking. It means that we may be outside the true fellowship of Christ even when we are ardent workers for some social improvement, if our crusade is carried on in an unloving way. Thus it is possible to have a burning zeal for race equality or for world peace that is really alien to Christ, provided the zeal allows us to be unloving or unfair to those who happen to differ from us on these particular issues. The paradox of the unloving pacifist, who condemns all of those in the armed forces and maligns his opponents, is one which we sometimes see in contemporary experience. It may be no worse than many other features of our religious life, but it stands out because the inconsistency of the position is so glaring. Christian pacifism is a great and needed witness, but whenever it is separated from the love of Christ it seems inevitably to become cruel and bitter. The crusade for racial justice, with absolute insistence upon equality of opportunity and equal justice, is one of the most urgent matters in the life of modern man, but if it is separated from love, even the demand for justice is debased. A Negro's hatred of white people, while understandable, is really no better than a white man's contempt for colored people. The task of the Church is to be a continual reminder of what the central matter is.[3]

A third area where love needs to be applied is the circumstance of facing social or political violence. An increasing number of Christians see the example of Jesus as the Suffering Servant relating directly to this area of life. John H. Yoder speaks to this area of application.

> As long as readers could stay unaware of the political/social dimension of Jesus' ministry (which most of Christendom seems to have done quite successfully), then it was also possible to perceive the "in Christ" language of the Epistles as mystical or the "dying with Christ" as psychologically morbid. But if we may posit—as after the preceding pages we must—that the apostles had and taught at least a core memory of their Lord's earthly

ministry in its blunt historicity, then this centering of the apostolic ethic upon the disciple's cross evidences a substantial, binding, costly social stance. There have perhaps been times when the issues of power, violence, and peoplehood were not at the center of ethical preoccupations; but in the waning twentieth century they certainly are, and the rediscovery of this ethic of "responsibility" or of "power" can no longer at the same time claim to be Christian and bypass the judgment or the promise of the Suffering Servant's exemplarity.[4]

Journaling Focus

Day One: Interact with the biblical, Anabaptist, and contemporary material you have just read. Your response v likely reflect your background teaching and experience. Be free to identify new insights, points of agreement, disagreement, or question.

Spiritual Exercise: Discerning the Spiritual Battle

The past several lessons have referred to the spiritual character of the conflict in which the church of Christ is involved. Lesson 18 discussed the kingdoms of Christ and Satan and the conflict between the two. When Satan attacks Christ, he does so by attacking the followers of Christ (Rev. 12). Lesson 19 presented the cross as a symbol of the suffering experienced by Christ and his followers in a world of evil and hostility. The conflict at the cross was not only physical, it was also spiritual. The powers of darkness were at work.

Now in Lesson 20, we observed that hostility is a spiritual as well as a physical reality and that it can be conquered only by the spiritual force of divine love.

All of these lessons assume that the Christian is involved in a spiritual battle. Furthermore, these lessons assume that the nature of the battle can be understood only through spiritual insight and victory ' in the battle can be achieved only through spiritual resources. It is therefore important that we reflect on this spiritual battle.

As Jesus began his public ministry he was tempted by the devil in the wilderness (Mt. 4:1f.). As he taught, Jesus frequently spoke about the devil and the conflict with him (Mt. 13:19, 39; 16:23; Jn. 8:44; 17:15).

Paul warned the believers to be alert to the work and ways of Satan (2 Cor. 11:14; Eph. 4:27; 1 Tim. 3:7; 4:1). His most detailed instructions were given to the Ephesians (Eph. 6:10-20). He pointed the Colossians to the cross of Christ as the source of victory (Col. 2:15).

John spoke about the need to test the spirits (1 Jn. 4:1). This is necessary when so many ideas and patterns appear to be on the edge between truth and error.

In his book *Called & Committed* David Watson has a helpful discussion of the "Spiritual Warfare." He discusses six tactics frequently used by the evil one in the history of God's people. These are (1) persecution, (2) accusations in the form of criticism or false reports, (3) carnality of Christians, (4) counterfeit movements, (5) temptation to worldly materialism, morality and values, and (6) demon-possession.[5]

It is important that we take seriously the warnings and instructions of the biblical writers noted earlier in this lesson so that we can identify the enemy and claim the victory already provided in Jesus Christ.

Day Two: In the *Contemporary Writings*, three areas were discussed in which love must be applied if we are to be children of peace. Identify the area in which you are experiencing the most conflict and reflect on how this lesson can influence your daily response.

Day Three: Identify the most intense spiritual battle in which you are now engaged. Then reflect on the tactics of Satan mentioned by Watson and the biblical references to the devil mentioned in this lesson. Now attempt to describe the spiritual realities of the battle. Look beyond the visible persons or circumstances to the unseen power at work, beyond the flesh and blood to the principalities and powers (Eph. 6:12).

Day Four: Refresh in your mind the exercise of *Day Three*, including the unseen power or Satan behind your battle. Then meditate on Ephesians 6:10-20. Is there some part of the spiritual armor you have been missing? If so, take all necessary steps to complete your protection.

Day Five: Your general journaling today can focus on your major item of concern or activity.

Discipling Session

The purpose of this session is to learn from each other concerning the meaning of redemptive love and the nature of the spiritual battle. The group experience should equip each member to more adequately and more effectively relate to the spiritual battle of disciples.

1. Share with your discipling partner your journaling on *Day One* and *Day Two*. Encourage honesty of response even though points of view may differ. You may also want to share from *Day Five*.

2. As a total group, reflect on your experience with the exercises of *Day Three* and *Day Four*. These can be shared as one total experience. Attempt to learn all you can from each other. Are there major questions or issues needing more attention?

3. Desired Discipling Skill: ability to discern spiritual conflicts. The area of spiritual conflicts may seem strange and difficult to grasp. It is important that we learn with other Christians so that our insights can be tested.

Lesson 21

Ministry to Human Need

Discipleship Theme: The Service of Charity

This lesson relates to, but goes beyond, two previous lessons. In Lesson 15, the focus was meeting material needs within the brotherhood. In this lesson we will look at meeting human need outside the church. In Lesson 20, we examined the response of love toward those who evidence hatred toward us. In this lesson we will reflect on the response of love toward persons who possess needs that we can meet. Love, therefore, not only determines our reactions (how we react toward hostility and violence); love also determines our actions (how we act toward persons needing the service of charity).

Biblical Teachings

The theme of service and charity finds broad support in the New Testament. Jesus supported the giving of alms when done with the proper motive (Mt. 6:2-4; Lk. 12:33). He instructed the rich young ruler to "sell what you have and give to the poor" (Mt. 19:21). In one of his most significant statements, Jesus identified meeting the needs of the hungry and thirsty, welcoming the stranger, clothing the naked, and visiting the sick and prisoners as a service done to him and as evidence of true Christianity (Mt. 25:31-40).

Paul also taught and practiced the importance of serving the needy. When James, Cephas, and John gave to Paul and

Barnabas the right hand of fellowship, they sent them to the Gentiles with the instructions that they should "remember the poor." Paul later reflected, "Which very thing I was eager to do" (Gal. 2:10). To the Ephesians Paul wrote, "Let the thief no longer steal, but rather let him labor, doing honest work with his hands, so that he may be able to give to those in need" (Eph. 4:28).

Timothy was instructed by Paul to charge the rich not to be proud or trust in their riches. Rather, "They are to do good, to be rich in good deeds, liberal and generous" (1 Tim. 6:18).

The Christian, then, is to view human need the way Jesus viewed human need and to respond with loving service as the servant of Jesus Christ.

Anabaptist Writings

The practice of mutual aid or meeting needs within the brotherhood was strongly practiced by the Anabaptists, as was noted in Lesson 15. But they also practiced the service of charity to those outside the brotherhood.

In his discussion "On Two Kinds of Obedience," Michael Sattler stated that "the filial is busy with the love of God and the neighbor."[1]

Sattler viewed the love of neighbor as the outworking of the Holy Spirit in the life of the believer. The divine order was teach, hear, believe, baptize, receive the Spirit, and produce good works.[2]

Hans Leopold, a minister of the Swiss Brethren in Augsburg who was martyred in 1528, said, "If they know of anyone who is in need, whether or not he is a member of their church, they believe it their duty, out of love to God, to render him help and aid."[3]

Menno Simons both taught and practiced this type of help and aid. We noted in Lesson 15 his description of true evangelical faith: "It clothes the naked; it feeds the hungry; it comforts the sorrowful; it shelters the destitute; it aids and consoles the sad; ... it binds up that which is wounded; it heals that which is diseased and it saves that which is sound."[4]

205 Ministry to Human Need

Menno also wrote concerning those who are born of God. "They show mercy and love, as much as they can. No one among them is allowed to beg. They take to heart the need of the saints. They entertain those in distress. They take the stranger into their houses. They comfort the afflicted; assist the needy; clothe the naked; feed the hungry; do not turn their face from the poor; do not despise their own flesh."[5]

Menno not only instructed his followers regarding charity, he practiced it as well. During the winter of 1553-54, Menno associated with a Mennonite congregation at Wismar on the Baltic seacoast. The congregation became involved in helping a group of refugees whose ship had frozen in the ice some distance from shore. John C. Wenger describes the incident.

> The year 1553 found Menno living in Wismar in Mecklenburg, one of the cities of the Hanseatic League. This was the year in which the Zwinglian Protestants of London got into difficulty and had to flee. Two ships carrying these Zwinglian refugees left London for the continent on September 15. They first sailed to Lutheran Denmark, hoping for an asylum. But when King Christian of Denmark learned that they were Zwinglians he ordered them to leave his land. One of the ships arrived at Wismar on December 21 but froze fast in the ice some distance from the shore. The Mennonites of Wismar went to the aid of the refugees, taking to them bread and wine for their refreshment. Poor as they were, the Wismar Mennonites also made up a purse of twenty-four *Thalers* for these people. But the Zwinglian leaders refused the gift, stating that all they wished was opportunity for employment. The Mennonites assisted them so far as it was in their power.[6]

The effort to help these people led to two theological debates between Menno Simons and Herman Backereel, the leader of the refugees, and Martin Micron from East Friesland.

Contemporary Writings

The concern for meaningful service as a part of the church's mission is receiving the attention of numerous contemporary writers. Donald G. Bloesch puts this concern in biblical perspective.

> *Diakonia* (service) is not merely a supplement to the spiritual mission of the church, but an integral element in it. We serve our fellow men with a

supernatural love and for the purpose of preparing them for a supernatural kingdom. Our service is not to be confused with humanitarianism, which often takes the form of condescension and social uplift. We view our neighbor not simply as someone in need but as one for whom Christ died. We give ourselves to our neighbor because Christ first gave Himself for us. We serve our neighbor because of our deep concern for his total welfare (both physical *and* spiritual). Only this kind of love is directed to the whole man; only this deserves to be called Christian love.

There is much talk today of helping the downtrodden and poverty stricken. This is a concern that certainly belongs in the church, and yet we must insist that this kind of ministry should seek to alleviate not merely material but also and above all spiritual poverty. Indeed *diakonia* as well as evangelism must have for its final aim the conversion of men to God. St. Teresa put this very profoundly: "The soul of the care of the poor is the care of the poor soul."[7]

Jim Wallis believes that progress is being made in moving our concern away from materialism and security to the needs of the poor. Does he express your point of view?

Three things are true of a growing number of Christians in this country. First, we no longer believe that our worth and identity as human beings depends on our consumption and possession of things. We are Christians who no longer believe the central lie of the economic system. We neither shun nor ignore material needs, but we meet them simply as we care for one another in our communities of faith. There is no longer a financial incentive in our lives; economic success is no longer a goal. Material goods now have only instrumental value.

Second, we do not feel the need for a nuclear arsenal to protect us. This is not simply a statement of our political position on peace. This is something we know in our hearts. We are not secretly glad that we can go to bed at night and know that nuclear weapons are there to protect us. Their presence makes it harder, not easier, to sleep. We don't recognize any need for the arms race.

Third, a change has come about in the way we tend to look at the world. Social questions, political decisions, and newspaper headlines are now viewed from the vantage point of how they affect poor people. For most of us, that is an entirely new starting point, a whole new perspective for how we think and act. Now, our first impulse is to ask, "How does this affect the poor?"[8]

Richard J. Foster helps to broaden our understanding of service when he identifies nine different types of service.[9]

First, there is the service of hiddenness. When our deeds of service are concealed, they have special value for us as well as the one being served.

Then there is the service of small things. Simple assistance in simple matters is the place to start one's service and the type of service that should continue to be practiced.

A third type of service is guarding the reputations of others. Bernard of Clairvaux called this the service of "charity."

There is also the service of being served. This is the type of service Jesus offered Peter when he wanted to wash his feet.

Fifth, there is the simple service of common courtesy. The word of thanks or the expression of appreciation while being simple is still a service to another.

Closely related is the service of hospitality. An open home is an invaluable service and is a requirement for the office of bishop (1 Tim. 3:2; Tit. 1:8).

Listening is an important and much needed service. One of the greatest gifts we can give another person is our full attention in a service of listening. To be heard and understood is a priceless experience.

The eighth service is bearing one another's burdens (Gal. 6:2). Entering into the sufferings, sorrows, and hurts of another person means that we too suffer, sorrow, and hurt. That is a service that "fulfills the law of Christ."

The final service identified by Foster is sharing the word of life. By this he means a fresh word from God. This is what should happen when believers meet together. Any member who has listened to God can serve the other members by sharing that word of life.

Journaling Focus

Day One: As you reflect on the biblical, Anabaptist, and contemporary readings related to service, describe the message they are speaking to you. Select one word that describes how you feel about yourself with respect to service and describe why you selected that particular word.

Spiritual Exercise: Meditation and Service

What is the relationship between our meditation or prayer and our service? Is there a direct relationship? Does meditation influence charity? Richard J. Foster has observed that there seems to be little attempt to relate the two in contemporary literature but that their relatedness is a distinguishing feature of classical literature.

> By now you may have grown weary of my constant stress upon this matter, but the need for such a holistic message today is as obvious as the lack of it is terrifying. It is by far the most distinguishing feature of the classical literature on this subject, and the most lacking feature in the contemporary literature. Take, for example, Francis de Sales' *Introduction to the Devout Life*, which has instruction on meditation, prayer, humility, and solitude combined with counsel on wealth, poverty, attire, and simplicity of speech. Or consider William Law's *A Serious Call to a Devout and Holy Life*, which has three chapters on economics set in the middle of a discussion on devotional exercises. Or think of Richard Baxter's *A Christian Directory*, which gives practical instruction on prayer and faith, love and submission, as well as condemning the sin of oppression and boldy setting forth a scheme of economic ethics.[10]

One contemporary writer who is an exception to Foster's observation is Henri Nouwen. In an article entitled "A Self-Emptied Heart," Nouwen describes the vocation of the Christian as following Christ in his downward path of compassion. This is the meaning of discipleship but it cannot be achieved without three disciplines: the church, the Book, and the heart (which he describes as personal prayer)

> Our vocation is to follow Christ on his downward path and become witnesses to God's compassion in the concreteness of our time and place. Our temptation is to let needs for success, visibility, and influence dominate our thoughts, words, and actions to such an extent that we are trapped in the destructive spiral of upward mobility and thus lose our vocation. It is this lifelong tension between vocation and temptation that presents us with the necessity of formation. Precisely because the downward mobility of the way of the cross cannot depend on our spontaneous responses, we are faced with the question, "How do we reach conformity to the mind and heart of the self-emptying Christ?"

To follow Christ requires the willingness and determination to let his Spirit pervade all the corners of our minds and hearts and there make us into other Christs. Formation is transformation, and transformation means a growing conformity to the mind of Christ, who did not cling to his equality with God but emptied himself.

Thus discipleship cannot be realized without discipline. Discipline in the spiritual life, however, has nothing to do with the discipline of athletics, academic study, or job training, in which physical fitness is achieved, new knowledge is acquired, or a new skill is mastered. The discipline of the Christian disciple is not to master anything, but rather to be mastered by the Spirit. True Christian discipline is the human effort to create the space in which the Spirit of Christ can transform us into his image.

We must pay careful attention to the disciplines of the spiritual life, for without discipline, discipleship degenerates into a spiritualized form of upward mobility, which is far worse than straightforward secular ambition to make it to the top.

I would like to call attention to three disciplines by which spiritual formation can take place. They are the discipline of the church, the discipline of the Book, and the discipline of the heart.[11]

Day Two: Reflect on the quotation by Nouwen and on your own life over the past year. Are you moving on the downward path of compassion or the upward path of self centeredness and power? Meditate prayerfully on Philippians 2:1-11. What does God seem to be saying to you?

Day Three: Read again the nine types of service identified by Richard J. Foster. Which of these have you exercised during the past month? Which types of service have you "passed by" even though the opportunity was available? Reflect on why you passed them by.

Day Four: Wait before God in silent prayer. After you have "centered down," ask God to show you one person who needs your service of love. It may be a family member, a community member, or some person beyond your community. Reflect on the deepest need of the person and the type of service that will best relate to that person's need. Decide how and when you will serve that person.

Day Five: For your general journaling, you may want to reflect on your most significant experience of giving or receiving charity.

Discipling Session

In this session the focus will be on our attitudes toward the service of charity and our willingness to express the love of Christ by serving the needs of others through deeds of service. The group experience should free us to share with others our own attitudes, actions, failures, and dreams, and to discuss these same areas in the lives of others.

1. Share with your discipling partner the essence of your journaling on *Day One* and *Day Four*. Try to reflect as accurately as possible where you are with respect to service.

2. As a total group, share your experiences with the exercises on *Days Two* and *Three*. If specific questions or problems are raised, take them seriously. As persons share, practice the service of listening. Do not report on your plans for service that developed on *Day Four* unless you need advice from others. Spend some time as a group in silent prayer holding before God your own needs and the person God is leading you to serve.

3. Desired Discipling Skill: ability to motivate service. Motivation which endures comes from the call of God, not the pressure of others. If we can help others hear that call, we are doing them a great service.

Lesson 22

Discipleship and Evangelism

Discipleship Theme: The Great Commission

In this lesson we will examine the centrality of evangelism for a life of faithful discipleship and the importance of evangelism in the ministry of the church. From the perspectives of world population, the commission of Jesus Christ and his expected return, the urgency of the evangelistic task is greater today than at any time in world history.

Biblical Teachings

Shortly before his ascension, Jesus gave a task to his followers which is frequently called the Great Commission—great because it extends to the ends of the earth and to the end of the age, and a commission because it comes to the church with the authority of the King. Matthew 28:18-20 is the teaching to which the followers of Christ have gone throughout the centuries to rediscover the task of the church, and from which they have gone to the nations of the earth.

The centrality of the Great Commission for the early church is seen by the fact that each of the four Gospels and Acts repeats this command of Christ. (See also Mk. 15:15-18; Lk. 24:44-49; Jn. 20:21-23; Acts 1:8.) It obviously lay behind the growth and dynamic of the early church. Acts begins with the resurrection version of the Great Commission (1:8) and it bursts forth like a four-stage rocket with the Gospel taking root in Jerusalem (2:41f.),

Judea (8:4f.), Samaria (8:6f.), and the ends of the earth (13:3—28:30).

A key person in this expansion was the apostle Paul whose testimony and sense of calling continued to reflect the Great Commission. He wrote: "Therefore, if any one is in Christ, he is a new creation; the old has passed away, behold, the new has come. All this is from God, who through Christ reconciled us to himself and gave us the ministry of reconciliation" (2 Cor. 5:17-18). (See also Rom. 1:16-17 and 1 Cor. 9:19-23.)

Peter likewise reflected the commission of Christ when he wrote: "The Lord is not slow about his promise as some count slowness, but is forbearing toward you, not wishing that any should perish, but that all should reach repentance" (2 Pet. 3:9).

The spread of the gospel as presented in the book of Acts is testimony to the missionary character of the early church. The Great Commission was their mission.

Anabaptist Writings

Pages 253 to 256 of Appendix 1 contain a discussion of the Anabaptists' participation in the Great Commission. Notice the following points:

First, they took the Great Commission very seriously, believing it applied to them just as it did to the apostles. Obedience to Christ included witnessing to the new life in Christ.

Second, their view of the universality of the church led to a universal missionary responsibility.

Third, their vision and efforts met with amazing success. The movement spread quickly to surrounding countries.

Fourth, eschatology was an important factor in their zeal. They expected to soon see the return of Christ. (This fact will receive additional attention in the next lesson.)

Pilgram Marpeck wrote about the Great Commission and emphasized the authority with which Christ spoke these words and its importance for his followers. He wrote:

For whoever believes that all authority has been given to Christ, attested to by His words (Mt. 28:18), moves, speaks, and acts not out of his own authority but by the authorization of Christ. . . .[1]

Marpeck also saw in the Great Commission the promise that believers would never be left orphans. Christ would be with them until the end of the world. In this was great comfort.[2]

When Menno Simons wrote about the Great Commission he did so with a note of urgency. He emphasized his great desire to see the gospel preached throughout the world and the price he was paying to help this come to pass.

> In the second place, we desire with ardent hearts even at the cost of life and blood that the holy Gospel of Jesus Christ and His apostles, which only is the true doctrine and will remain so until Jesus Christ comes again upon the clouds, may be taught and preached through all the world as the Lord Jesus Christ commanded His disciples as a last word to them while He was on earth. Matt. 28:19; Mark 16:15.[3]
>
> My writing and preaching is nothing else than Jesus Christ. I seek and desire nothing (this the Omniscient One knows) but that the most glorious name, the divine will, and the glory of our beloved Lord Jesus Christ may be acknowledged throughout the world. I desire and seek sincere teachers, true doctrines, true faith, true sacraments, true worship, and an unblamable life. For this I must pay dearly with so much oppression, discomfort, trouble, labor, sleeplessness, fear, anxiety, care, envy, shame, heat and cold, and perhaps at last with torture, yes, with my blood and death.[4]

Contemporary Writings

One of the primary concerns of contemporary authors writing about evangelism has to do with the goal of evangelism. Some missiologists such as C. Peter Wagner have criticized evangelism for stopping short of the goal of church growth. Wagner believes that "presence evangelism" and "proclamation evangelism" are inadequate and that there must also be "persuasion evangelism." To these types Howard A. Snyder adds "propagation evangelism" or the formation of Christian community. Snyder states:

> In this process, propagation or reproduction feeds into a continuous cycle which, empowered by the Holy Spirit, makes the Church a dynamic, living organism. The goal of evangelism therefore is the formation of the Christian community, the *koinonia* of the Holy Spirit. This is not a total definition of evangelism, because it does not include the many possible mo-

tives and means involved. There may be various legitimate motives for evangelism. Still, the goal must always be the formation of the biblical Church. This is necessary in order to reach the really ultimate goal of evangelism: the glorification of God.[5]

Other authors confirm community as the goal of evangelism. David Watson says:

When the church commits itself to a pattern of corporate life based on radical biblical principles, it will immediately challenge the moral, political, economic, and social structures of the world around it. Thus by its very existence, the church becomes both prophetic and evangelistic, and only in this way will the proclamation of the gospel make much impact among the vast majority of people who, at this moment, are thoroughly disillusioned with the church as an institution. For this reason it is impossible to separate the call to discipleship, the call to community, and the call to mission. Without a strong commitment to discipleship, there can be no authentic Christian community; and without such a community, there can be no effective mission.[6]

Jim Wallis calls for the fellowship of the new community.

To convert means to commit our lives unreservedly to Jesus Christ, to join his new order, and to enter into the fellowship of the new community. Our sins are forgiven, we are reconciled to God and to our neighbor, and our destiny becomes inextricably bound to the purposes of Christ in the world.[7]

Waldron Scott, writing from the international perspective of world missions, speaks a similar message.

A major objective of discipleship evangelism, then, is to make disciples who are committed not only to Christ but also to the Body of Christ, the Church. This is in line with Jesus' expressed goal: "I will build my church" (Matthew 16:18). Since the apostles were to be the means of building his church, Jesus banded them together from the very beginning. By doing so he gave them experience in community living (albeit a mobile community) which they would draw upon later in establishing congregations in many cities and towns in the Roman Empire, beginning at Jerusalem.[8]

Donald G. Bloesch writes that in order to carry out the Great Commission "our ministry will involve *didache* (teaching) and *diakonia* (service) as well as *kerygma* (proclamation). Since the convert cannot mature except in the community of the family of God, we need also to give serious attention to *koinonia* (fellowship)."9

In further clarifying his position, Bloesch states:

> We advocate not physical or monastic withdrawal as a general strategy but rather an interior life of devotion—what Bonhoeffer called an arcane or hidden discipline. Our prayer life must give rise to active involvement in the concerns of the world. This involvement should be expressed in social action as well as in charity to our neighbor. It should also take the form of proclamation. We are to be not only servants but also heralds of the message of salvation. Just as the basis of the Christian life is the hearing of the gospel so one of its primary fruits should be the preaching of the gospel.10

Journaling Focus

Day One: In your journaling reflect on the biblical, Anabaptist, and contemporary readings regarding evangelism. Describe your feelings about evangelism and important new insights.

Day Two: Describe your experience in evangelism about which you felt the most comfortable and which was most "successful."

Spiritual Exercise: Fasting

In the quotation from Donald Bloesch, he advocated "an interior life of devotion—what Bonhoeffer called an arcane or hidden discipline. Our prayer life must give rise to active involvement in the concerns of the world." Evangelism that flows out of interior devotion or the hidden discipline of prayer is evangelism God can use.

In previous lessons, we have reflected on and practiced prayer. In this lesson we will focus on the companion spiritual exercise, fasting. There are many motives for fasting and many activities associated with fasting. I am recommending fasting for the purpose of prayer and that the focus of prayer be evangelism. In *Celebration of Discipline,* Richard Foster has a helpful dis-

cussion of "The Discipline of Fasting." Several key quotations are
listed below. For a fuller discussion read the entire chapter.

> In Scripture the normal means of fasting involved abstaining from all
> food, solid or liquid, but not from water. In the forty-day fast of Jesus, we
> are told that "he ate nothing" and toward the end of the fast that "he was
> hungry" and that Satan tempted Him to eat, indicating that the abstaining
> was from food but not from water (Lk. 4:2ff.). From a physical standpoint,
> this is what is usually involved in a fast.
>
> Sometimes there is described what could be considered a partial fast;
> that is, there is a restriction of diet but not total abstention. Although the
> normal fast seemed to be the custom with the prophet Daniel, there was an
> occasion where for three weeks he "ate no delicacies, no meat or wine
> entered my mouth, nor did I anoint myself at all" (Dan. 10:3). We are not
> told the reason for this departure from his normal practice of fasting;
> perhaps his governmental tasks precluded it.
>
> There are also several examples in Scripture of what has rightly been
> called an "absolute fast," or an abstaining from both food and water. It ap-
> pears to be a desperate measure to meet a dire emergency. Upon learning
> that execution awaited herself and her people, Esther instructed Mordecai,
> "Go, gather all the Jews . . . and hold a fast on my behalf, and neither eat
> nor drink for three days, night or day. I and my maids will also fast as you
> do" (Esther 4:16). Paul engaged in a three-day absolute fast following his
> encounter with the living Christ (Acts 9:9). Since the human body cannot
> go without water much more than three days, both Moses and Elijah en-
> gaged in what must be considered supernatural absolute fasts of forty days
> (Deut. 9:9, 1 Kings 19:8). It must be underscored that the absolute fast is
> the exception and should never be engaged in unless one has a very clear
> command from God, and then for not more than three days.[11]
>
> Modern men and women are largely ignorant of the practical aspects
> of fasting. Those who desire to fast need to acquaint themselves with this in-
> formation.
>
> As with all the Disciplines, a progression should be observed; it is wise
> to learn to walk well before we try to run. Begin with a partial fast of
> twenty-four hours' duration; many have found lunch to lunch to be the best
> time. This would mean that you would not eat two meals. Fresh fruit juices
> are excellent. Attempt this once a week for several weeks. In the beginning
> you will be fascinated with the physical aspects, but the most important
> thing to monitor is the inner attitude of worship. Outwardly you will be
> performing the regular duties of your day, but inwardly you will be in
> prayer and adoration, song and worship. In a new way, cause every task of
> the day to be a sacred ministry to the Lord. However mundane your duties,
> they are for you a sacrament. Cultivate a "gentle receptiveness to divine
> breathings." Break your fast with a light meal of fresh fruits and vegetables
> and a good deal of inner rejoicing.[12]

In the daily exercises which follow, you will relate fasting, prayer, and evangelism.

Day Three: For the exercise today, observe a one-meal fast. Select a meal that you will miss. Spend that time meditating on the biblical writings at the beginning of this lesson that relate to evangelism. Let these passages saturate your mind. Then reflect on your own practice of evangelism. Are you satisfied with your evangelistic activity? If not, what new practice do you feel led to follow? Describe the practice in your journaling.

Day Four: In your general journaling, you may want to reflect prayerfully on the congregation where you participate. What changes are needed for it to become an evangelistic community? What will you do to the congregation to help bring about the change?

Day Five: Today you are to fast for two meals, as recommended by Foster. This may depend on your work demands. Spend your fasting time in intercessory prayer for a person to whom you feel led to witness. Then describe in your journaling your experience of fasting and praying. (If fasting has been meaningful to you, you may want to lengthen the experience following the guidelines of Foster.)

Discipling Session

This session is to provide a setting to discuss your feelings about evangelism and your approach to witnessing. Also, you will share and learn from others about fasting and prayer for the purpose of evangelism. This will increase your ability to help other persons practice these disciplines.

1. Share with your discipling partner your experience with the exercises on *Day One* and *Day Two.* Practice your listening skills as you listen to another person share feelings which might be clear or mixed.

2. As a total group share about your experience with fasting and praying. What did you experience physically, spiritually, and psychologically? Was your experience of prayer with fasting any

different than prayer without fasting? If there was a difference, describe it.

3. Share your own experience with evangelism. What pattern have you been following and what pattern do you plan to follow in the future?

4. Desired Discipling Skill: ability to motivate fasting and evangelism. Motivating fasting and evangelism begins with our discovering the value of fasting and its relationship to intercessory prayer. Only then are we prepared to motivate other persons.

Lesson 23

The Motivation of Eschatology

Discipleship Theme: The Return of Christ

In Lesson 18, we noticed that the kingdom of God is both present and future. It is related to both time and eternity, this age and the age to come. Lesson 23 expands the future aspect of the kingdom with a focus on the end of this age and the age to come. The anticipation of the return of Christ and related events, such as judgment and rewards (eschatology), motivated the early church to faithful discipleship. This same conviction has motivated believers since that day, including the Anabaptists and present-day Christians.

Biblical Teachings

The New Testament abounds with references to the return of Christ. These references speak about the belief concerning Christ's return and the motivation which this belief should create. In this discussion, I will identify a selected group of passages and their stated motivation.

Matthew 24 records Jesus' teachings about future events preceeding and associated with his return. He states that there will be an end to this age (Mt. 24:14), and that the end is associated with the coming of the Son of Man (Mt. 24:27). This knowledge should motivate followers to live with an attitude of "watching" because the exact time of his coming has not been revealed to them (Mt. 24:42).

In Matthew 25 Jesus motivates his followers to continue watching for his return (Mt. 25:13) and to view ministry to human need as a ministry both to others and to Christ (Mt. 25:31-46).

The Gospel of John records Jesus' promise that he will return for his followers and this should motivate them to a life of peace in the midst of perplexity (Jn. 14:1-3).

After Pentecost, the disciples spoke about their belief in the return of Christ. They shared this conviction and saw it as a motivation to repentance and preparation for Christ's return (Acts 3:19-21).

Paul describes the future glory of creation as a motivation to endure present suffering (Rom. 8:18-23). Writing to the church at Thessalonica, Paul describes the return of Christ in order to motivate them to a life of hope when facing the realities of death (1 Thess. 4:13—5:5).

Peter sees the return of Christ as motivation to living with the expectation of a new age, to calling persons to repentance, and to holy living (2 Pet. 3:1-13).

John likewise views the expected coming of Christ as the motivation for purity of life (1 Jn. 3:1-3).

For the New Testament writers belief in the return of Christ motivated them and the church to the attitude of watchfulness, ministry to human suffering, calling persons to repentance, the attitudes of peace and hope, and lives of purity and holiness.

Anabaptist Writings

The Anabaptists lived with a strong sense of eschatology. In this respect they were not alone. The social and religious turmoil of the sixteenth century led many to believe they were living in the end time. The Anabaptists, however, believed that the second coming of Christ was near at hand and that their religious movement was related to the future working and plans of God. God was gathering again his faithful people to accomplish his purposes. Eschatology provided a strong motivation for their mission. In fact, eschatology motivated much that they experienced in their life of discipleship.

Pages 251 and 255 of Appendix 1 contain additional discussion of the Anabaptists' eschatological convictions. Three results should be noted.

First, these convictions sustained them in the face of suffering and martyrdom. They believed that death would usher them into a new life with Christ

Second, they were motivated to mission by the expectation of Christ's imminent return. They wanted to prepare people to meet God.

Third, these convictions motivated their search for God's truth and God's righteousness. They wanted to rightly understand God and correctly follow his will for his people

Balthasar Hubmaier expected the return of Christ soon and that there would then be judgment and rewards. He wrote:

> I also believe and confess that you will come to judge the quick and the dead in the day of the last judgment, which, to all godly men, will be a chosen day, rich in joy. Then shall we see our God and Saviour face to face in his great glory and majesty, coming in the clouds of heaven. Then our carnal, sinful and godless life will have an end. Then will every man receive the reward of his works. Those who have laboured well will go into eternal life; those who have done evil into everlasting fire. O my Lord Jesus Christ, hasten that day and come down to us soon . . . . [1]

Menno Simons lived with a strong anticipation of the return of Christ. This motivated his appeal to those he felt were not following Christ and it became the basis of hope for those enduring suffering for Christ.

At the conclusion of Menno's "Epistle to Micron" (Micron was a Dutch Reformation leader), Menno wrote the following:

> I pray that no person will think that I write this way to render Micron evil for evil. Ah, no. I leave vengeance to Him who is Judge of all the world. I have done this to the service of Micron and all the erring ones so that they may be converted and give becoming praise and honor to Christ, the Son of God. The truth is set before them by the grace of God in such power and clearness that no man can undo it with the Scriptures nor contradict it with reason. Therefore it would be well if our opponents would see more clearly so that they may with all the saints flee from the future judgment and that they may in the day of His appearance stand before the throne of His Majesty in eternal joy. [2]

Writing to believers who were suffering for the cause of Christ, Menno encouraged them to be faithful because the day of their release was at hand. He wrote:

> Yes, dear brethren, the desirable day of your release is at hand; the day in which you shall stand with great constancy against those who have afflicted you, and have taken away your sweat and your toil, yes, your blood and your life. Then shall all those who pursue us be as ashes under the souls of our feet and they shall acknowledge too late that emperor, king, duke, prince, crown, scepter, majesty, power, sword, and mandate, were nothing but earth, dust, wind, and smoke.
>
> With this day in view, all afflicted and oppressed Christians who now labor under the cross of Christ are comforted in the firm hope of the life to come; and they leave all tyrants with their heathenish mandates to God and His judgment. But they continue unmovable with Christ Jesus and His holy Word, and they construe all their doctrine, faith, sacraments, and life accordingly; and not in all eternity according to any other doctrine or mandate, even as the Father has commanded it from heaven and as Christ Jesus together with His holy apostles taught in all clarity and bequeathed it to all devout and pious children of God.[3]

Contemporary Writings

The theme of the return of Christ does not appear to receive major attention in contemporary writings. Eschatology does not seem to be a major motivator of the church in its ministry. However, the theme is mentioned by some authors as a perspective that should be kept in mind.

Howard A. Snyder writes:

> The Kingdom of God in its fullness will probably not come tomorrow. Or next week. For the time being, more important than cocking an ear toward the skies for the trumpet call is listening carefully for the cries of the lost and the people without hope, and looking after the children too weak to cry because they have no food.
>
> And certainly we should look to Jesus—risen, seated at God's right hand and sure to return. But we must also remember that Jesus walked this earth and died on the cross.
>
> Think of Jesus on the cross. What does his suffering mean for us in this interim before the Kingdom fully comes? Should his body, the Church on earth today, be like he himself was two millennia ago?[4]

Donald G. Bloesch, speaking of the Christian life as a pilgrimage of faith, states:

In the mind of Paul and of the entire New Testament, the hope of the Christian is centered in the consummation of the kingdom of God. Our hope is to be focused upon the coming again of Jesus Christ in power and glory in order to set up the kingdom that shall have no end. Then—at the second advent—the veil that separates us from the invisible world will fall away. In the words of Paul: "For now we see in a mirror dimly, but then face to face" (I Cor. 13:12). Then we shall know even as we are known. Then faith or indirect cognition will be replaced by the beatific vision or direct cognition. Then a reason that has been merely converted or redirected will be superseded by a glorified and transfigured reason.[5]

David Watson dares to speak forthrightly about the believer's hope and its meaning for our day. He provides a fitting conclusion to this discussion.

More than ever today we need to hold fast to this hope. Christ warned his disciples that before the close of the age false teaching would lead many astray. Other cataclysmic events would also precede that day: "There will be signs in sun and moon and stars, and upon the earth distress of nations in perplexity at the roaring of the sea and the waves, men fainting with fear and with foreboding of what is coming on the world; for the powers of the heavens will be shaken. And then they will see the Son of man coming in a cloud with power and great glory. Now when these things begin to take place, look up and raise your heads, because your redemption is drawing near." We cannot say precisely what these words refer to, nor can we interpret dogmatically Peter's description of the Day of the Lord when "the heavens will pass away with a loud noise, and the elements will be dissolved with fire, and the earth and the works that are upon it will be burned up." Such words are not inconsistent with a nuclear holocaust, and the possibility of this frightful form of total human suicide increases every year.[6]

The call to discipleship, however, is also a call to God's promised glory. In view of the urgency of the times, we are to live lives that honor Christ, that heal the wounds within his body, and that hasten the coming of the day of God. This is not a day in which to play religious games. Time is running out fast. Christ looks for disciples who are unashamed of him, bold in their witness, obedient to his Word, united in his love and filled with his Spirit. Joy and woe will be woven fine; tears, pain and sweat will be mingled with radiant love and inexpressible joy. Christ wants disciples who will not only have hope, but give hope. Whatever we receive we are to give away, that others may rise up through the darkness that covers the earth. "Arise, shine; for your light has come, and the glory of the Lord has risen upon you." Like St. Francis of Assisi, we need to pray that where there is hatred, we may give love; where there is injury, pardon, where there is doubt, faith; where there is despair, hope; where there is sadness, joy; where there is darkness, light. "Grant that we may not seek so much to be consoled, as to console; to be understood, as to understand; to be loved, as to love; for in giving we receive, in pardoning, we are pardoned, and dying we are born to eternal life."

The disciple of Christ cannot lose: when he gives all, he gains all; when he loses his life, he finds it. Jim Elliot, martyred as a missionary to the Aucas in South America in 1956, summed it up like this: "He is no fool who gives what he cannot keep, to gain what he cannot lose."[7]

Journaling Focus

Day One: —Reflect on what you have read in the biblical, Anabaptist, and contemporary writings concerning the return of Christ and its motivation for mission. What new insights have you gained?

Spiritual Exercise: Motivated by the Future

The Scriptures frequently point to the future as a way of influencing the present. This principle was observed in a number of Scriptures noted earlier in this lesson. This principle is also seen in the lives of some outstanding Bible characters.

On several occasions, Paul received a glimpse of the eternal world or the world to come. The book of Acts records Paul's encounter with the risen Christ who appeared to him from heaven while on his way to Damascus. This encounter changed many things about Paul's life including his life's purpose (Acts 9:1-16). In later years he referred to this event as a reorienting life experience (Acts 22:6-16; 26:12-18).

Paul wrote to the church at Corinth to defend his apostolic authority. As a part of this discussion, he reported his experience of being "caught up into Paradise—whether in the body or out of the body I do not know, God knows, and he heard things that cannot be told, which man may not utter" (2 Cor. 12:3-4).

Without a doubt Paul's glimpse of the future greatly affected the way he lived the present. He saw the present life through the perspective of the future life. His present life was motivated by eschatology.

The Apostle John had a similar experience which is recorded in the book of Revelation. At the conclusion of this letter to the seven churches, John seems to address all Christians of this age encouraging them to read the letter and to then live with an awareness of the age to come. Gaining some awareness of the future life will affect the present life. A study of Revelation would suggest that Christ wants all of his followers to be motivated by eschatology. He wants all of us to experience living into the future because that will influence our living in the present.

Day Two: Read chapters 20-22 of Revelation. Record the words or phrases that indicate the nature of life in eternity. Reflect on the quality of life described in these chapters and the nature of eternity. What motivations are stirred within you?

Day Three: Reflect on what you have learned through a study of these twenty-three lessons. List your most important learnings in the order of priority for you.

Day Four: During the total discipling experience, you have made a number of commitments to each other such as prayer support and accountability. You have also studied and discussed spiritual and material sharing.

Spend some time reflecting on whether you would like to make a continuing commitment to the group. If so, describe in writing this commitment.

Day Five: Review your general journaling to increase your self-understanding. Did you repeatedly struggle with the same issues? Is there evidence of growth?

Discipling Session

In this final session, you will share your response to the future realities of eschatology and the motivation this creates. Also, you will decide whether you wish to continue a group commitment.

1. Share with your discipling partner your experience with the exercises on *Day One* and *Day Two*

2. Share with the total group your list of learnings identified

on *Day Three.* What new areas of growth do you want to pursue?

3. Discuss as a total group the question of a continuing group commitment. After you come to agreement on the matter, enter into your commitment if this is your decision.

4. Desired Discipling Skill: ability to see the present through the future. Persons who have received a glimpse of the age to come have a different perspective on this age. Let us pray that God, through the Scriptures, will give us this view.

Looking Ahead

Now that you have completed this series of studies, you may wish to lead a group of persons through this discipling experience. I would suggest the following:

1. Prayerfully select a group of from six to eight persons who are genuinely interested in growing in their practice of discipleship.

2. Invite them to an introductory meeting. Explain the nature of the lessons, what they can expect to learn about discipleship, discipling and spiritual exercises, and the necessary time commitment.

3. If they agree to enter the study, determine the best time for the weekly meetings and the beginning date, after copies of the handbook are secured.

4. At the first meeting, you will want to spend some time reflecting on the introduction to the handbook. This will provide important background understanding.

5. As leader you will want to support all group members in regular prayer and walk with them in the discipling experience.

Appendices

Appendix 1

The Anabaptist Concept of Discipleship and Its Application In Discipling

Introduction

The Purposes of the Study

This study has two primary purposes. The first purpose is to describe the early Anabaptists' concept of discipleship. Several Anabaptist scholars have already identified their understanding of the Anabaptist view of discipleship. However, since this study was foundational for the handbook on discipleship and discipling, I felt the need to clarify my own understanding by developing a description based on my reading and research.

The second purpose of the study is to describe my findings on the Anabaptist approach to discipling. I wanted to discover how the early Anabaptists helped people to understand and practice discipleship. The discipling pattern in Anabaptist life has not been researched so this aspect of the study involved an examination of primary resources.

The Scope of the Study

In this study, I gave primary attention to the period 1524-1560, which has been called "the formative period of Anabaptism ending with the death of Menno Simons."[1] The Anabaptist church began on January 21, 1525, but writings have been preserved from certain of the founding leaders which were written in 1524. Menno Simons died in 1561.

The major primary resources are the writings of Conrad Grebel (c. 1498-1526), Michael Sattler (c. 1490-1527), Pilgram Marpeck (149?-1556), and Menno Simons (c. 1496-1561). Conrad Grebel was nurtured in the Zwinglian Reformation and became one of the founding Anabaptist leaders. Key second-generation leaders were Menno Simons in the North and Pilgram Marpeck in the South. Bridging the founding leaders and the second-generation leaders was Michael Sattler and the *Seven Articles of Schleitheim* which provided the "transition between birth and consolidation."[2]

Basing a study on these primary resources creates certain difficulties because Anabaptism "was a vast and variegated movement, borrowing freely from many sources in pre-Reformation mysticism, in pre-Reformation dissent, in renaissance humanism, and in the Protestant Reformation."[3] However, I have observed a broad unity in these writings on the essence of discipleship and their approach to discipling. From this study, I identified the twenty-three themes developed in the handbook.

Definition of Terms

The term "Anabaptist" refers to a group of Christians in the sixteenth century who baptized again or practiced believer's baptism. In this study, the term refers primarily to the thought and life of the above-mentioned leaders who were related to the Swiss Brethren, the South and Central German Anabaptists, and the Dutch and Northwest German Anabaptists. It does not include the revolutionary Münsterites or the communitarian Hutterites, although they were related to the Anabaptist movement.

The term "discipleship" is not a New Testament term but it is clearly a New Testament concept. Behind the concept of discipleship is the term "disciple" which designated "those who followed Jesus and is used around 225 times in the gospels."[4] Disciple (mathētēs) means a learner or a follower. It identifies one who has heard the call of Jesus and become his follower. The concept of following Jesus or discipleship is expressed in 1 Peter 2:21, "For to this you have been called, because Christ also suffered for you, leaving you an example, that you should follow in his steps."

For the Anabaptists, the German term *Nachfolge Christi* "Following Christ," or "discipleship," was central to their understanding of the Christian life. Robert Friedmann has identified the inner dynamic of this concept by noting that "once the reborn person comes to know that God has revealed to him His will, there is but one thing for him to do: to obey."[5] In fact, Friedmann observes that the term "obedience" is used more frequently in Anabaptist writings than the term "discipleship."[6] An often-quoted Scripture was Paul's admonition "to bring into captivity every thought to the obedience of Christ" (2 Cor. 10:5). In this study, the term "discipleship" refers to the daily pilgrimage of following Christ by bringing the whole of one's life under his Lordship.

The term "discipling" is not used in the New Testament nor was it used by the Anabaptists. However, the concept or reality can easily be found in the Scriptures and in Anabaptist history. "Discipling" in this study refers to the process of helping disciples (Christians) understand and follow the call of Christ in their total lives as members of his body. It assumes that those being discipled seriously want to follow Jesus and that they are joined to other disciples who recognize Jesus as their Lord.

1. The Anabaptist Concept of Discipleship

There is general agreement among Anabaptist scholars that discipleship was one of the central concepts of Anabaptist faith and theology, and some scholars view discipleship as the central concept of Anabaptism. Furthermore, Anabaptist scholars understand discipleship to mean following Christ or bringing all of life under his lordship.

In this section of the study, I will describe discipleship as viewed by a select group of Anabaptist scholars and leaders, and will then identify six consequent applications of this concept in Anabaptist life.

In his classic essay, *The Anabaptist Vision*, Harold S. Bender states that "fundamental in the Anabaptist vision was the conception of the essence of Christianity as discipleship. It was a concept which meant the transformation of the entire way of life of the individual believer and of society so that it should be fashioned after the teachings and example of Christ."[1] The inner experience of repentance needed to be expressed outwardly by new behavior.

In the article on "Discipleship" in *The Mennonite Encyclopedia*, Bender writes that in the Anabaptist understanding, "the individual responds to the call of Christ, forsakes his life of sin and self, receives a new nature, comes under the lordship of Christ, and takes Christ's life and teaching as normative for himself and for the church, and indeed ultimately for the whole social order."[2]

Bender enlarges this concept in his article on "The Anabaptist Theology of Discipleship," which appeared in *The Mennonite Quarterly Review*. He indicates that behind the Anabaptist view of discipleship lays a particular view of Christ. Classic Protestant theology and Calvinism in particular tended to "think of Christ primarily as a prophet or moral teacher, one who brings intellectual truth out of which to build a system of thought, theological or ethical, with answers to the meaning of life or existence."[3] Catholicism, both Greek and Roman, tended to "think of Christ primarily as a being to be worshiped."[4] Orthodox theology of Christ was combined with liturgical and sacramental worship which elicited adoration and for some a Christ-mysticism. Lutheranism viewed Christ primarily as Savior. When Christ is viewed with this narrow focus, "Justification by faith becomes so great and so wonderful, that sanctification of life and obedience to Christ, and transformation after His image, are in effect minimized and neglected. The Lordship of Christ is in effect set aside."[5]

Bender sees in Anabaptism a view of Christ which makes him "Prophet, Saviour, *and* Lord, and makes the believer His disciple."[6] In the words of the Apostle Paul, Christ is to be "formed" in the life of the disciple. The major ideas of Anabaptism derive from this view of Christ. The Anabaptist view of discipleship is summarized by Bender in the following words:

> In essence the discipleship which the Anabaptists proclaimed was simply the bringing of the whole of life under the Lordship of Christ, and the transformation of this life, both personal and social, after His image. From this point of view they subjected not only the church but the whole social and cultural order to criticism, rejected what they found to be contrary to Christ, and attempted to put into actual practice His teachings as they understood them both ethically and sociologically.[7]

In his book, *The Theology of Anabaptism*, Robert Friedmann reports on a conversation he had with Harold S. Bender in which Bender defended the concept of a "theology of discipleship" because "the Anabaptists embraced a form of theology in which discipleship and all it implies had a central and normative function, as compared with the theology of mainline Protestantism, which in its concern for personal salvation has no organic place for the 'brother.' "[8]

Robert Friedmann sees the Anabaptist view of discipleship related to their view of " 'existential Christianity' where there existed no basic split between faith and life. . . ."[9] It was not existential in the sense of being an experience of despair but rather in the sense of being an experience of certainty which led to certain consequences. It was "the *certainty* of resting in God's gracious hands, of being called and able to respond to this call. Such a believer is intent on being obedient to God's commands and is willing to accept the possible price."[10]

In reflecting on the Anabaptist vision of discipleship, J. Lawrence Burkholder says that the key question for the Anabaptists was: "What does it mean to follow Christ? Or, what does it mean to submit life in its totality to the claims of the kingdom of God?"[11] While this question may sound simple, it was a unique and radical question. For as Burkholder indicates, the Greek Orthodox church has seen its task as uniting heaven and earth or being a bridge between time and eternity. The Roman church has viewed the problem of sin as its primary concern and its answer has been sacramentalism. Lutheranism has been primarily concerned with man's alienation from God and his need for forgiveness.[12]

"The uniqueness of Anabaptism," says Burkholder, "lies in its conviction that Christianity is much more than reflection upon Christ as the divine Being who invaded time, and it is more than the appropriation of benefits of the divine drama of the cross. Christianity is the concrete and realistic 'imitation' of Christ's life and work in the context of the kingdom of God."[13]

Walter Klaassen provides an appropriate, final perspective in this brief survey of how Anabaptist scholars understand discipleship from an Anabaptist point of view. "A major feature of Anabaptist Christology was the weight placed on the function of Jesus as model and example. That involved an emphasis on his human life with his actions and words as described in the Gospels."[14] The Anabaptists did not minimize his divine nature but emphasized his human life because he called disciples to follow him (Mk. 1:16-20).

Turning now to several Anabaptist leaders and their view of discipleship, we see the theme of following Jesus to be quite central. Michael Sattler wrote a didactic hymn on the theme of discipleship. It contains thirteen verses and appears in Appendix 2. Verse one says that when Christ gathered his little flock, he told them that they must with patience follow him daily, bearing his cross. In verse two he told them to follow his teachings. The rest of the verses describes the price of suffering which will come from following Christ but also Christ's faithfulness to those who are faithful to him.

Pilgram Marpeck emphasized both the deity and humanity of Christ and the implications of his humanity for the Christian life and the church. Marpeck states his understanding in these words: "He, the Man Jesus Christ (who alone accomplishes in the believers the good pleasure of the Father), He the Lord, a true Son of Man, is Lord, Ruler, Leader, and Director of His saints."[15]

In his writings, Menno Simons illustrated his commitment to the teachings of Jesus and the apostles and appealed to all persons to follow them. In "Foundation of Christian Doctrine," he points out that "in the New Testament we are directed to the Spirit, Word, Counsel, admonition, and usage of Christ. What these allow we are free to do, but what He forbids we are not free to do. To this all true Christians should conform...."[16]

Menno also wrote a hymn that has been entitled "Hymn of Discipleship." It is found in Appendix 3. The hymn speaks primarily of the suffering that comes to those who faithfully follow Jesus. This was the experience of Old Testament saints, of Jesus himself, and of those that "begin to walk life's narrow way."

Since the Anabaptists rejected a split between their faith and their life, their understanding of discipleship needed to have concrete expression. We turn now to six of the consequent applications of their view of discipleship.

Believer's Baptism

The Anabaptists were called to submit to believer's baptism as a sign of repentance and regeneration, and as a mark of membership in a covenant community or church.

It is appropriate to look first at believer's baptism because all of the early Anabaptist leaders recognized the importance of this issue. In his discussion of the close relationship between baptism and discipleship among the Anabaptists, William R. Estep notes that Felix Manz wrote a pamphlet on baptism, Hubmaier penned six books or pamphlets on the issue, Pilgram Marpeck, Menno Simons, and Dirk Philips wrote monographs on the subject, and believer's baptism was frequently a key subject at Anabaptist disputations and in confessions. Estep notes that "understanding the place of baptism in Anabaptist life may well be the key to interpreting the Anabaptist views of discipleship and the church."[17]

The earliest statement on the Anabaptist view of baptism is found in a letter which Conrad Grebel wrote to Thomas Müntzer in 1524. Grebel first commended Müntzer for his rejection of infant baptism and then discussed the view of the Swiss Brethren on issues such as the Lord's Supper and baptism. Regarding baptism, Grebrel wrote:

> We understand that even an adult is not to be baptized without Christ's rule of binding and loosing. The Scripture describes baptism for us thus, that it signifies that, by faith and the blood of Christ, sins have been washed away for him who is baptized, changes his mind, and believes before and after; that it signifies that a man is dead and ought to be dead to sin and walks in newness of life and spirit, and that he shall certainly be saved if, according to this meaning, by inner baptism he lives his faith; so that the water does not confirm or increase faith, as the scholars at Wittenberg say, and [does not] give very great comfort [nor] is it the final refuge on the deathbed. Also baptism does not save, as Augustine, Tertullian, Theophylact, and Cyprian have taught, dishonoring faith and the suffering of Christ in the case of the old and adult, and dishonoring the suffering of Christ in the case of the unbaptized infants.[18]

Reflecting on the reinstitution of believer's baptism, Estep suggests that it was "probably the most revolutionary act of the Reformation."[19] The Anabaptists recognized the danger involved in breaking with the religious and social system but they believed it to be the will of God and therefore willingly took that risk and encouraged others to take it.

Michael Sattler had a key role in describing the Anabaptist belief on believer's baptism. In a booklet attributed to Sattler, *On Distinguishing Scripture*, "Sattler" stated that "Scripture demonstrated the divinely ordained order: (1) teach, (2) hear, (3) believe, (4) baptise, (5) receive the Spirit, and (6) produce good works."[20]

The Schleitheim Confession was adopted by a group of Anabaptists on February 24, 1527. This very significant confession was written by Sattler and the first of seven articles concerns baptism. It reads as follows:

> I. Notice concerning baptism. Baptism shall be given to all those who have been taught repentance and the amendment of life and [who] believe truly that their sins are taken away through Christ, and to all those who desire to walk in the resurrection of Jesus Christ and be buried with Him in death, so that they might rise with Him; to all those who with such an understanding themselves desire and request it from us; hereby is excluded all infant baptism, the greatest and first abomination of the pope. For this you have the reasons and the testimony of the writings and the practice of the apostles. We wish simply yet resolutely and with assurance to hold to the same.[21]

After Sattler was burned at the stake on May 20, 1527, Wolfgang Capito, who knew Sattler personally from discussions at Strasbourg, wrote the following about him:

> Now we were not in agreement with him as he wished to make Christians righteous by their acceptance of articles and an outward commitment. This we thought to be the beginning of a new monasticism. We desired rather to help the believing life to progress by contemplation of the mercies of God, as Moses bases his exhortations to good works, on the reminder of divine favors and of the fatherly disciplining of the people by God (Deut. 8); which is the order of salvation.[22]

The "outward commitment" of believer's baptism and all that it symbolized set the Anabaptists apart from the other Reformers.

Pilgram Marpeck further developed the theology of believer's baptism by seeing it related to a covenant theology (1 Pet. 3:21). He referred to baptism as "the covenant seal," which must be preceded by circumcision of the heart or the new birth which comes through faith in Christ. Without faith in Christ there can be no true baptism. Marpeck wrote, "Where there is no faith, there is nothing but nothing and baptism is no baptism."[23] Marpeck also refers to baptism as "the commitment to a holy covenant"[24] and that "it is the true and correct Christian baptism only if it happens according to the command of Christ."[25]

For Marpeck baptism is the entrance and the gate to the church, not in the sense of being a sacramental work but as an act of the church.

> No one belongs to this church unless he has the holiness of faith and of love, praises the name of God, and is inclined, from the heart, toward serving his fellowman. Baptism shall serve this end, that Christ's church, through baptism, be joined together, *formed,* and united in one body of love. Consequently, anyone given entrance into the holy church, *the community of Christian believers,* must deny and disown the devil, the world, and all that is a part of it, *as well as die to all vanity, pride, and all lusts of the flesh.* Then, upon verbal confession of the sound of faith which he believes with his heart, he shall be baptized, in God's name ... and in Christ's, when he is cleansed of sin by repentance and faith, and enters into an unblemished, obedient way of life. So shall the holy church be gathered through baptism, and those who do not enter and do not draw near to Christ will also not be reckoned by Christ as belonging to His church, nor will they be accepted.[26]

In summary, baptism for Marpeck was a sign of entering the new covenant, a symbol of a new and holy life of discipleship and an entrance into the visible church or community of believers.

Menno Simmons wrote extensively regarding believer's baptism. For him the issue was not adult baptism versus infant baptism but rather the baptism of believers versus the baptism of unbelievers. This was the key issue because of Menno's emphasis on repentance and regeneration. The divine order of the Christian life was the new birth from above making us children of God, baptism signifying obedience as God's children, and the communion of the Holy Spirit, assuring us of God's grace, forgiveness, and everlasting life.[27] (See Jn. 1:14; Mt. 28:20; Acts 2:37-38.)

Menno frequently stressed the nonsacramental nature of believer's baptism. In his book *Christian Baptism* he stated that "we are not cleansed in baptism of our inherited sinful nature which is in our flesh, so that it is entirely destroyed in us, for it remains with us after baptism.... We declare in the baptism we receive that we desire to die unto the inherent, sinful nature, and destroy it, so that it will no longer be master in our mortal bodies (Rom. 6:12)...."[28]

Baptism, then, was seen as an act of obedience to the command of Christ and the apostles, a sign of regeneration, and a pledge of discipleship. Menno spoke most eloquently of the life of regenerated believers (see Appendix 4). Baptism was a symbol of a new quality of life and a pledge for life.

Anabaptist scholars express in various ways the significance of believer's baptism for the Anabaptists and its centrality in their theology. Ethelbert Stauffer says that "the Anabaptists not only renewed the mode of baptism of the early Christians, they also renewed the old ideas of baptism as death ... and death as baptism...."[29] They believed that baptism was the beginning of a way that would end in martyrdom.

Robert Friedmann points out that one of the terms used in connection with baptism was "sealing," which was a "vow to discipleship, somewhat comparable to monastic vows."[30] A commonly used phrase was "baptism is the sealing of a new life" (Rev. 7:3).

Walter Klaassen believes that baptism focused on both the beginning and nature of the Christian life. In addition it was the "external act by which Anabaptists expressed their rejection of the sacramental church of Rome and the territorial churches of Protestantism."[31] The result was severe persecution based on the "old imperial Roman law providing the death penalty for rebaptism."[32]

In spite of their rejection of the Roman church, there are indications that the Anabaptists accepted certain monastic concepts in their view of baptism and the church. We have already noted the statement by Capito accusing Sattler of beginning a new monasticism, and the observation of Friedmann relating the concept of baptism as "sealing" to monastic vows.

Kenneth Davis points out that there were two primary church models in existence at the time of the Reformation: the state church model and the monastic model. The Anabaptists adopted a modified monastic model borrowing from the ascetic tradition (stress on moral virtue) as expressed in the Franciscan Tertiaries and the Brethren of the Common Life.[33] Davis sees in the practice of believer's baptism a retaining of the threefold monastic vow of poverty, chastity, and obedience.

> The Anabaptists repeatedly interpret baptism as a pledge or initiatory vow involving the acceptance of the new life of purity and devotion to Christ; their expression of chastity. It was also a pledge of submission to brotherhood discipline; their vow of obedience. It included a renunciation of private possessions in favor of either the Christian stewardship of or the community of goods; their vow of poverty.[34]

Thus believer's baptism represented both a rejection of a powerful religious system and the acceptance or reshaping of certain aspects of the system. Both of these realities must be kept in mind to understand the radical significance of baptism for the Anabaptists.

Life in the Body of Christ

Anabaptists were called to share life in the body of Christ ministering to the spiritual and physical needs of one another.

We have noticed that baptism marked their entrance into the visible church and that the visible church was viewed as a community of believers, the people of God, the body of Christ. Anabaptists understood the church as people (believers), not as an institution. This understanding called for a shared life among the members which touched both the spiritual and material areas of life.

Menno Simons instructed pastors to take diligent care of their sheep and to exhort them to love, to good works, and to godly, unblamable conduct.[35] Parents were to teach and instruct their children. Members were to help one another walk in newness of life. The church needed to exercise congregational discipline over the spiritual life of its members, and this discipline was the task of the brotherhood, not the state

Congregational discipline was based on the rule of Christ (Mt. 18:15-17). It involved fraternal admonition and binding and loosing. Communal discipline in some form was practiced by the various Anabaptist groups and was considered a sign of the true church.

The purpose and goal was to achieve a level of life consistent with New Testament standards which was tragically rare in the sixteenth century. The level of life envisioned by the Anabaptists was well stated in Menno Simons' classic description of true evangelical faith.

True evangelical faith is of such a nature that it cannot lie dormant, but manifests itself in all righteousness and works of love; it dies unto the flesh and blood; it destroys all forbidden lusts and desires; it seeks and serves and fears God; it clothes the naked; it feeds the hungry; it comforts the sorrowful; it shelters the destitute; it aids and consoles the sad; it returns good for evil; it serves those that harm it; it prays for those that persecute it; teaches, admonishes, and reproves with the Word of the Lord; it seeks that which is lost; it binds up that which is wounded; it heals that which is diseased and it saves that which is sound; it has become all things to all men. The persecution, suffering, and anguish which befalls it for the sake of the truth of the Lord is to it a glorious joy and consolation.[36]

Sharing life in the body of Christ also involved physical concerns and needs. In fact, they looked after the welfare of each other because they were members of one body (1 Cor. 12:13; 10:17; Eph. 4:5-6). The love of Christ prepared them to "serve their neighbors, not only with money and goods, but also after the example of their Lord ... with life and blood."[37] Walter Klaassen concludes that "the majority of Anabaptists believed that property could be held privately, but that it could never be absolutely private. Property was viewed as a trust from God ... and should always be available to sisters and brothers in need."[38]

Documents of the Marburg Anabaptists indicate that persons requesting baptism were asked the following question: "If need should require it, are you prepared to devote all your possessions to the service of the brotherhood and do you agree not to fail any member who is in need and you are able to help?"[39] Davis sees this question as another example of the broad meaning of baptism and the close relationship between Anabaptist baptism and monastic initiation vows.

Holy Living

Anabaptists were called to live a holy life filled with the fruits of righteousness and separated from sin and evil.

The Anabaptists had a dream of rediscovering original Christianity which included true faith and fruits of righteousness. Conrad Grebel's letter to Thomas Müntzer of 1524 represents the earliest statement of this dream.

> Just as our forebears fell away from the true God and from the one true, common, divine Word, from the divine institutions, from Christian love and life, and lived without God's law and gospel in human, useless, unchristian customs and ceremonies, and expected to attain salvation therein, yet fell far short of it, as the evangelical preachers have declared, and to some extent are still declaring, so today too every man wants to be saved by superficial faith, without fruits of faith, without baptism of trial and probation, without love and hope, without right Christian practices, and wants to persist in all the old manner of personal vices, and in the common ritualistic and anti-Christian customs of baptism and of the Lord's Supper, in disrespect for the divine Word and in respect for the word of the pope and of the antipapal preachers, which yet is not equal to the divine Word nor in harmony with it. In respecting persons and in manifold seduction there is grosser and more pernicious error now than ever has been since the beginning of the world. In the same error we too lingered as long as we heard and read only the evangelical preachers who are to blame for all this, in punishment for our sins. But after we took Scripture in hand too, and consulted it on many points, we have been instructed somewhat and have discovered the great and harmful error of the shepherds, of ours too, namely, that we do not daily beseech God earnestly with constant groaning to be brought out of this destruction of all godly life and out of human abominations, to attain to the true faith and divine practice.[40]

Why did the Anabaptists view the Reformers as falling short of New Testament faith and life? A partial answer can be found in the contrast between the Reformed and the Anabaptist understanding of law and gospel. Richard C. Detweiler has done a comparative study of law and gospel in the writings of Martin Luther and Menno Simons. Detweiler points out that Luther makes a sharp distinction between law and gospel, locating the gospel in heaven and the law on earth. Law relates to man's condition of sin. There is a time to hear the gospel and receive forgiveness. However, when outward duties must be performed, you are obligated to listen to the law. The Christian thus lives a divided life.[41]

For Menno, law and gospel function "more separately and successively, the Law operating first, and then the Gospel, rather than the Law coming to sinful man, as it were, in the Gospel."[42] The gospel for Luther provided declared righteousness. The gospel for Menno provided life-changing power.[43] The Anabaptists had a dream of a church whose members would have changed lives, changed from sin and evil to holiness and righteousness.

Harold S. Bender has written vividly of the Anabaptist view of a changed life.

> To profess the new birth meant a new life. To take the name of Christ meant to take His spirit and His nature. To promise obedience to Him meant actually to live out and carry through His principles and do His works. To claim the cleansing and redemption from sin which baptism symbolized, meant to leave off the sins and lusts of the flesh and the spirit and to live a holy life. To take up the cross daily meant to go out into conflict with the world of sin and evil and fight the good fight of faith, taking gladly the blows and buffetings of the world. To be a disciple meant to teach and to observe all things whatsoever the Master had taught and commanded.[44]

Article IV of *The Schleithem Confession*, written by Michael Sattler, focuses on the Anabaptist view of the world and the need for separation from evil. It reads as follows:

> IV. We have been united concerning the separation that shall take place from the evil and the wickedness which the devil has planted in the world, simply in this; that we have no fellowship with them, and do not run with them in the confusion of their abominations. So it is; since all who

have not entered into the obedience of faith and have not united themselves with God so that they will to do His will, are a great abomination before God, therefore nothing else can or really will grow or spring forth from them than abominable things. Now there is nothing else in the world and all creation than good or evil, believing and unbelieving, darkness and light, the world and those who are {come] out of the world, God's temple and idols, Christ and Belial, and none will have part with the other.

To us, then, the commandment of the Lord is also obvious, whereby He orders us to be and to become separated from the evil one, and thus He will be our God and we shall be His sons and daughters.

Further, He admonishes us therefore to go out from Babylon and from the earthly Egypt, that we may not be partakers in their torment and suffering, which the Lord will bring upon them.

From all this we should learn that everything which has not been united with our God in Christ is nothing but an abomination which we should shun. By this are meant all popish and repopish works and idolatry, gatherings, church attendance, winehouses, guarantees and commitments of unbelief, and other things of the kind, which the world regards highly, and yet which are carnal or flatly counter to the command of God, after the pattern of all the iniquity which is in the world. From all this we shall be separated and have no part with such, for they are nothing but abominations, which cause us to be hated before our Christ Jesus, who has freed us from the servitude of the flesh and fitted us for the service of God and the Spirit whom He has given us.

Thereby shall also fall away from us the diabolical weapons of violence—such as sword, armor, and the like, and all of their use to protect friends or against enemies—by virtue of the word of Christ:—"you shall not resist evil."[45]

Did the teachings of this confession find expression in life? Wolfgang Capito, writing about Sattler shortly after his martydom, viewed him as a sincere and influential leader. According to Capito, Sattler "demonstrated at all times an excellent zeal for the honor of God and the church of Christ, which he desired to see righteous and honorable, free of vices, irreproachable, and to be by their righteous life a help to those who are without."[46] The influence of Sattler and his following was noted when Capito wrote that "the poor people have undertaken to avoid lascivious playing, drinking, gluttony, adultery, war, murder, gossip, living according to fleshly lusts, and to flee what is of the world and according to the flesh."[47]

Menno Simons frequently wrote about his desire for a holy

church. He wanted "an irreproachable church without spot and without wrinkle, one which serves the Lord with all its power and which conforms itself to His Word...."[48] He seemed to have viewed the church as more divine than human as he appeals to the church to become the pure bride of God. "Although thou art pure, make thyself purer still; although thou art holy, make thyself holier still; although thou art righteous, make thyself more righteous still."[49]

Robert Friedmann relates holiness of life to the baptismal vow when he writes that "baptism meant a solemn vow 'not to sin any more,' as Jesus admonished."[50] Friedmann also provides helpful insight when he observes that the Anabaptists lived by a kingdom theology with a "Christ/world" dualism rather than by traditional theology with a "gospel/law" dualism.[51] The dualism of the Anabaptists and their view of holiness as separation from the world are closely related.

The perspective of Kenneth Davis is again helpful when he notes that the Anabaptists' doctrine of the church relates closely to a theology of ascetic holiness. Holy living was not merely the goal for members; it was the requirement for participation in the church.[52]

An ascetic theology of holiness holds that Christlikeness in spirit and conduct is possible and intended by God, that salvation requires some level of otherworldly perfection, and that the pursuit of holiness must become the interpretive principle of Christian doctrine and practice.[53] While the Anabaptists did not identify their position as ascetic theology, they did revive and exhibit its concern for holiness.

Redemptive Love

Anabaptists were called to an ethic of redemptive love, thus renouncing physical violence and the sword.

The earliest statement regarding the Anabaptist view of violence appears in the 1524 letter of Conrad Grebel to Thomas Müntzer. Grebel, speaking for the Swiss Brethren, wrote as follows:

Moreover, the gospel and its adherents are not to be protected by the sword, nor are they thus to protect themselves. . . . True Christian believers are sheep among wolves, sheep for the slaughter; they must be baptized in anguish and affliction, tribulation, persecution, suffering, and death; they must be tried with fire, and must reach the fatherland of eternal rest, not by killing their bodily, but by mortifying their spiritual, enemies. Neither do they use worldly sword or war, since all killing has ceased with them. . . .[54]

The Schleitheim Confession of 1527 restates the Anabaptists' opposition to the use of the sword either for self-protection or for the purposes of war. In addition it rejects the use of the sword by the church as a way of dealing with heretics or those that need to be excommunicated from the church. The state church could only remove such persons from the church by death. The Anabaptists, having a free church model, removed such persons by using the ban. Article six of *The Schleitheim Confession* reads, in part, as follows:

VI. We have been united as follows concerning the sword. The sword is an ordering of God outside the perfection of Christ. It punishes and kills the wicked, and guards and protects the good. In the law the sword is established over the wicked for punishment and for death, and the secular rulers are established to wield the same.

But within the perfection of Christ only the ban is used for the admonition and exclusion of the one who has sinned, without the death of the flesh, simply the warning and the command to sin no more.

Now many, who do not understand Christ's will for us, will ask: whether a Christian may or should use the sword against the wicked for the protection and defense of the good, or for the sake of love.

The answer is unanimously revealed: Christ teaches and commands us to learn from Him, for He is meek and lowly of heart and thus we shall find rest for our souls. Now Christ says to the woman who was taken in adultery, not that she should be stoned according to the law of His Father (and yet He says, "what the Father commanded me, that I do") but with mercy and forgiveness and the warning to sin no more, says: "Go, sin no more." Exactly thus should we also proceed, according to the rule of the ban.[55]

Pilgram Marpeck, writing in 1544, identifies the source of strength for nonviolence when he directs his readers toward the love of God or supernatural love. This love is for all faithful hearts and is the mark of the true church.[56]

In an earlier writing, Marpeck supported a position similar to Grebel and *The Schleitheim Confession* noting the difference between the Old and New Testaments.

> Thus, revenge is no longer permitted in the New Testament for, through patience, the Spirit can now more powerfully overcome enemies than it could in the Old Testament. Therefore, Christ forbade such vengeance and resistance (Lk. 9, 21; Mt. 5), and commanded the children who possessed the Spirit of the New Testament to love, to bless (c ii) their enemies, persecutors, and opponents, and to overcome them with patience (Mt. 5; Lk. 6),[57]

Menno Simons added his strong support to the rejection of violence and the sword. In one of his early writings (1527) he described regenerate persons stating that "hatred and vengeance they do not know, for they love those who hate them; they do good to those who despitefully use them and pray for those who persecute them."[58] He adds, "They are the children of peace who have beaten their swords into plowshares and their spears into pruning hooks, and know war no more."[59]

There can be no doubt but that the Anabaptists lived their convictions of nonviolent love and paid for those convictions with their own blood. The hundreds and thousands who died in the years 1527-60 in Switzerland, Germany, and the Low Countries is historic evidence to this fact.

On what did their convictions rest? First, they believed that the essential nature of Christianity was the transformed life. This was a contrast to Roman Catholicism (receiving divine grace) and to Lutheranism (enjoying the inner experience of grace).[60]

Furthermore, the Anabaptists believed that the church was a "brotherhood of love in which the fulness of the Christian life ideal is to be expressed."[61] Again this was a contrast to Catholicism (an institution), Lutheranism (a place to proclaim the divine Word), and Pietism (a resource for individual piety).

Their convictions of nonviolence were the logical application of their beliefs concerning discipleship, baptism, and the church which were discussed earlier in this section.

The perspective of Davis is also helpful in providing an

understanding of the context out of which the Anabaptists rejection of the sword emerged. Their view of the church as a "separated brotherhood-community through which the kingdom of God finds expression on earth"[62] is seen by Davis as a laicized expression of monasticism. The Anabaptists practiced a partial withdrawal from society in the areas of worship, conduct, social fellowship, and civic obligations. This pattern resembled the ascetic principle of separation from the world which was granted to monastic orders.

Davis describes these privileges as "exemption from the duties of political officeholding, from bearing and use of weapons in military service, and from the taking of oaths. In varying degrees, in varying localities and times, these exemptions were also extended to the laicized forms of monasticism, especially to the tertiaries."[63] When the Anabaptists espoused these same exemptions, they were expressing "their basic ascetic ideals of dualistic separation of the carnal from the spiritual, and of the church from the world."[64]

Cross Bearing

Anabaptists were called to bear the cross of Christ, and to willingly suffer in the spirit of Christ.

In his essay on "The Anabaptist Vision of Discipleship," J. Lawrence Burkholder sees the Anabaptists' acceptance of suffering, "not as incidental but as essential to discipleship."[65] For them baptism was a baptism unto death. The Anabaptist martyrs constantly had on their lips the words of Jesus, "I have a baptism to be baptized with" (Lk. 12:50).

What lay behind this view of discipleship? Did the earliest Anabaptists expect a life of suffering or did it come as a surprise with a theology of suffering developing later in the movement?

Again we turn to Grebel's letter to Müntzer and a section quoted in this study. "True Christian believers," wrote Grebel, "are sheep among wolves, sheep for the slaughter; they must be baptized in anguish and affliction, tribulation, persecution, suffering, and death."[66] Also, he accused the reformers of preaching a "sinful sweet Christ."[67] These words were written in 1524, before the movement began.

By 1527 persecution had begun and the likelihood of death for some, especially the leaders, was anticipated. Thus article five of *The Schleitheim Confession,* which concerns shepherds in the church, directs that "if the shepherd should be driven away or led to the Lord by the cross, at the same hour another shall be ordained in his place, so that the little folk and the little flock of God may not be destroyed, but be preserved by warning and be consoled."[68]

Pilgram Marpeck, writing against the position of Caspar Schwenckfeld about 1530, argues that being a disciple means following the "ceremonies of Christ, such as baptism, the Lord's Supper, teaching, the ban, and the laying on of hands...."[69] He refutes Schwenckfeld's spiritualistic interpretation that the suffering experienced by those who employ these ceremonies "is not the cross of Christ, but rather a punishment from God."[70]

Some fifteen years later, Marpeck wrote the following concerning service and suffering:

> Whatever we serve in this life, we serve under the sweet yoke of Christ and whatever we suffer in the flesh, we suffer in Christ's stead.... Our service is to Christ's members. In them, we make up whatever is lacking of Christ's sufferings, and we do so in all patience and faith.[71]

The suffering of the Christian was a familiar theme for Marpeck. He wrote that Christians will rule with Christ, "but only after they have gone through the depth of tribulation with Him."[72] In the meantime, Christ called them to live with hearty joy released "from the fear of death in which you were imprisoned."[73]

The theme of suffering runs throughout the writings of Menno. When Menno was invited by some of the brethren to accept the office of elder and bishop of the brotherhood, he was troubled in heart. He sensed his own limitations and the physical dangers of becoming an appointed leader. He later wrote about his fear of "the indescribably heavy cross which, if I began to preach, would be the more felt."[74]

In some of his early writings, Menno asked, "And who is it that would be above his Lord? Is it not he that would not suffer as Christ suffered?"[75] Further, he wrote that everyone should remember "that he has not learned Christ except by suffering."[76] Again, he said that "none can rejoice with Christ unless he first suffer with Him. For this is a sure word, says Paul, If we be dead with him, we shall also live with him; if we suffer, we shall also reign with him."[77]

One of Menno's most moving writings is *The Cross of the Saints*. In it, he describes the persecutors, their reasons for persecuting Christians, persecution as the lot of the people of God, the excuses of the persecutors, the blessings of bearing the cross for Christ's sake, and promises for those bearing the cross. The need for such a booklet of encouragement becomes obvious when the nature of their persecution is understood. Menno penned the following description:

> How many pious children of God have we not seen during the space of a few years deprived of their homes and possessions for the testimony of God and their conscience; their poverty and sustenance written off to the emperor's insatiable coffers. How many have they betrayed, driven out of city and country, put to the stocks and torture? How many poor orphans and children have they turned out without a farthing? Some have they hanged, some have they punished with inhuman tyranny and afterward garroted them with cords, tied to a post. Some they have roasted and burned alive. Some, holding their own entrails in their hands, have powerfully confessed the Word of God still. Some they beheaded and gave as food to the fowls of the air. Some have they consigned to the fish. They have torn down the houses of some. Some have they thrust into muddy bogs. They have cut off the feet of some, one of whom I have seen and spoken to. Others wander aimlessly hither and yon in want, misery, and discomfort, in the mountains, in deserts, holes, and clefts of the earth, as Paul says. They must take to their heels and flee away with their wives and little children, from one country to another, from one city to another—hated by all men, abused, slandered, mocked, defamed, trampled upon, styled "heretics." Their names are read from pulpits and town halls; they are kept from their livelihood, driven out into the cold winter, bereft of bread, pointed at with fingers. Yes, whoever can wrong a poor oppressed Christian thinks he has done God a service thereby, even as Christ says.[78]

Such inhuman treatment could only be endured because, as Menno had discovered, "The Lord is your strength, your comfort and refuge; He sits with you in prisons and dungeons; He flies with you to foreign lands; He accompanies you through fire and water: He will never leave you nor forsake you."[79]

This was the experience of suffering. What was their theology of suffering? Ethelbert Stauffer has probed this question deeply and shows that the Anabaptists had a theology of martyrdom. Located in the New Testament, this theology "found its very center in the Cross which gives meaning and order to all this suffering."[80] There is throughout history a struggle between God and anti-God, and the death of Christ is the central event in this struggle. "The fact of the Cross soon became the principle of the Cross which from now on determines the life and fate of the disciples."[81] Those who follow God become involved in the struggle symbolized by the cross. Jesus called his dying a baptism. Paul applied the reality to his own life and called baptism a dying.

The Anabaptist theology of martyrdom had three themes, according to Stauffer. First, martyrdom has been the path of the people of God through history. The Scriptures and church history indicate that the true church has been a suffering church. The "imitation" of Christ included experiencing the cross of Christ. He "lived under the Cross before he died on the Cross."[82]

A second theme was the apocalyptic interpretation of persecution. The Anabaptists believed that "the present extremity is not just one stage on the path of martyrdom through history but it is its very last stage...."[83] They believed that the end of history was at hand; therefore, their suffering was a "sign of divine election."[84]

The third theme was the place of baptism, confession of faith, and defenselessness in their martyr theology. As indicated earlier, they renewed the mode of baptism practiced by the early church and their understanding of baptism as death. Holding true to their confession of faith was extremely important because that revealed whether they were of the "truth." Sealing one's confession with blood was evidence that they were of the "truth." Defenselessness in the face of persecution was based on *Geslassenheit* (resignation, yieldness). It was the attitude that

Jesus exemplified and that he asked of his followers. Therefore, the gospel and those that follow the gospel do not need to be protected by the sword. Truth will finally be victorious.

In summary, the theology of martyrdom held that "the path of discipleship of Christ remains for the entire span between Calvary and the end a way of martyrdom."[85]

The significance of the theology of martyrdom becomes evident when contrasted with the theology of the cross, a term used by Thomas Müntzer and Martin Luther. It was the contrast between the concepts of a suffering church that experienced conflict with the world of evil, and the concept of the individual suffering of inner despair as one struggles with guilt and gives up claims to personal righteousness in submission to the gospel. In a sense it was the contrast between external and internal suffering. Or to use a different terminology, it was the contrast between the "bitter Christ" and the "sweet Christ."[86]

This discussion on the Anabaptist concept of cross bearing still needs the perspective of Davis. He observes that Stauffer roots the theology of martyrdom in Judaism, the New Testament, and the early church Fathers, but then "relegates the concept almost exclusively to the 'underground' movements through medieval times up to the Reformation."[87] Davis sees the theology of martyrdom continuing through the Desert Fathers and the whole monastic tradition. Furthermore, it was related during that period of time, to the "imitation of Christ" motif. The theme of "cross-bearing" was prominent in primitive monastic literature and there was a desire to imitate Christ in his death.[88]

From his point of view, Davis sees the Anabaptist view of suffering related to penitential exercises. Why? Because submissive acceptance of suffering was a means of sanctification and mortification of the flesh.[89] Furthermore, it was a way of imitating Christ in his suffering and therefore related to salvation.[90] Finally, it was "an actual continuation of Christ's atonement,"[91] Christ was still suffering in his members (Col. 1:24).

The insights of Davis would suggest that the concept of cross bearing or imitating Christ in his suffering was a part of the Christian tradition from the time of the early church to the Reformation. The Anabaptists took a familiar theological concept and found in it a fresh application and meaning.

Great Commission

Anabaptists were called to participate in the Great Commission, sharing Christ's call to repentance and faith, and the hope of Christ's return.

The Anabaptists were the missionaries of the Reformation. No religious group took the Great Commission as seriously as they did. Franklin H. Littell says that "no words of the Master were given more serious attention by His Anabaptist followers than His final command: 'Go ye therefore, and teach all nations, baptizing them in the name of the Father, and of the Son, and of the Holy Ghost: teaching them to observe all things whatsoever I have commanded you....' "[92]

What lay behind their unique missionary role in an era of strong spiritual awakening? One factor was their distinctive interpretation of the Great Commission. Charles W. Ranson states that the Protestantism of the Reformation was blind to their universal missionary obligation. "The prevailing view with regard to foreign missions at the beginning of the Protestant era was that the command to preach the Gospel to all nations was given only to the original apostles and expired with them. This view was to persist within Protestantism for three centuries and more."[93] The Anabaptists saw the Great Commission as the mandate of Christ on the church in every generation.

Another factor contributing to the missionary zeal of the Anabaptists was their concept of the nature of the church. For them the church was to be universal. For the Reformers the church was territorial. Littell summarizes the contrast when he writes:

> The gathering of small congregations by believers' baptism went on apace, and Anabaptism spread in many areas closed to the state churches by their acceptance of the principle of territorialism. The Anabaptists represent thereby an early Protestant vision of a world mission unrestricted by terri-

torial limitations, and in a unique fashion foreshadow the later concept of the Church as a community of missionary people.[94]

The Anabaptists assumed that the "Christian" culture of Europe which had experienced Christian teaching for a thousand years needed to hear the gospel. Furthermore, this task became the responsibility of all true believers, not only the professionals.

Their zeal and "success" is documented historically; Sebastian Franck, an opponent of the Anabaptists, wrote in 1531 that their teachings covered the land and that they baptized thousands. Some Reformers feared that most of the common people would join this radical movement. Zwingli himself said that his struggle with the Anabaptists was more difficult than his struggle with the Catholics.[95]

The Anabaptist leaders spoke frequently about their mission convictions. Conrad Grebel, in 1524, urged Thomas Müntzer to "go forward with the Word and establish a Christian church with the help of Christ and his rule...."[96] Immediately after the beginning of the Anabaptist movement in 1525, the leaders moved out from Zurich, calling their hearers to repentance and faith. On August 20, 1527, a number of Anabaptist leaders and missionaries met to plan their missionary strategy. The land was divided and Brethren were sent to designated countries and centers to preach the gospel and make disciples. This historic meeting has been called the Martyr Synod because most of those attending died as martyrs within a few years.

Menno Simons labored with fearless courage for twenty-five years (1535-1560) as a bishop and evangelist. He combined missionary zeal and pastoral concern. Because of his conviction he preached and wrote: "I can no longer hold my tongue, the truth must be told, so that its righteousness may go forth as a light and its salvation burn as a torch, and that all men may know the righteousness of the Lord and all tongues, generations, and people confess His glory."[97] This statement appeared in his booklet on *Why I Do Not Cease Teaching and Writing* (1539). In the same booklet, he wrote, "We desire with ardent hearts even at the cost of life and blood that the holy Gospel of Jesus Christ and His apostles . . . may be taught and preached through all the world as the Lord Jesus Christ commanded His disciples as a last word to them while He was on earth. Matt. 28:19; Mark 16:15."[98]

Menno felt constrained by God to be his witness and share his message as the following quotations reveal:

> This is my only joy and heart's desire: to extend the kingdom of God, reveal the truth, reprove sin, teach righteousness, feed hungry souls with the Word of the Lord, lead the straying sheep into the right path, and gain many souls to the Lord through His Spirit, power, and grace. So would I carry on in my weakness as He has taught me who purchased me, a miserable sinner, with His crimson blood, and has given this mind, by the Gospel of His grace, namely, Jesus Christ. To Him be praise and glory and the eternal kingdom. Amen.[99]
>
> Therefore, we preach, as much as possible, both by day and by night, in houses, and in fields, in forests and wastes, hither and yon, at home or abroad, in prisons and in dungeons, in water and in fire, on the scaffold and on the wheel, before lords and princes, through mouth and pen, with possessions and blood, with life and death. We have done this these many years, and we are not ashamed of the Gospel of the glory of Christ. Rom. 1:16. For we feel His living fruit and moving power in our hearts, as may be seen in many places by the lovely patience and willing sacrifices of our faithful brethren and companions in Christ Jesus.
>
> We could wish that we might save all mankind from the jaws of hell, free them from the chains of their sins, and by the gracious help of God add them to Christ by the Gospel of His peace. For this is the true nature of the love which is of God.[100]

Contributing to their missionary zeal was a strong sense of eschatology. The cover letter that was circulated with *The Schleitheim Confession* concluded by quoting Titus 2:11-14. Paul here admonishes his hearers to await "the same hope and the appearing of the glory of the great God and of our Saviour Jesus Christ."

They felt they were in the stream of a fresh working of God in history. Littell says, "The Anabaptists believed that they were forerunners of a time to come, in which the Lord would establish His people and His Law throughout the earth."[101]

In his letter to the Anabaptists at Horb, Michael Sattler well expressed the urgency with which they lived, and the hope with which they died. "Pray that reapers may be driven out into the harvest, for the time of threshing has come near.... The world has arisen against those who are redeemed from its error. The gospel is testified to before all the world for a testimony. According to this the day of the Lord must no longer tarry."[102]

Davis helps provide a fitting conclusion to this section. He points out that "both medieval asceticism in its monastic and lay expressions and Anabaptism saw the primary goal of the Christian life as a conscious, responsible pursuit of holiness, perfection, or Christlikeness...."[103] Both movements called on their followers to renounce worldliness and the evils of the flesh, and to discipline the material and physical aspects of life. Salvation required the desire for holiness of life and progress in its development.

It appears that Anabaptism built on certain commonly held monastic concepts, giving them fresh interpretation and meaning. The result was a religious form that was readily accepted by the common people but that in turn changed them into a vital religious movement. The methods by which they discipled members in their walk of discipleship will be explored in the next section of this study.

2. The Anabaptist Approach to Discipling

In the Introduction I indicated that a number of scholars have researched the Anabaptist concept of discipleship, but that little attention has been given to their approach to discipling. In this section, I will report my findings regarding how the early Anabaptists helped members to understand and practice discipleship.

The Process of Discipling

The process of discipling happened as a result of intense congregational life. My research indicates that the Anabaptists did not have a "planned program" for discipling. Rather, their view of the Christian life and of the church resulted in an intense form of congregational life. Discipling took place within that setting and as a result of those activities.

Reference has been made to *The Schleitheim Confession* of 1527. Circulated with that confession was a document concerning congregational order. It reveals the intense character of their congregational life. The introduction states that

... according to the command of the Lord and the teachings of His apostles ... we should observe the new commandment in love one toward another, so that love and unity may be maintained, which all brothers and sisters of the entire congregation should agree to hold to as follows:

1. The brothers and sisters should meet at least three or four times a week, to exercise themselves in the teachings of Christ and His apostles and heartily to exhort one another to remain faithful to the Lord as they have pledged.

2. When the brothers and sisters are together, they shall take up something to read together. The one to whom God has given the best understanding shall explain it, the others should be still and listen, so that there are not two or three carrying on a private conversation, bothering the others. The Psalter shall be read daily at home.

3. Let none be frivolous in the church of God, neither in words nor in actions. Good conduct shall be maintained by them all also before the heathen.

4. When a brother sees his brother erring, he shall warn him according to the command of Christ, and shall admonish him in a Christian and brotherly way, as everyone is bound and obliged to do out of love.

5. Of all the brothers and sisters of this congregation none shall have anything of his own, but rather, as the Christians in the time of the apostles held all in common, and especially stored up a common fund, from which aid can be given to the poor, according as each will have need, and as in the apostles' time permit no brother to be in need.

6. All gluttony shall be avoided among the brothers who are gathered in the congregation; serve a soup or a minimum of vegetable and meat, for eating and drinking are not the kingdom of heaven.

7. The Lord's Supper shall be held, as often as the brothers are together, thereby proclaiming the death of the Lord, and thereby warning each one to commemorate, how Christ gave His life for us, and shed His blood for us, that we might also be willing to give our body and life for Christ's sake, which means for the sake of all the brothers.[1]

Notice should be made of their frequency of meeting, the importance of teaching and admonition, and the active participation of each member. The frequency and focus of the Lord's Supper is also significant. Christ gave his life for them and they were to be willing to give body and life for the sake of their brothers and sisters.

In 1527 or 1528, an Anabaptist congregation in Tyrol, Austria, adopted a similar statement entitled "Discipline of the Church: How a Christian Ought to Live." The introduction states that all of the brethren and sisters unanimously agreed to keep the rule of discipline, but if a better rule of discipline is produced by a brother or sister, it shall be accepted at any time. There are twelve articles. Several should be noted that reflect their intense life together. Article one states that when they meet together "they shall sincerely ask God for grace that He might reveal His divine will and help us to note it . . . and when the brethren part they shall thank God and pray for all the brethren and sisters of the entire brotherhood. . . ."[2]

Article two states that they are to "admonish one another in the Lord to remain constant. . . . To meet often, at least four or five times, and if possible . . . even at midweek. . . ."[3]

In article four each member is to "yield himself in God to the brotherhood completely with body and life, and hold in common all gifts received of God. . . ."[4]

Article seven states that "in the meeting one is to speak and the others listen and judge what is spoken, and not two or three stand together. . . ."[5]

According to article nine, a person interested in the faith but not yet converted shall be taught the gospel before meeting in the brotherhood. When he has learned and "agrees to the content of the Gospel, he shall be received by the Christian brotherhood as a brother or a sister, that is, as a fellow member of Christ. . . ."[6]

Article eleven states that when they keep the Lord's Supper, "each one shall be admonished to become conformed to the Lord in the obedience of the Father. . . ."[7]

Werner O. Packull describes an Anabaptist meeting held in Augsburg in 1529. "The candlelight service lasted all night with between sixty and one hundred persons in attendance. . . . Besides reading and preaching they celebrated the Lord's Supper together."[8]

In *The Admonition of 1542*, Pilgram Marpeck calls for instruction before and after baptism. Baptism stands in the middle. The first instruction is being "taught and enlightened in the knowledge and the will of God."[9] If the Holy Spirit touches that heart and the person believes the gospel, his new birth is witnessed in baptism. After baptism, "they are taught to observe all that Christ has commanded, as is fitting for obedient children, and at all times to seek to do the will of their Father."[10]

The combination of an intense pattern of teaching and study led to an unusual knowledge of the Bible. Robert Friedmann notes that "they read assiduously from cover to cover, including the Apocrypha. To them it was an open book, and they claimed to have experienced a spirit akin to it. They read it as people seeking divine guidance."[11]

The emergence of such intense congregational life did not happen in a vacuum. There was in Europe a deep desire for reform and voices were calling for repentance. Davis observes that many accepted the Protestant Reformation as the fulfillment of their expectations but it failed to increase the piety of the people. Anabaptism emerged as an "alternative, reform movement."[12]

Davis further notes that the ascetic theology of holiness in the sixteenth century contained elements such as "spiritual exercises (praying, Bible study, and worship), fasting, work, simplicity, plainness or poverty, foot washing, communal discipline, and deeds of charity. . . ."[13] Many of these elements were incorporated into the congregational life of the Anabaptists.

The Basis of Discipling

The basis of discipling was the rule of Christ and the baptismal vow. For the Anabaptists the rule of Christ (Mt. 18:15-18) was the directive and pattern for discipling and the baptismal vow was the basis for discipling.

In section I we noticed the close similarity between the monastic vow of chastity, poverty, and obedience, and the Anabaptist baptismal vow. The character of that vow was basic to the quality of mutual admonition that took place after baptism.

Balthasar Hubmaier wrote a tract entitled *On Fraternal Admonition* (1527). In it, he states that the right to admonish one another comes "from the baptismal commitment, which a man gave before receiving water baptism, in which he subjected himself, according to the order of Christ, to the church and all her members."[14]

Hubmaier also wrote a catechism. His answer to the question, What is the baptismal pledge? has a similar emphasis on the relationship between the vow at baptism and the admonition which was expected to follow baptism.

Q. What is the baptismal pledge?

A. It is a commitment which man makes to God publicly and orally before the church, in which he renounces Satan, all his thoughts and works. He pledges as well that he will henceforth set all his faith, hope and trust alone in God, and direct his life according to the divine Word, in the power of Jesus Christ our Lord, and in case he should not do that, he promises hereby to the church that he desires virtuously to receive from her members and from her fraternal admonition, as is said above.[15]

Hubmaier summarized his understanding when he wrote: "Where water baptism is not given according to the order of Christ, there it is impossible to accept fraternal admonition from one another in a good spirit."[16]

These statements by Hubmaier fit well with his view of the three stages of the Christian life. These stages are (1) a transformation of the spirit and soul or inner baptism, (2) placing yourself in the care and discipline of a brotherhood or outer baptism, and (3) suffering and persecution or a baptism of blood.[17]

The relationship between the monastic vow and the baptismal vow noted earlier may also be reflected in the term "rule of Christ." Davis points out that each monastic order had its "Rule." The details of that rule vary between the various orders but it included their relationship of obedience to the abbot and how they would function as a family. The Brethren of the Common Life became a link between the monastery and ordinary life in that they followed the monastic vows in modified form. Their rule was less rigid.[18]

It may be that the Anabaptists were therefore using a familiar concept but with special meaning when they spoke about the rule of Christ. They were saying that they were committing themselves to live under the rule of Christ rather than under the rule of an abbot, and that Matthew 18:15-18 was the Christ-given "Rule" on how they would live together as the family of God, the body of Christ.

It is significant to notice that all of the Anabaptist leaders used the term "rule of Christ" or "command of Christ" for Matthew 18:15-18 and related it to the manner of their life together as believers who had taken the vow of baptism.

In Grebel's letter to Müntzer, he said that "an adult is not to be baptized without Christ's rule of binding and loosing."[19] The Lord's Supper "should not be used without the rule of Christ in Matthew 18:15-18, otherwise it is not the Lord's Supper, for without that rule every man will run after the externals."[20]

Michael Sattler, in *The Schleitheim Confession* and in the "Congregational Order," used the term "command of Christ" when referring to Matthew 18.

Pilgram Marpeck wrote that those who have been baptized have authority "so that whatever they loose on earth is loosed and free in heaven, and what they have bound on earth is bound in heaven."[21]

Menno Simons spoke of the two heavenly keys which were the key of binding and key of loosing. These keys were given to the church by Christ and were the basis of the church's authority expressed in Matthew 18.

John Howard Yoder's article "Binding and Loosing" shows how the Matthew 18 passage was understood in the New Testament period and by groups such as the Anabaptists. He clearly indicates its importance in Anabaptist life.

For the Anabaptists believer's baptism was totally voluntary but it carried with it a strong commitment to a life of discipleship. The instructions of Christ in Matthew 18 became an important part of that process.

The Responsibility for Discipling

One of the earliest statements identifying the role of leaders among the Anabaptists was *The Schleitheim Confession* of 1527. Article five concerns the shepherds in the church of God. The use of the term "shepherd" immediately suggests a role of caring for and nurturing the people rather than administering an institutional church. The description of the shepherd's task bears out this suggestion.

> The shepherd in the church shall be a person according to the rule of Paul, fully and completely, who has a good report of those who are outside the faith. The office of such a person shall be to read and exhort and teach, warn, admonish, or ban in the congregation, and properly to preside among the sisters and brothers in prayer, and in the breaking of bread, and in all things to take care of the body of Christ, that it may be built up and developed, so that the name of God might be praised and honored through us, and the mouth of the mocker be stopped.[22]

In 1532, Pilgram Marpeck wrote a confession or defense of his faith. In it, he states his desire "that the Lord will have mercy on us all, and convert us to the pleasure of His divine will, that we may obey His voice and Word."[23] Marpeck was appealing for true discipleship. He went on to indicate how true discipleship would be achieved and his commitment to that task. "May we also warn, admonish, teach, discipline, hear, and understand one another in integrity and truth, and live in obedience to the Word in faith. For this reason, I have surrendered to God and all true believers, and try to serve all men with whatever I have and can accomplish through His Son Christ Jesus. Amen."[24]

Menno Simons was not only a pastor to members of churches but he was also a pastor to pastors or a bishop. He frequently wrote concerning the task of pastors, teachers or shepherds. In his *Foundation of Christian Doctrine*, he wrote that "shepherds who are sent of God and have been rightly called, teach the Word of God unfalsified, keep in its holy ordinances, live unblamably in their little power, for they are born of God, are taught and moved by His Holy Spirit. . . . [They will] preach the word of repentance and grace aright, so that they may win many souls, and that at the

risk of name and fame, house and property, person and life."[25]
Every preacher and teacher, said Menno, was to "teach, exhort,
reprove, root up, and build in the name of the Lord."[26]

Near the end of Menno's life (1558), he wrote one of his most
eloquent statements concerning the task of those to whom the
Word of the Lord is committed. Various terms and phrases are
used to describe the scope of the leader's role in discipling the believers. It reads as follows:

> Once more, arm yourselves, for true teachers are called in the Scrip-
> tures, the angels of the Lord, and valiant soldiers. Therefore be men; keep
> the commandment of God; hold fast and waver not.
>
> Watchmen and trumpeters are they. Therefore, blow your trumpet on
> the right note; watch diligently over the city of God; watch, I say, and
> neither slumber nor sleep.
>
> Spiritual pillars are they. Oh, stand fast in the truth, bear your burden
> willingly, waver not, neither be faint.
>
> Messengers of peace are they called. Ah, brethren, live up to your
> name, walk in peace, promote it, and break it not.
>
> Bishops and overseers are they called. Oh, take great care of the flock
> of Christ. Take great care of them, I say, and neither destroy nor neglect
> them.
>
> Shepherds are they called. Oh, keep and feed the lambs of Christ;
> leave them not nor disdain them.
>
> Teachers are they called. Make known the Word and truth of Christ
> and neither hide it nor keep silence. Spiritual nurses and fathers are they.
> Oh, nourish and cherish your young children. Neither grieve nor thrust
> them away. Spiritual mother hens in Christ are they called. In Christ gather
> the little chicks and neither scatter them nor peck at them. Stewards of God
> are they called. Ah, dispense the mysteries of God aright; neither abuse nor
> disgrace them.
>
> The light of the world are they called. Shine forth in full glory and con-
> ceal not the brightness of your virtue.
>
> The salt of the earth are they called. Oh, let the salt penetrate through
> and through to stay worms and decay.
>
> Ministers are they called in Christ's stead. Ah, brethren, serve but do
> not lord it.
>
> Let no man glory in any gift, I beseech you. We are receivers, not
> givers, of grace; it is not of ourselves. Observe; we are servants and not
> lords. Ah, brethren, bow and submit yourselves.[27]

But the responsibility for discipling was also extended to individual members. They were to be a "kingdom of priests."

The "Congregational Order" circulated with *The Schleit-heim Confession* called for frequent meetings of the brothers and sisters "to exercise themselves in the teaching of Christ and His apostles and heartily to exhort one another. . . ."[28]

When Michael Sattler was in prison facing death, he wrote to the believers at Horb expressing his pastoral concern for them and encouraging them to be faithful in their suffering. He admonishes them against blaming God for their circumstances or forgetting to love each other. He refers to those who have fallen short in their love stating that "they have not wanted to build up one another in love. . . ."[29]

Throughout Sattler's brief but significant ministry, he stressed the importance of individual members discipling one another. In his pamphlet, "How Scripture Should Be Discerningly Exposited," he concludes with a discussion on how they should seek God's truth together. It reads, in part, as follows:

> Now he who presents himself to the Lord Christ, [ready] for all obedience and for the discipline and admonition of the Holy Spirit, will soon find a Peter, Paul, Ananias, Apollos, a servant of God and brother of the fellow believers, so that he might not remain in error, and so that on that day he will have no excuse to plead.[30]

Pilgram Marpeck served as the spiritual leader of a scattered group of churches. In a letter to saints in Moravia, which was delivered by two brethren, he states that the brothers are making the journey to become acquainted with them and their knowledge of Christ, "and also that you may receive from them both a spoken and a written testimony to the truth of the state of our life in order that all of us may have received the same comfort, peace, and joy and bear the same compassion in the tribulation of Christ in the fellowship of His body."[31] Members were not only built in faith through the teaching of Scripture but also as they shared the truth of the state of their lives.

Early in Menno Simons' ministry, he expressed the need for brotherly admonition. In fact, he invited it for himself. "If I err in some things," he wrote, ". . . I pray everyone for the Lord's sake, lest I be put to shame, that if anyone has stronger and more convincing truth he through brotherly exhortation and instruction might assist me."[32]

On several occasions, Menno encouraged parents to teach their children in the way of truth. In his tract "The Nurture of Children," he appeals to parents to "instruct your children thus, from youth up, and daily admonish them with the Word of the Lord, setting a good example. Teach and admonish them, I say, to the extent of their understanding."[33] Prayers at mealtime was a part of the nurturing by parents. Menno encouraged prayer before and after meals. In fact, he wrote "A Christian Grace Before Meals" and "A Christian Grace or Prayer of Thanksgiving After Meals." These were suggested prayers for use in the home.

In one of his strongest appeals for discipling by individual members, Menno commanded his readers "diligently to observe each other unto salvation, in all becoming ways teaching, instructing, admonishing, reproving, warning, and consoling each other as occasion requires . . . in accordance with the Word of God and in unfeigned love, until we increase in God and become united in faith. . . ."[34]

For the Anabaptists discipling was a major responsibility of leaders and members. Through this process, they could be the visible church.

The Context for Discipling

The context for discipling was both the gathered congregation and conversation between individuals. We have already noticed the intense congregational life of the Anabaptists, intense not simply because they met frequently but due to the personal, life-related concerns on which they reflected when they met together. Davis points out that the brotherhood was a special agency for spiritual progress. Their gathered life was a setting for progress in sanctification.[35]

Matthew 18 was the basis for brotherhood discipline and correction which to some Anabaptists was the mark of the true church. (Of course, the Matthew 18 process started with conversation between individuals.) In her doctoral dissertation on "Communal Discipline in the Early Anabaptists Communities of Switzerland, South and Central Germany, Austria, and Moravia, 1525-1550," Jean Ellen Goodban Runzo describes the communal discipline practiced by each of these Anabaptist communities. Even though there was a range of specific beliefs and practices, all of these communities based their discipline on Matthew 18:15-17. Further, they believed that Christ's demand for discipleship and a morally pure church could be achieved only through the practice of congregational discipline.[36]

However, the congregation was also the setting where there was instruction, inspiration, and worship which "contributed to the believer's progress in sanctification from justification."[37] According to Davis, "sermonizing . . . retained its vital place in the Christian life of the church,"[38] even though printed Scriptures were widely distributed. The sermon aided in sanctification as it helped the worshipers reflect on the life and teachings of Jesus and on the need for mutual love. After the sermon, individual members frequently shared words of correction and encouragement.

In his last letter to the congregation at Horb, Michael Sattler instructed them not to forget "the assembly, but apply yourselves to coming together constantly and that you may be united in prayer for all men . . . ."[39]

Since the responsibility for the discipling applied to individual members, this process also took place outside of the gathered community. One of the most vivid descriptions of how this might have taken place is found in the tract *On Fraternal Admonition* by Balthasar Hubmaier. He entitled this section "How to Admonish One Another." Note the appeal to the baptismal vow of brotherly admonition and to the steps outlined in Matthew 18.

> Brother! It stands written that men must give an account on the judgment day for every vain word that they have spoken. Now dear brother you made a baptismal pledge to Christ Jesus our Lord. You committed yourself to Him in such way, and publicly pledged it before the church, that you

would henceforth desire to direct and rule your life according to His Holy Word (to which scripture testifies); and that if you should not do so, you would willingly let yourself be admonished according to the command of Christ. Thereupon you received water baptism and were numbered in the membership of the Christian community.

Now you are using much vain language and frivolous speech, whereby good morals are seriously destroyed, as is not fitting for a Christian man. I therefore remind you of your baptismal pledge, my dearest brother, that you would call to memory what you promised to God, and I beg you for the sake of God and of the salvation of your soul henceforth to avoid such frivolous talk and to improve your life, thus doing the will of God.

If now your brother ceases to sin, you have won a precious jewel. If he does not, then take two or three witnesses with you and try once more in the same words. If he will not hear them either, then say to the congregation, which will know how to proceed. Deal in the same way with all other sins.[40]

It should not be assumed that conversation between individuals for the purpose of discipling had only a discipline character. There were also words of encouragement and nurture as we have observed earlier in this study. But there was a deep concern that brothers and sisters live in obedience to the Word of God and that they practice the obedience of faith. Therefore, the spiritual life of fellow members was the concern of all members, and they discipled one another when they met as a group and when they met individually.

The Procedure for Discipling

The procedure for discipling was relating biblical teachings to the lives of individuals with the awareness that Jesus was among them. In his discussion of Anabaptism, Walter Klaassen observes the central importance of the Bible as the guide and norm for their lives. While this approach caused some problems in overemphasizing details, it did provide an unchanging norm in a society of biblical unfaithfulness and gross ignorance and neglect of biblical teachings.[41] Again the words in Michael Sattler's "Congregational Order" are relevant when he instructed the brothers and sisters "to exercise themselves in the teaching of Christ and His apostles...."[42] Menno Simons gave similar instructions in his writings. In the *Meditation on the Twenty-fifth Psalm,* Menno admonished his readers "to examine this Psalm with care, word by word, with a submissive humble heart."[43]

Pilgram Marpeck frequently referred to the relationship of the Scriptures to daily life. In a letter to Swiss and Alsatian brethren intended to promote a greater unity among the various Anabaptist groups, Marpeck wrote the following:

> My dearly beloved in God the Father and the Lord Jesus Christ. Especially in this critical time of great danger, my fervent prayer, wish, and desire, now and always, is that one of these days, before my end, God might open the way to [come to] you all. There, together, we might rejoice in the way, truth, and life which is Jesus Christ, discuss His will, mind, and Spirit which are given in word, deed, and act, and share our delight in the love and truth of the gospel of Christ.[44]

In his letter "Judgment and Decision," Marpeck concludes by indicating that "Christ, Moses, the prophets, and the apostles used divine and biblical Scriptures in three ways."[45] The first is teaching for those who know nothing of God and his Word. The second is admonition and warning to those who have been taught. Finally, there are commandments and prohibitions for those that transgress God's commandments, the purpose of which is to lead to repentance. In another letter, Marpeck speaks of the "Scriptures which men test, learn, experience, witness to, and judge to the praise of God and their own salvation, and from them judge themselves and others."[46] This is a good description of the role of Scripture in the discipling process.

Behind this process of discipling were two important assumptions. One was the activity of the Holy Spirit in making the Scriptures alive and understandable. Marpeck wrote that "the Word does not ignite itself where God does not make it alive...."[47] The task of explaining and applying the Scriptures did not depend totally on them. The Holy Spirit also was at work.

A second assumption was the presence of Jesus when they gathered in his name. This understanding was crucial for their view of the church and the nurturing task of the church. The key passage was Matthew 18:19-20 and it is therefore fitting to see Matthew 18:15-20 as a central passage for the Anabaptists combining the rule of Christ and the presence of Christ. The following quotations express this view.

> Christ will be with His own until the end of the world, and will not leave them orphans. And where, on this basis, two or three are gathered in His name, there He is in the midst of them. And whatever they will agree to ask of the heavenly Father in His name and according to His will, that He will do or give.[48]
>
> The true saints of God and children of Christ are those whose ruler is the Holy Spirit in the Word of truth. Where two or three are gathered in His name, He is among them.... I pray God my heavenly Father that He will not allow me to be separated from such a gathering and fellowship of the Holy Spirit, it makes no difference who they are or where they gather in the whole world. I hope to be in their fellowship and to submit myself to the rule of the Holy Spirit of Christ in the obedience of faith.[49]

For the Anabaptists the norm by which they discipled was the Scriptures as they understood them. But truth taking root in the lives of individuals happened supernaturally. They planted and watered but God gave the increase.

The Methods of Discipling

The methods of discipling included writing, teaching, preaching, individual admonition, and Bible study and prayer. The Anabaptists used a variety of methods to communicate their message and nurture one another in the faith. In addition to the above-mentioned methods, they also participated in public debates; however, their purpose in the debates was primarily to explain or defend their point of view before the Reformers rather than disciple Anabaptists.

Looking briefly at the discipling methods of various leaders, we recall the very significant letter of Conrad Grebel to Thomas Müntzer urging him to move forward with the Word and "establish a Christian church."

Balthasar Hubmaier wrote nineteen printed works in about two years. His writings helped develop the concept of the believers' church.

Michael Sattler wrote tracts and letters during his short but intense ministry. Perhaps his most significant writing was the

Seven Articles or *The Schleitheim Confession.* In his letter to the church at Horb, he called on the readers to "Pray without ceasing for all prisoners."[50]Sattler was also active in teaching and preaching.

Pilgram Marpeck, in addition to teaching and preaching, wrote numerous letters to individuals, epistles to churches and books for instructing believers in their faith and life. The writings of Marpeck that have been preserved total over 500 pages.

Menno Simons was the most influential of the early Anabaptist leaders due partly to his many years of ministry and his untiring activity. Harold S. Bender sees Menno's greatness in "his character, his writings, and his message."[51] His letters and tracts to individuals, letters to congregations, and tracts and books to instruct believers in the faith total over 1000 pages. He was a tireless teacher, preacher, and defender of the faith.

He also encouraged others to study the Scriptures and follow their teachings. Reference has already been made to his instructions to examine the twenty-fifth Psalm "with care, word by word, with a submissive humble heart."[52] In the *Foundation of Christian Doctrine,* he appealed to his readers to "examine the Scriptures correctly. . . ."[53] He provided some indication of what it meant to study the Bible correctly when he wrote in *Christian Baptism* about those that "tear a fragment from the holy Scriptures. . . ."[54] "They do not regard that which is written before or after, by which we may ascertain the right meaning. . . ."[55] For Menno discipling through Bible study involved the proper study of the Bible.

Menno's zeal in making disciples and flexibility in methods was expressed in his *Reply to Gellius Faber* when he wrote the following:

> And I am still willing and prepared, at all times, as long as I have breath or sense, and can sit on a wagon or lie in a ship to appear before Gellius or anybody, verbally to defend the foundation of our faith, and to testify to the truth of Jesus Christ, just so it takes place under safe conduct, in good faith, and in Christian fidelity, to the praise of our God, to the extension of His church, to the promulgation of His holy Word, and to the sal-

vation of our neighbors. This is the main desire of my heart, my joy and desire, to preach and publish His great, adorable name, teach His Word, seek His gain, honor, and praise to the best of my humble ability.[56]

The Scope of Discipling

At the beginning of this study, we noted the centrality of discipleship in the Anabaptist view of the Christian life. A true disciple was to bring all of life under the lordship of Christ. The specific meaning of this broad concept was developed in section one. In section two we have been identifying the various aspects of the discipling process.

In this brief discussion, I am noting the fact that the concept and scope of discipling was as broad as the concept of discipleship. In the discipling process, all aspects of discipleship received attention. Discipling was a comprehensive concept reflecting a concern for one's total life. It was much broader than the need for discipline, or than the needs of young Christians. The brotherhood's concern included positive encouragement and the need for growth. It applied to those mature in the faith as well as to babes in Christ. Why? Because as Menno said, Christ "has taught and left unto His followers an example of pure love, and a perfect life."[57] This held before the Anabaptists an ideal which they could not fully achieve but toward which they attempted to move. Discipleship was a lifelong pilgrimage and discipling was a lifelong process.

One example of the inclusive scope of discipling was Marpecks' concern that the gifts of the body be discerned, appreciated, and exercised. In his letter "On the Inner Church," Marpeck rejoiced in the fact that the treasures given to us by God have become new in Christ and useful to each other.

> We should see and observe the pleasure of the temple of His body and thus comfort and make glad our souls. Indeed, we should fall into wonderment, and thank our God and Father for it. We should frequently contemplate the gifts, for we should pay more attention to the giver than to the gifts. Such is the giver's intention. He who does not contemplate the gifts cannot understand either the gift or the giver. Nor may he love either of them properly, nor can he truly thank the giver.

All gifts are given us by God, and they are given for two reasons. First, in them we can learn to know our Creator, God, and Father and thus, with a pure heart, we may glorify, praise, and thank Him. Second, we are to use the gifts to serve each other, and not to lord it over each other.[58]

The gifts in every single member must be heard and seen. There can be no unendowed member who has not been given something of the treasures of Christ, such as virtues and the fruits of the Holy Spirit on the body of Christ.[59]

In his pastoral letter "The Servants and Service of the Church," Marpeck explained how the Holy Spirit's gifts are to function in the body.

In this body the gifts of the Holy Spirit are manifest in each member according to the measure of faith in Jesus Christ for service in the growth of the body of Christ. By this service the weakest, least, and smallest members are strengthened, comforted, led, guided, and pastured by the strong, leading, and most able members. Thus they are trained, preserved, increased, and nourished until they reach the full maturity of Christ. For whoever would be the greatest must be the vassal and servant and not the ruler of all the others, says the Lord. Their service is not compelled or forced not for the sake of shameful gain; rather it flows voluntarily from an affectionate disposition. They do not rule over the heritage of God but become an example to the flock, says Peter.[60]

This description is a fitting explanation and definition of discipling—members helping each other become mature in Christ. When maturity in Christ is achieved, members are fully living a life of discipleship.

The Content of Discipling

The biblical content of discipling was primarily the teaching and examples of Christ and the apostles. A distinctive of Anabaptist hermeneutics was the concept of progressive revelation within the Scriptures. They held to a "non-flat" view of the Bible which was in contrast to the view of the Reformers. (Zwingli accused them of rejecting the Old Testament.) For the Anabaptists the whole of Scripture was divine and an essential part of God's revelation. However, they rejected the equality of the Old and New Testaments for their faith and life. For them the

New Testament stood above the Old and the culmination of revelation was found in Christ. This was important in their approach to church-state relations and ethics.

The priority given to the New Testament was expressed in the frequently used phrase, "the doctrine of Christ and the apostles." In the introduction to Sattler's' "Congregational Order," he speaks about "the command of the Lord and the teachings of the apostles."[61] The first statement called for the members to meet "at least three or four times a week, to exercise themselves in the teaching of Christ and His apostles. . . ."[62] The Old Testament, in the minds of the Anabaptists, belonged primarily to the Jewish people. This did not mean its rejection but rather an acceptance of only those teachings that agreed with "the doctrine of Christ and the apostles."[63] This was their interpretive principle and it was expressed in their use of the Bible. It has been observed that "Menno Simons cites the New Testament 3½ times more often than the Old, and 40 percent of the New Testament citations are from the Gospels."[64]

Looking more closely at their use of the New Testament, Robert Friedmann points out that among the New Testament Epistles, the Anabaptists showed a preference for the writings of Peter. Frequently quoted passages were 1 Peter 3:21; 2:9; 3:15; 4:7; 4:8; 4:13; and 2 Peter 3:13 and 3:16. These spoke to issues such as baptism, the priesthood of all believers, suffering for Christ, and being ready to give a reason for the hope that is in you.[65]

This brief discussion supports the conclusion of Davis that the Anabaptist movement had "an essentially ascetic and ethical conception of Christianity."[66] The goal was holiness and the means was the "imitation of Christ."[67]

The Abuse of Discipling

The abuse of discipling was shunning. Earlier in this section, we noticed the importance of the rule of Christ (Mt. 18:15-18) and the concepts of binding and loosing. Loosing meant to forgive and was exercised at baptism with the opening of the door of membership, or when they received again a penitent sinner. Binding meant to withhold fellowship and was used when communion was withheld or when there was excommunication from membership. To exercise binding was called the ban. Article II of *The Schleitheim Confession* concerns the ban. It reads as follows:

> II. We have been united as follows concerning the ban. The ban shall be employed with all those who have given themselves over to the Lord, to walk after [Him] in His commandments; those who have been baptized into the one body of Christ, and let themselves be called brothers or sisters, and still somehow slip and fall into error and sin, being inadvertently overtaken. The same [shall] be warned twice privately and the third time be publicly admonished before the entire congregation according to the command of Christ (Mt. 18). But this shall be done according to the ordering of the Spirit of God before the breaking of bread so that we may all in one spirit and in one love break and eat from one bread and drink from one cup.[68]

The Swiss Brethren used the ban primarily with reference to communion but also used it for excommunication. Runzo states that they viewed the ban as an "essential sign of the true church"[69] and that they had a corporate approach to discipline. It was a communal concern and activity.

It is interesting to notice that Article VI of *The Schleitheim Confession*, which deals with the sword, states that "within the perfection of Christ only the ban is used for admonition and exclusion of the one who has sinned, without the death of the flesh, simply the warning and the command to sin no more."[70] Marpeck stated the same understanding when he wrote that "we are not to be like those who maintain the ban, banning people from the face of the earth. . . . "[71]

Both of these statements refer to the Catholic and Protestant approach to church discipline. In a society where church and world were one, the only way to get rid of a heretic was to put him to death. The ban of the state church was to "ban people from the face of the earth." Thousands of Anabaptists died under this ban. The persecution of the Anabaptists was the church discipline of the Catholics and Protestants. The Anabaptists held to a doctrine of two distinct kingdoms: church and world. Their use of the ban was putting a person back into the world rather than out of the world through death. Understood in this way, the Anabaptists' exercise of the ban was an act of mercy rather than inhuman judgment.

However, there were times when the Anabaptists used the ban in legalistic, unredemptive ways. In fact, Marpeck wrote several letters to the Swiss Brethren appealing to them to be less harsh and legalistic in their exercise of discipline. His primary emphasis was on admonition or the first stages of "the rule of Christ" rather than on excommunication which he felt should happen only rarely.

The most severe use of Matthew 18 happened among the Dutch Anabaptists. Their desire to maintain the purity, unity, and integrity of the church led to excessive legalism. Frequently the first stages of the rule of Christ was ignored, and discipline quickly became a public process. In addition, shunning or social avoiding was required after excommunication or the ban. Menno Simons taught the shunning of one's marriage partner when the spouse was under discipline.

This abusive extreme led to hostility and dissension rather than restoration. Walter Klaassen indicates that they rejected physical violence but practiced psychological violence. The end result was tragic for many congregations and leaders. Congregations were divided and greatly weakened. Attempts to bring unity failed. In 1558 Menno wrote the following to his brother in law, Reyn Edes:

> O my brother Reyn! If I could only be with you even a half day and tell you something of my sorrow, my grief and heartache, and of the heavy burden which I carry for the future of the church. . . . If the mighty God had not strengthened me in the past year, as He is now doing also, I would have lost my reason. There is nothing on earth that I love so much as the church; yet just in respect to her must I suffer this great sorrow.

The perspective of history would suggest that when the rich concept of discipling is narrowed to the concept of discipline and/

or the practice of shunning is added to the ban, then a potential for good becomes an instrument for evil and the body of Christ is harmed rather than enriched.

Conclusion

This study revealed that within the broad stream of Anabaptism, there was general agreement on the essence of discipleship. As the study has shown, there were differences in the application of principles which led to vigorous discussions within various groups and between the various groups. However, they approached these discussions from a broad common base.

Researching the Anabaptist approach to discipling was both rewarding and exciting. The most significant discovery was that discipling happened in the intensity of their congregational life. While I did not uncover a sixteenth-century program of discipling that can be copied today, my findings do support the need for developing patterns of discipling since they are largely absent in Mennonite churches today. Certain principles inherent in Anabaptist discipling have been included in the handbook.

This study was conducted simultaneously with a study on spirituality and discipling skills. This combination led to an unexpected benefit—the interaction of Roman Catholic spirituality and Anabaptist discipleship. This interaction has resulted in both a clearer understanding of the uniqueness of Anabaptism and of Anabaptist borrowings from Catholicism. *Anabaptism and Asceticism* by Kenneth Davis was the key aid in this process.

Appendix 2

When Christ with His Teaching True

Michael Sattler

1. When Christ with His teaching true
   Had gathered a little flock
   He said that each with patience
   Must daily follow Him bearing his cross.

2. And said: You, my beloved disciples,
   Must be ever courageous
   Must love nothing on earth more than Me
   And must follow My teaching.

3. The world will lie in wait for you
   And bring you much mockery and dishonor;
   Will drive you away and outlaw you
   As if Satan were in you.

4. When then you are blasphemed and defamed
   For My sake persecuted and beaten
   Rejoice; for behold your reward
   Is prepared for you at heaven's throne.

5. Behold Me: I am the Son of God
   And have always done the right.
   I am certainly the best of all
   Still they finally killed Me.

6. Because the world calls Me an evil spirit
   And malicious seducer of the people
   And contradicts My truth
   Neither will it go easy with you.

7. Yet fear not such a man
   Who can kill only the body
   But far more fear the faithful God
   Whose it is to condemn both.

8. He it is who tests you as gold
   And yet is loving to you as His children
   As long as you abide in My teaching
   I will nevermore forsake you.

9. For I am yours and you are Mine
   Thus where I am there shall you be,
   And he who abuses you touches My eye,
   Woe to the same on that day.

10. Your misery, fear, anxiety, distress, and pain
    Will be great joy to you there
    And this shame a praise and honor,
    Yea, before the whole host of heaven.

11. The apostles accepted this
    And taught the same to everyman;
    He would follow after the Lord,
    That he should count on as much.

12. O Christ, help Thou Thy people
    Which follows Thee in all faithfulness,
    That though through Thy bitter death
    It may be redeemed from all distress.

13. Praise to Thee, God, on Thy throne
    And also to Thy beloved Son
    And to the Holy Ghost as well.
    May He yet draw many to His kingdom.

From *The Legacy of Michael Sattler*, translated and edited by John H. Yoder, pp. 141-145.

Appendix 3

Hymn of Discipleship

Menno Simons

1

My God, where shall I wend my flight?
  Ah, help me on upon the way;
The foe surrounds both day and night
  And fain my soul would rend and slay.
    Lord God, Thy Spirit give to me,
    Then on Thy ways I'll constant be,
    And, in Life's Book, eternally!

2

When I in Egypt still stuck fast,
  And traveled calm broad paths of ease,
Then was I famed, a much sought guest,
  The world with me was quite at peace;
    Enmeshed was I in Satan's gauze,
    My life abomination was,
    Right well I served the devil's cause.

3

But when I turned me to the Lord,
  And gave the world a farewell look,
Accepted help against the evil horde,
  The lore of Antichrist forsook;
    Then was I mocked and sore defamed,
    Since Babel's councils I now disdained;
    The righteous man is e'er disclaimed!

4

As one may read of Abel, famed,
  Zacharias too—recall it well—
And Daniel too, whom bad men framed
  So that he among fierce lions fell;
    So were the prophets treated, all,
    Christ Jesus too—it is good to recall—
    Nor were the prophets spared this call

5

I'd rather choose the sorrow sore,
  And suffer as of God the child,
Than have from Pharaoh all his store,
  To revel in for one brief while;
    The realm of Pharaoh cannot last,
    Christ keeps His kingdom sure and fast;
    Around His child His arm He casts.

6

In the world, ye saints, you'll be defamed,
  Let this be cause for pious glee;
Christ Jesus too was much disdained;
  Whereby He wrought to set us free;
    He took away of sin the bill
    Held by the foe. Now if you will
    You too may enter heaven still!

7

If you in fires are tested, tried,
  Begin to walk life's narrow way,
Then let God's praise be magnified,
  Stand firm on all He has to say;
    If you stand strong and constant then,
    Confess His Word in the sight of men,
    With joy he extends the diadem!

8

Come hither, bride, receive the crown,
  And neckpiece wrought of burnished gold;
Put on that white and costly gown.
  Thy years shall nevermore grow old.
    From death to life thou didst arise;
    All tears shall vanish from thine eyes;
    No grief nor sorrow more shall rise!

9

Now standest thou, Zion, in fairest hue,
  A crown to thee, of grace, is given;
The name of God and Jerusalem new
  Upon thy sides are deeply graven.
    Thou wert abused, yes, stripped quite bare,
    But now art decked in garment fair;
    Art entered to the rest that is there.

10

Then evil men shall, frightened, see
  As they behold thy splendor mounted,
That these are they—Where shall we flee?—
  Whose life by us was glibly counted
    For folly and for ravings wild;
    We judged these people were beguiled,
    Who live forever, reconciled!

11

He who this hymn for us did write,
  And to God's praise sang gladly,
Had conflict oft; with flesh did fight;
  Was tempted sore and sadly.
    Pray God that love in him may rise,
    Let him with Babel ne'er fraternize;
    Then the Home awaits him, in the skies!

From *The Complete Works of Menno Simons,* translated by Leonard
Verduin and edited by John Christian Wenger, pp. 1065-1067.

Appendix 4

The Regenerated

Menno Simons

These regenerated people have a spiritual king over them who rules them by the unbroken sceptre of His mouth, namely, with His Holy Spirit and Word. He clothes them with the garment of righteousness, of pure white silk. He refreshes them with the living water of His Holy Spirit and feeds them with the Bread of Life. His name is Christ Jesus.

They are the children of peace who have beaten their swords into plowshares and their spears into pruning hooks, and know war no more. They give to Caesar the things that are Caesar's and to God the things that are God's.

Their sword is the sword of the Spirit, which they wield in a good conscience through the Holy Ghost.

Their marriage is that of one man and one woman, according to God's own ordinance.

Their kingdom is the kingdom of grace, here in hope and after this in eternal life.

Their citizenship is in heaven, and they use the lower creations such as eating, drinking, clothing, shelter, with thanksgiving and to the necessary support of their own lives, and to the free service of their neighbor, according to the Word of the Lord.

Their doctrine is the unadulterated Word of God, testified through Moses and the prophets, through Christ and the apostles, upon which they build their faith, which saves our souls. Everything that is contrary thereto, they consider accursed.

Their baptism they administer to the believing according to the commandment of the Lord, in the doctrines and usages of the apostles.

Their Lord's Supper they celebrate as a memorial of the favors and death of their Lord, and an incitement to brotherly love.

Their ban or excommunication descends on all the proud scorners—great and small, rich and poor, without any respect of persons, who once passed under the Word but have now fallen back, those living or teaching offensively in the house of the Lord—until they repent.

They daily sigh and lament over their poor, unsatisfactory evil flesh, over the manifest errors and faults of their weak lives. Their inward and outward war is without ceasing. Their sighing and calling is to the most High. Their fight and struggle is against the devil, world, and flesh all their days, pressing on toward the prize of the high calling that they may obtain it. So they prove by their actions that they believe the Word of the Lord, that they know and possess Christ in power, that they are born of God and have Him as their Father.

From *The Complete Writings of Menno Simons*, translated by Leonard Verduin and edited by John Christian Wenger, pp. 94-95.

Notes

Introduction

1. Marlin Jeschke, *Discipling the Brother* (Scottdale: Herald Press, 1972).

2. Larry Richards and Norm Wakefield have written a four-volume series called Discipling Resources. The titles are *Basic Christian Values, First Steps for New and Used Christians, Fruit of the Spirit,* and *The Good Life* (Grand Rapids: Zondervan, 1981).

3. Donald A. McGavran and Win Arn, *How to Grow a Church* (Glendale, Calif. Gospel Light, 1973), p. 80.

4. *Ibid.*, p. 102.

5. Donald A. McGavran, *Understanding Church Growth* (Grand Rapids: Eerdmans, 1970), p. 212.

6. *Ibid.*, p. 310.

7. Juan Carlos Ortiz, *Disciple* (Carol Stream, Ill.: Creation House, 1975), p. 113.

8. Leroy Eims, *The Lost Art of Disciple Making* (Grand Rapids: Zondervan, 1978).

9. Walter A. Henrichsen, *Disciples Are Made—Not Born* (Wheaton: Victor Books, 1974).

10. Allen Hadidian, *Successful Discipling* (Chicago: Moody Press, 1979).

11. Waylon B. Moore, *Multiplying Disciples: The New Testament Method For Church Growth* (Colorado Springs: Navpress, 1981.)

12. Billie Hanks, Jr., and William A. Shell, eds., *Discipleship* (Grand Rapids: Zondervan, 1981).

13. Waldron Scott, *Bring Forth Justice* (Grand Rapids: Eerdmans, 1980).

14. Richards and Wakefield, *op. cit.*

15. *Ibid.*, back cover.

16. James W. Fowler, *Stages of Faith* (San Francisco: Harper & Row, 1981), p. 11.

17. John H. Yoder, trans. and ed., *The Legacy of Michael Sattler,* Classics of the Radical Reformation, (Scottdale: Herald Press, 1973), p. 7

Lesson 1
    1. Harold S. Bender, "The Anabaptist Theology of Discipleship," *The Mennonite Quarterly Review*, 24 (January 1950), 27.
    2. For a fuller discussion see *The Mennonite Encyclopedia*, vol. 2: s.v. "Half-Anabaptists," by Robert Friedmann.
    3. Bender, *op. cit.*, pp. 29-31.
    4. *The Complete Writings of Menno Simons*, trans. Leonard Verduin and ed. John Christian Wenger (Scottdale: Herald Press, 1956), p. 225. Hereafter referred to as CWMS.
    5. Dietrich Bonhoeffer, *The Cost of Discipleship*, trans. R. H. Fuller (New York: Macmillan, 1953), pp. 31-32.
    6. Craig R. Dykstra, *Vision and Character: A Christian Educator's Alternative to Kohlberg* (New York: Paulist Press, 1981), p. 90.
    7. Kenneth Ronald Davis, *Anabaptism and Asceticism*, Studies in Anabaptist and Mennonite History, No. 16 (Scottdale: Herald Press, 1974), p. 134.

Lesson 2
    1. John R. Martin, *Keys to Successful Bible Study* (Scottdale: Herald Press, 1981), pp. 108-109.
    2. Bender, *op. cit.*, pp. 27-29.
    3. William Klassen and Walter Klaassen, trans. and ed. *The Writings of Pilgram Marpeck*, Classics of the Radical Reformation, No. 2, (Kitchener and Scottdale: Herald Press, 1978), pp. 507-510.
    4. Bonhoeffer, *op. cit* ., pp. 51-52.
    5. Morton T. Kelsey, *Adventure Inward* (Minneapolis: Augsburg, 1980).

Lesson 3
    1. *The New International Dictionary of New Testament Theology*, (Vol. 1): s.v. "ἀκολουθέω" by Christian Blendinger.
    2. *Ibid.*
    3. *Ibid.*
    4. Jack Dean Kingsbury, "The Verb *Akolouthein* ("To Follow") as an index of Matthew's View of His Community," *Journal of Biblical Literature*, Vol. 97, no. 1 (March 1978), pp. 57-58.
    5. *The New International Dictionary of New Testament Theology* (Vol. 1): s.v. "μιμέομαι" by Wolfgang Bauder.
    6. Leonhard Schiemer, "A Letter to the Church at Rattenberg," quoted in Walter Klaassen, ed., *Anabaptism in Outline* (Kitchener and Scottdale: Herald Press, 1981), pp. 90-91.
    7. Christian leaders of the fourth and fifth centuries who went to the deserts of Egypt, Palestine, and Syria to practice a spirituality which emphasized martyring the fake self and doing battle with the devil.
    8. Bonhoeffer, *op. cit.*, p. 51.
    9. Kelsey, *op. cit.*, pp. 131-132.

Lesson 4
    1. *The New International Dictionary of New Testament Theology*, (Vol. 1): s.v. "μαθητή's" by Dietrich Müller.
    2. Hans Denck, "The Contention that Scripture Says," quoted in Walter Klaassen, ed., *Anabaptism in Outline* (Kitchener and Scottdale: Herald Press, 1981), p. 87.

3. Walter Klaassen, *Anabaptism: Neither Catholic nor Protestant* (Waterloo: Conrad Press, 1973), p. 40.

4. *Ibid.*, p. 45.

5. Elton Trueblood, *A Place to Stand* (New York: Harper & Row, 1969), p. 50.

6. Jim Wallis, *The Call to Conversion* (San Francisco: Harper & Row, 1981), pp. 13-14.

7. *Ibid.*, pp. 155-156.

8. Paul Roy, S. J., *Building Christian Communities for Justice* (New York: Paulist Press, 1981), p. 26.

9. Damien Isabell, O.F.M., *The Spiritual Director* (Chicago: Franciscan Herald Press, 1976), pp. 54-55.

Lesson 5

1. John Christian Wenger, *Introduction to Theology* (Scottdale; Herald Press, 1954), pp. 272-273.

2. *Ibid.*, p. 278.

3. *Ibid.*, p. 279.

4. Harold S. Bender, "Walking in the Resurrection," *The Mennonite Quarterly Review,* 35 (April 1961) p. 96.

5. Hans Hotz, quoted in Leland Harder, *Sources of Swiss Anabaptism,* (Scottdale: Herald Press, 1984), p. 521.

6. CWMS, p. 53.

7. *Ibid.*, p. 93.

8. *Ibid.*, p.101.

9. *Ibid.*, p. 300.

10. Wallis, *op. cit.*, p. 1.

11. J. R. W. Stott, *Basic Christianity* (Grand Rapids: Eerdmans, 1958), pp. 111-115.

12. The image of "ladder" was used by the Desert Fathers to describe the steps of spirituality. John of the Cross (1542-1591) developed the ladder of ascent consisting of the following ten steps which are found in Holmes, *op. cit .,* p. 100.

1. The soul becomes sick for the glory of God.
2. The soul searches for God unceasingly.
3. The soul is moved to do works for God.
4. The soul suffers, the flesh is conquered, and God gives joy.
5. The soul has an impatient desire and longing for God.
6. The soul runs swiftly toward God and senses his touch.
7. The soul acquires an ardent boldness.
8. The soul lays hold of God as the beloved.
9. The soul burns gently with love.
10. The soul is assimilated to God, apparently after death.

13. For many Anabaptists these three steps had some similarities with stages three, four, and five of Fowler's stages of faith. Fowler's stage three would be similar to the adults who had grown up in the Catholic Church and culture. His stage four would be similar to the acceptance of the Anabaptist faith or the Anabaptists' stage two. Stage five in Fowler's system would have some similarities with stage three of Anabaptism.

14. Paul M. Miller, *Peer Counseling in the Church* (Scottdale: Herald Press, 1978), pp. 24-26.

15. *Ibid.*, p. 26.

Lesson 6
1. Wenger, *op. cit.*, pp. 273-275.
2. *Ibid.*, p. 275.
3. In his Foreword to *The Concept of Grace in the Radical Reformation,* George H. Williams affirms the radical difference between Martin Luther and the Anabaptists in their understanding of grace. Williams writes: "Because grace within the Anabaptist perspective means the ontological change within the believer, that is, a clear motion toward personal and group sanctification and discipline, rather than the state of one declared righteous forensically by virtue of the Work of Christ, discipleship, in which the life of Jesus Christ serves as the model for the life of every earnest Christian, becomes not only a possibility but also a requirement—much as in the pre-Constantinian Church. This demand led Anabaptists on their particular quest for a Christocentric hermeneutic, pivotal for almost all groupings, and with it the renunciation of coercion in matters of faith. Inevitably this emphasis upon religious voluntarism, both personal and ecclesiological, shaped the Anabaptist modalities for relating their churches with other churches and the structures of society at large, notably the magistracy." Alvin J. Beachy, *The Concept of Grace in the Radical Reformation* (Nieuwkoop: B. de Graaf, 1977), p. xiv.
4. For the purpose of this study, faith is being defined in the more narrow biblical sense (which goes beyond assent to propositions) rather than in broad terms such as values (Tillich), or visions and values (Niebuhr), or quality of human life (Smith). For further discussion of definitions of faith, see Fowler, *op. cit.*, pp. 3-15. In light of the Anabaptist view of discipleship, faith can be defined as confidence in God's love as revealed in Jesus which is expressed in following him.
5. John H. Yoder, trans. and ed., *The Schleitheim Confession* (Scottdale: Herald Press, 1973), p. 12.
6. Pilgram Marpeck, quoted in Harold S. Bender, "Walking in the Resurrection," *The Mennonite Quarterly Review,* 35 (April 1961), p. 101.
7. CWMS, p. 225.
8. John H. Yoder, trans. and ed., *The Legacy of Michael Sattler,* Classics of the Radical Reformation. (Scottdale: Herald Press, 1973), pp. 121-122.
9. Bender, "Walking in the Resurrection," p. 104.
10. Dirk Philips, quoted in Bender, *op. cit.*, p. 100.
11. CWMS, pp. 396-397.
12. Bonhoeffer, *op. cit.*, p. 56.
13. Davis, *op. cit.*, pp. 174-175.
14. *Ibid.*, p. 175.
15. CWMS, p. 1052.
16. Davis, *op. cit.*, p. 174.
17. Tilden H. Edwards, *Spiritual Friend* (New York: Paulist Press, 1980), p. 126.

Lesson 7
1. John Christian Wenger, *Separated unto God* (Scottdale: Mennonite Publishing House, 1951), p. 42.
2. *Ibid.*, p. 59.
3. Yoder, *The Schleitheim Confession,* pp. 16, 18.
4. CWMS, p. 679.
5. *Ibid.*, p. 113.
6. *Ibid.*, p. 221.

7. Bender, "Walking in the Resurrection," pp. 108-109.
8. Stott, *op. cit.*, pp. 139-140.
9. Bonhoeffer, *op. cit.*, p. 134.
10. *Ibid.*, p. 136.
11. CWMS, p. 70.
12. Martin, *op. cit.*, p. 70.
13. *Ibid.*, pp. 65-75.

Lesson 8
1. Klassen and Klaassen, *op. cit.*, pp. 182-183.
2. *Ibid.*, pp. 165-166.
3. Donald G. Bloesch, *The Crisis of Piety* (Grand Rapids: Eerdmans, 1968), p. 131.
4. *Ibid.*, pp. 68-69.
5. Robert Friedmann, *The Theology of Anabaptism*, Studies in Anabaptist and Mennonite History, No. 15 (Scottdale: Herald Press, 1973), p. 36.
6. Carl F. H. Henry, ed., *Revelation and the Bible* (Philadelphia: Presbyterian and Reformed Publishing Company, 1958), p. 206.

Lesson 9
1. Conrad Grebel, "Letters to Thomas Müntzer," *Spiritual and Anabaptist Writers*, ed. George H. Williams, The Library of Christian Classics, No. 25, (Philadelphia: The Westminster Press, 1957), p. 79.
2. Bernhard Rothmann, "Restitution," quoted in Walter Klaassen, ed., *Anabaptism in Outline* (Kitchener and Scottdale: Herald Press, 1981), pp. 106, 107.
3. Dirk Philips, "Refutation of Two Letters of Sebastian Frank," *ibid.*, p. 115.
4. CWMS, pp. 742-743.
5. Wallis, *op. cit.*, p. 113.
6. David Watson, *Called & Committed* (Wheaton: Harold Shaw, Publishers, 1982), p. 18.
7. Howard Snyder, "Holding a Mirror to the Contemporary Church," *Christianity Today*, September 17, 1982, pp. 22-23.
8. Andrew Murray, quoted in Wilbur M. Smith, *Profitable Bible Study* (Boston: W. A. Wilde Co., 1953), p. 63.
9. Dietrich Bonhoeffer, *Life Together*, trans., John W. Doberstein (San Francisco: Harper & Row, 1954), p. 83.
10. Martin, *op. cit.*, pp. 76-90.

Lesson 10
1. Paul S. Minear, *Images of the Church in the New Testament* (Philadelphia: The Westminster Press, 1960).
2. Harold S. Bender, *These Are My People* (Scottdale: Herald Press, 1962), p. 25.
3. *Ibid.*, p. 29.
4. *Ibid.*, pp. 33-34.
5. Klassen and Klaassen, *op. cit.*, p. 385.
6. *Ibid.*, pp. 331-332.
7. CWMS, pp. 93-94.
8. Howard A. Snyder, *The Community of the King* (Downers Grove, Ill:

InterVarsity Press, 1977), pp. 55-56.
    9. Bonhoeffer, *op. cit.*, p. 21.
    10. *Ibid.*, pp. 25-26.
    11. Richard J. Foster, *Celebration of Discipline* (San Francisco: Harper & Row, 1978), pp. 24-25.
    12. Isabell, *op. cit.*, p. 15.

Lesson 11
    1. Balthasar Hubmaier, "A Form for Baptism," quoted in Walter Klaassen, ed. *Anabaptism in Outline* (Kitchener and Scottdale: Herald Press, 1981), p. 168.
    2. Bender, *These Are My People*, pp. 74-75.
    3. David P. Scaer, "The Conflict over Baptism," *Christianity Today*, April 14, 1967, p. 8.
    4. Foster, *op. cit.*, p. 25.
    5. Bonhoeffer, *Life Together*, pp. 83-84.

Lesson 12
    1. Yoder, *The Schleitheim Confession*, p. 11. (This concept of communion led to the practice of "closed communion" or communing only with likeminded believers.)
    2. Balthasar Hubmaier, *Schriften*, ed. by G. Westin and T. Bergsten, Gütersloher, 1962, pp. 355, 361-363.
    3. Klassen and Klaassen, *op. cit.*, p. 148.
    4. CWMS, pp. 515-516.
    5. Bonhoeffer, *Life Together*, pp. 120-121.
    6. Wallis, *op. cit.*, pp. 154-155, 158.
    7. Dietrich Bonhoeffer, *Psalms: the Prayer Book of the Bible*, trans. James H. Burtness (Minneapolis: Augsburg, 1970), p. 19.
    8. *Ibid.*, pp. 14-15.
    9. Bonhoeffer, *Life Together*, pp. 47-48.

Lesson 13
    1. Encourage: also means to comfort or console.
    2. Admonish: means to put in mind, to warn, to exhort. A contemporary term might be "carefront."
    3. Bonhoeffer, *Life Together*, pp. 103-104.
    4. *Ibid.*, pp. 105-106.

Lesson 14
    1. John Howard Yoder, "Binding and Loosing," *Concern No. 14* (n.p., February 1967).
    2. Hans Denck, "Concerning True Love," quoted in Walter Klaassen, ed. *Anabaptism in Outline* (Kitchener and Scottdale: Herald Press, 1981), pp. 215-216.
    3. Klassen and Klaassen, *op. cit.*, p. 325.
    4. *Ibid.*, pp. 356-357.
    5. CWMS, pp. 411-412.
    6. *Ibid.*, p. 413.
    7. *Ibid.*, p. 472.
    8. Watson, *op. cit.*, p. 61.
    9. Bonhoeffer, *Life Together*, p. 107.

10. Foster, *op. cit.*, pp. 127-128.
11. *Ibid.*

Lesson 15
1. Bender, *These Are My People*, p. 46.
2. *Ibid.*, p. 52.
3. J. Winfield Fretz, "Brotherhood and the Economic Ethic of the Anabaptists," *The Recovery of the Anabaptist Vision*, ed., Guy F. Hershberger (Scottdale: Herald Press, 1957), pp. 195-197.
4. Klassen and Klaassen, *op. cit.*, pp. 278-279.
5. CWMS, p. 558.
6. "An Evangelical Commitment to Simple Lifestyle," included in David Watson, *Called & Committed* (Wheaton: Harold Shaw, Publishers, 1982), p. 201.
7. Wallis, *op. cit.*, pp. 67-68.

Lesson 16
1. Watson, *op. cit.*, pp. 75-78.
2. CWMS, p. 99.
3. *Ibid.*, p. 189.
4. *Ibid.*, p. 146.
5. Snyder, *The Community of the King*, p. 57.
6. Gordon Cosby, *Handbook for Mission Groups* (Waco: Word Books, 1975), p. 72.
7. *Ibid.*, p. 75.
8. *Ibid.*, p. 73.
9. Snyder, "Holding a Mirror to the Contemporary Church," p. 23.
10. Elizabeth O'Connor, *Eighth Day of Creation* (Waco: Word Books, Publisher, 1971), pp. 17-18.
11. *Ibid.*, p. 55.

Lesson 17
1. John H. Yoder, *The Politics of Jesus* (Grand Rapids: Eerdmans, 1972), pp. 115-130.
2. *The Mennonite Encyclopedia*, vol. 4: s.v. "Ethics" by J. Lawrence Burkholder.
3. Klaassen, *Anabaptism: Neither Catholic nor Protestant*, p. 22.
4. Harold S. Bender, *The Anabaptist Vision* (Scottdale: Herald Press, 1944), pp. 34-35.
5. Watson, *op. cit.*, p. 178.
6. Yoder, *op. cit.*, pp. 133-134.

Lesson 18
1. See as examples Psalm. 145:13, and Daniel 2:44.
2. Bender, *These Are My People*, pp. 112-113.
3. Friedmann, *op. cit.*, p. 41.
4. Yoder, *The Schleitheim Confession*, p. 11.
5. *Ibid.*, p. 12
6. CWMS, p. 554.
7. Snyder, *The Community of the King*, p. 14.
8. *Ibid.*, p. 16.

9. *Ibid.*, p. 28.

10. *Ibid.*, pp. 12-13.

11. Waldron Scott, *Bring Forth Justice* (Grand Rapids: Eerdmans, 1980), p. 196.

12. *Ibid.*, p. 212.

13. *Ibid.*, p. 214.

14. Orlando E. Costas, *World Missions—Building Bridges or Barriers* (Bangalore: WEF Missions Commission, 1979), p. 36. Quoted in Scott, *op. cit.*, p. 217.

Lesson 19

1. Bonhoeffer, *The Cost of Discipleship*, p. 71.

2. Snyder, *The Community of the King*, p. 30.

3. *Ibid.*, p. 190.

4. *Ibid.*, pp. 187-188.

5. Watson, *op. cit.*, p. 24.

6. Jacques Ellul, *The Presence of the Kingdom* (New York: Seabury Press, 1948), p. 9.

7. It is debatable whether the only choices are to "dominate others" or "accept . . . domination."

8. *Ibid.*, p. 11.

Lesson 20

1. Yoder, *The Legacy of Michael Sattler*, pp. 59-60.

2. Catherine Marshall, *Adventures in Prayer* (New York: Ballantine Books, 1975), p. 91.

3. Elton Trueblood, *The Company of the Committed* (New York: Harper & Row, 1961), pp. 98-99.

4. Yoder, *The Politics of Jesus*, pp. 130-131.

5. Watson, *op. cit.*, pp. 127-134.

Lesson 21

1. Yoder, *The Legacy of Michael Sattler*, p. 122.

2. *Ibid.*, p. 151.

3. J. Kuhn, *Toleranz und Offenbarung*, 231, quoted in John Horsch, "The Faith of the Swiss Brethren," *MQR* (April 1931) 5:139.

4. CWMS, p. 307.

5. *Ibid.*, p. 558.

6. *Ibid.*, p. 836.

7. Bloesch, *op. cit.*, p. 53.

8. Wallis, *op. cit.*, pp. 133-134.

9. Foster, *op. cit.*, pp. 117-122.

10. Richard J. Foster, *Freedom of Simplicity* (San Francisco: Harper & Row, 1981), p. 148.

11. Henri Nouwen, "A Self-Emptied Heart," *Sojourners*, Vol. 10 (August 1981), p. 20.

Lesson 22

1. Klassen and Klaassen, *op. cit.*, p. 77.

2. *Ibid.*, p. 91.

3. CWMS, p. 303.

4. *Ibid.*, p. 311.
5. Snyder, *The Community of the King*, p. 104.
6. Watson, *op. cit.*, p. 23.
7. Wallis, *op. cit.*, p. 16.
8. Scott, *op. cit.*, p. 183.
9. Bloesch, *op. cit.*, p. 52.
10. *Ibid.*, pp. 134-135.
11. Foster, *Celebration of Discipline*, p. 43.
12. *Ibid.*, p. 49.

Lesson 23
1. Bathasar Hubmaier, "Twelve Articles," quoted in Walter Klaassen, ed., *Anabaptism in Outline* (Kitchener and Scottdale: Herald Press, 1981), p. 320
2. CWMS, p. 942.
3. *Ibid.*, p. 613.
4. Snyder, *The Community of the King*, p.187.
5. Bloesch, *op. cit.*, p. 142.
6. Watson, *op. cit.*, pp. 196-197.
7. *Ibid.*, pp. 197-198.

Appendix 1

Introduction
1. Walter Klaassen, ed., *Anabaptism in Outline*, Classics of the Radical Reformation, No. 3 (Kitchener and Scottdale: Herald Press, 1981), p. 12
2. John H. Yoder, trans. and ed., *The Legacy of Michael Sattler*, Classics of the Radical Reformation, (Scottdale: Herald Press, 1973), p. 7.
3. *Ibid.*
4. Edward Blaine Stoltzfus, "Grace and Discipleship" (Th.M. thesis, Princeton Theological Seminary, 1963), p. 134.
5. Robert Friedmann, *The Theology of Anabaptism*, Studies in Anabaptist and Mennonite History, No. 15 (Scottdale: Herald Press, 1973), p. 44.
6. *Ibid.*

1. The Anabaptist Concept of Discipleship
1. Harold S. Bender, *The Anabaptist Vision* (Scottdale: Herald Press, 1944), p. 20.
2. *The Mennonite Encyclopedia*, vol. 4: s.v. "Discipleship," by Harold S. Bender.
3. Harold S. Bender, "The Anabaptist Theology of Discipleship," *The Mennonite Quarterly Review*, 24 (January 1950), p. 27.
4. *Ibid.*, p. 28.
5. *Ibid.*
6. *Ibid.*, p. 29.
7. *Ibid.*
8. Friedmann, *op. cit.*, p. 19
9. *Ibid.*, p. 27.
10. *Ibid.*, p. 29.

11. J. Lawrence Burkholder, "The Anabaptist Vision of Discipleship," *The Recovery of the Anabaptist Vision*, ed., Guy F. Hershberger (Scottdale: Herald Press, 1957), p. 136.

12. *Ibid.*, p. 135.

13. *Ibid.*, p. 137.

14. Klaassen, *Anabaptism in Outline*, p. 23.

15. William Klassen and Walter Klaassen, trans. and ed., *The Writings of Pilgram Marpeck*, Classics of the Radical Reformation, No. 2, (Kitchener and Scottdale: Herald Press, 1978), pp. 509-510.

16. *The Complete Writings of Menno Simons*, trans., Leonard Verduin, and ed., John Christian Wenger (Scottdale: Herald Press, 1956), p. 186. Henceforth referred to as CWMS.

17. William R. Estep, *The Anabaptist Story* (Nashville: Broadman Press, 1963), p. 145.

18. Conrad Grebel, "Letters to Thomas Müntzer," *Spiritual and Anabaptist Writers*, ed., George H. Williams, The Library of Christian Classics, No. 25 (Philadelphia: The Westminster Press, 1957), pp. 80-81.

19. Estep, *Anabaptist Story*, p. 145.

20. Werner O. Packull, *Mysticism and the Early South German-Austrian Anabaptist Movement, 1525-1531* (Scottdale: Herald Press, 1977), p. 145.

21. John H. Yoder, trans. and ed., *The Schleitheim Confession*, (Scottdale: Herald Press, 1973), p. 10.

22. Yoder, *Legacy of Michael Sattler*, p. 87.

23. Estep, *Anabaptist Story*, p. 164.

24. Klassen and Klaassen, *op. cit.*, p. 172.

25. *Ibid.*

26. *Ibid.*, pp. 294-295.

27. CWMS, p. 243.

28. *Ibid.*, p. 245.

29. Ethelbert Stauffer, "Anabaptist Theology of Martyrdom," *The Mennonite Quarterly Review*, 19 (July 1945), p. 205.

30. Friedmann, *op. cit.*, p. 135.

31. Klaassen, *Anabaptism in Outline*, p. 162.

32. *Ibid.*, p. 163.

33. Kenneth Ronald Davis, *Anabaptism and Asceticism*, Studies in Anabaptist and Mennonite History, No. 16 (Scottdale: Herald Press, 1974), p. 197.

34. *Ibid.*, p. 199.

35. CWMS, p. 947.

36. *Ibid.*, p. 307.

37. *Ibid.*, p. 558.

38. Klaassen, *Anabaptism in Outline*, p. 232.

39. Davis, *op. cit.*, p. 206.

40. Grebel, *op. cit.*, p. 74.

41. Richard C. Detweiler, "The Concept of Law and Gospel in the Writings of Menno Simons, Viewed Against the Background of Martin Luther's Thought," *The Mennonite Quarterly Review*, 43 (July 1969), p. 193.

42. *Ibid.*, p. 201.

43. *Ibid.*, p. 211.

44. Bender, "Anabaptist Theology of Discipleship," p. 31.

45. Yoder, *Schleitheim Confession*, pp. 11-13.

46. Yoder, *Legacy of Michael Sattler*, p. 87.

47. *Ibid.*, p. 89.
48. CWMS, p. 299.
49. *Ibid.*, p. 221.
50. Friedmann, *op. cit.*, p. 28.
51. *Ibid.*, p. 41.
52. Davis, *op. cit.*, p. 210.
53. *Ibid.*, p. 130.
54. Grebel, *op. cit.*, p. 80..
55. Yoder, *Schleitheim Confession*, p. 14.
56. Klassen and Klaassen, *op. cit.*, pp. 390-391.
57. *Ibid.*, p. 63.
58. CWMS, p. 93
59. *Ibid.*, p. 94.
60. Bender, "Anabaptist Theology of Discipleship," p. 33.
61. *Ibid.*, p. 34.
62. Davis, *op. cit.*, p. 197.
63. *Ibid.*, p. 200.
64. *Ibid.*
65. Burkholder, *op. cit.*, p. 146.
66. Grebel, *op. cit.*, p. 80.
67. *Ibid.*, pp. 78-79.
68. Yoder, *Schleitheim Confession*, pp. 13-14.
69. Klassen and Klaassen, *op. cit.*, p. 71.
70. *Ibid.*
71. *Ibid.*, p. 415.
72. *Ibid.*, p. 412.
73. *Ibid.*, p. 410.
74. CWMS, p. 15
75. *Ibid.*, p. 45.
76. *Ibid.*, p. 49.
77. *Ibid.*, p. 54.
78. *Ibid.*, pp. 599-600.
79. *Ibid.*, p. 621.
80. Stauffer, *op. cit.*, p. 180.
81. *Ibid.*
82. *Ibid.*, p. 196.
83. *Ibid.*, p. 197.
84. *Ibid.*, p. 199.
85. *Ibid.*, p. 214.
86. Friedmann, *op. cit.*, p. 86.
87. Davis, *op. cit.*, p. 177.
88. *Ibid.*, p. 46.
89. *Ibid.*, p. 178.
90. *Ibid.*, p. 179.
91. *Ibid.*, p. 180.
92. Franklin H. Littell, *The Anabaptist View of the Church* (1952), quoted in J. Lawrence Burkholder, "The Anabaptist Vision of Discipleship," *The Recovery of the Anabaptist Vision*, ed., Guy F. Hershberger (Scottdale: Herald Press, 1957), p. 138.
93. Charles W. Ranson, *That the World May Know* (1953), quoted in J. D. Graber, "Anabaptism Expressed in Missions and Social Service," *The Recovery*

of the Anabaptist Vision, ed., Guy F. Hershberger (Scottdale: Herald Press, 1957), p. 157.

94. Franklin H. Littell, *The Anabaptist View of the Church* (1952), quoted in J. D. Graber, "Anabaptism Expressed in Missions and Social Service," *The Recovery of the Anabaptist Vision*, ed., Guy F. Hershberger (Scottdale: Herald Press, 1957), p. 154.

95. Bender, "Anabaptist Theology of Discipleship," p. 6
96. Grebel, *op. cit.*, p. 79.
97. CWMS, p. 298
98. *Ibid.*, p. 303.
99. *Ibid.*, p. 189.
100. *Ibid.*, p. 633.
101. Littell quoted in Graber, *op. cit.*, p. 155.
102. Yoder, *Legacy of Michael Sattler*, p. 61.
103. Davis, *op. cit.*, p. 201.

2. The Anabaptist Approach to Discipling

1. Yoder, *Legacy of Michael Sattler*, pp. 44-45.
2. William R. Estep, Jr., ed., *Anabaptist Beginnings* (Nieuwkoop: B. de Graaf, 1976), p. 128.
3. *Ibid.*
4. *Ibid.*
5. *Ibid.*
6. *Ibid.*, p. 129.
7. *Ibid.*
8. Packull, *op. cit.*, p. 123.
9. Klassen and Klaassen, *op. cit.*, p. 182.
10. *Ibid.*
11. Friedmann, *op. cit.*, p. 36.
12. Davis, *op. cit.*, p. 64.
13. *Ibid.*, p. 134.
14. Balthasar Hubmaier, "On Fraternal Admonition," *Concern No. 14*, (n.p., February 1967), p. 41.
15. John Howard Yoder, "Binding and Loosing," *Concern No. 14*. (n.p., February 1967),p. 16
16. Hubmaier, *op. cit.*, p. 43.
17. Davis, *op. cit.*, p. 143.
18. *Ibid.*, p. 48-53.
19. Grebel, *op. cit.*, p. 80.
20. *Ibid.*, p. 77.
21. Klassen and Klaassen, *op. cit.*, p. 112.
22. Yoder, *Schleitheim Confession*, p. 13
23. Klassen and Klaassen, *op. cit.*, p. 149.
24. *Ibid.*
25. CWMS, p. 168
26. *Ibid.*, p. 170.
27. *Ibid.*, p. 996-997.
28. Yoder, *Legacy of Michael Sattler*, p. 44
29. *Ibid.*, p. 59-60.
30. *Ibid.*, pp. 173-174.
31. Klassen and Klaassen, *op. cit.*, p. 550.

32. CWMS,p. 65
33. *Ibid.*, p. 951.
34. *Ibid.*, p. 411.
35. Davis, *op. cit.*, p. 183.
36. Jean Ellen Goodban Runzo, "Communal Discipline in the Early Anabaptist Communities of Switzerland, South and Central Germany, Austria, and Moravia, 1525-1550," (Ph.D. dissertation, The University of Michigan, 1978), p. 2
37. Davis, *op. cit.*, p. 184
38. *Ibid.*
39. Yoder, *Legacy of Michael Sattler*, p. 62
40. Hubmaier, *op. cit.*, pp. 40-41.
41. Walter Klaassen, *Anabaptism: Neither Catholic nor Protestant* (Waterloo: Conrad Press, 1973), p. 34
42. Yoder, *Legacy of Michael Sattler*, p. 44.
43. CWMS, p. 66.
44. Klassen and Klaassen, *op. cit.*, p. 429.
45. *Ibid.*, pp. 357-358.
46. *Ibid.*, p. 505.
47. *Ibid.*, p. 144.
48. *Ibid.*, p. 385.
49. *Ibid.*, pp. 331-332.
50. Yoder, *Legacy of Michael Sattler*, p. 63.
51. CWMS, p. 29
52. *Ibid.*, p. 66.
53. *Ibid.*, p. 188.
54. *Ibid.*, p. 268.
55. *Ibid.*
56. *Ibid.*, p. 636.
57. *Ibid.*, p. 108.
58. Klassen and Klaassen, *op. cit.*, p. 437.
59. *Ibid.*, p. 442.
60. *Ibid.*, p. 550.
61. Yoder, *Legacy of Michael Sattler*, p. 44
62. *Ibid.*
63. Klaassen, *Anabaptism in Outline*, p. 140
64. Davis, *op. cit.*, p. 216.
65. Friedmann, *op. cit.*, pp. 37-38.
66. Davis, *op. cit.*, p. 216.
67. *Ibid.*, p. 51.
68. Yoder, *Schleitheim Confession*, pp. 10-11.
69. Runzo, *op. cit.*, p. 61.
70. Yoder, *Schleitheim Confession*, p. 14.
71. Klassen and Klaassen, *op. cit.*, p. 275.
72. Klaassen, *Anabaptism in Outline*, p. 212
73. CWMS, p. 27.

Bibliography

Primary Anabaptist Sources
Estep, William R., Jr. *Anabaptist Beginnings*. Nieuwkoop: B. de Graaf, 1976.
Grebel, Conrad. "Letters to Thomas Müntzer," 1524. Edited by George H. Williams, *Spiritual and Anabaptist Writers*. The Library of Christian Classics, No. 25. Philadelphia: The Westminster Press, 1957.
Harder, Leland. *Sources of Swiss Anabaptism*. Scottdale: Herald Press, 1984.
Hubmaier, Balthasar. "On Fraternal Admonition," 1527. *Concern No. 14*. n.p., February 1967.
——————— *Schriften*. ed. G. Westin and T. Bergsten. Gutersloh, 1962.
Klaassen, Walter, ed. *Anabaptism in Outline*. Classics of the Radical Reformation, No. 3. Kitchener and Scottdale: Herald Press, 1981.
Klassen, William and Klaassen, Walter, trans. and ed. *The Writings of Pilgram Marpeck*. Classics of the Radical Reformation, No. 2. Kitchener and Scottdale: Herald Press, 1978.
Kuhn, J. *Toleranz und Offenbarung*. 231. "The Faith of the Swiss Brethren," *The Mennonite Quarterly Review*. April 1931.
Peachey, Shem and Peachey, Paul. "Answer of Some Who Are Called (Ana) Baptists Why They Do Not Attend the Churches: A Swiss Brethren Tract," *The Mennonite Quarterly Review*. January 1971.
The Complete Writings of Menno Simons, trans. by Leonard Verduin and ed. by John Christian Wenger. Scottdale: Herald Press, 1956.
Yoder, John H., trans. and ed. *The Legacy of Michael Sattler*. Classics of the Radical Reformation. Scottdale: Herald Press, 1973.
——————— , trans. and ed. *The Schleitheim Confession*. Scottdale: Herald Press, 1973.

Secondary Anabaptist Sources

Beachy, Alvin, J. *The Concept of Grace in the Radical Reformation.* Nieuwkoop: B. de Graaf, 1977.

Bender, Harold S. "The Anabaptist Theology of Discipleship," *The Mennonite Quarterly Review,* 24. January 1950.

_____. *The Anabaptist Vision.* Scottdale: Herald Press, 1944.

_____. "The Anabaptist Vision," ed. Guy F. Hershberger, *The Recovery of the Anabaptist Vision.* Scottdale: Herald Press, 1957.

_____. *These Are My People.* Scottdale: Herald Press, 1962.

_____. "Walking in the Resurrection," *The Mennonite Quarterly Review,* 35. April 1961.

Burkholder, J. Lawrence. "The Anabaptist Vision of Discipleship," ed. Guy F. Hershberger, *The Recovery of the Anabaptist Vision.* Scottdale: Herald Press, 1957.

Davis, Kenneth Ronald. *Anabaptism and Asceticism.* Studies in Anabaptist and Mennonite History, No. 16. Scottdale: Herald Press, 1974.

Detweiler, Richard C. "The Concept of Law and Gospel in the Writings of Menno Simons, Viewed Against the Background of Martin Luther's Thought," *The Mennonite Quarterly Review,* 43. July 1969.

Estep, William R. *The Anabaptist Story.* Nashville: Broadman Press, 1963.

Fretz, J. Winfield. "Brotherhood and the Economic Ethic of the Anabaptists," ed. Guy F. Hershberger, *The Recovery of the Anabaptist Vision.* Scottdale: Herald Press, 1957.

Friedmann, Robert. *The Theology of Anabaptism.* Studies in Anabaptist and Mennonite History, No. 15. Scottdale: Herald Press, 1973.

Graber, J. D. "Anabaptism Expressed in Missions and Social Service," ed. Guy F. Hershberger, *The Recovery of the Anabaptist Vision.* Scottdale: Herald Press, 1957.

Holmes, Urban T., III. *A History of Christian Spirituality.* New York: Seabury Press, 1981.

Klaassen, Walter. *Anabaptism: Neither Catholic nor Protestant.* Waterloo: Conrad Press, 1973.

Packull, Werner O. *Mysticism and the Early South German-Austrian Anabaptists Movement 1525-1531.* Studies in Anabaptist and Mennonite History, No. 19. Scottdale: Herald Press, 1977.

Runzo, Jean Ellen Goodban. "Communal Discipline in the Early Anabaptist Communities of Switzerland, South and Central Germany, Austria, and Moravia, 1525-1550." Ph.D. dissertation, The University of Michigan, 1978.

Stauffer, Ethelbert. "Anabaptist Theology of Martyrdom," *The Mennonite Quarterly Review,* 19. July 1945.

Stoltzfus, Edward Blaine. "Grace and Discipleship." Th.M. thesis, Princeton Theological Seminary, 1963.

The Mennonite Encyclopedia. Vol. 4. Scottdale: Mennonite Publishing House, 1957.

Yoder, John Howard. "Binding and Loosing." *Concern No. 14.* n.p., February 1967.

───────── *The Politics of Jesus.* Grand Rapids: Eerdmans, 1972.

Discipleship and Spirituality Sources

A Monk of New Clairvaux. *Don't You Belong to Me?* New York: Paulist Press, 1979.

Bloesch, Donald G. *The Crisis of Piety.* Grand Rapids: Eerdmans, 1968.

Bonhoeffer, Dietrich. *Life Together.* trans. John W. Doberstein. San Francisco: Harper & Row, 1954.

───────── *Psalms: The Prayer Book of the Bible,* trans. James H. Burtness. Minneapolis: Augsburg, 1970.

───────── *The Cost of Discipleship,* trans. R. H. Fuller. New York: Macmillan, 1953.

Cosby, Gordon. *Handbook For Mission Groups.* Waco: Word Books, 1975.

Cosgrove, Francis M., Jr. *Essentials of Discipleship.* Colorado Springs: Navpress, 1980.

Devers, Dorothy C. *Faithful Friendship.* Washington, D.C.: The Church of the Saviour, 1979.

Dyckman, Katherine Marie and Carroll, L. Patrick. *Inviting the Mystic, Supporting the Prophet.* New York: Paulist Press, 1981.

Dykstra, Craig R. *Vision and Character: A Christian Educator's Alternative to Kohlberg.* New York: Paulist Press, 1981.

Edwards, Tilden H. *Spiritual Friend.* New York: Paulist Press, 1980.

Eims, Leroy. *The Lost Art of Disciple-Making.* Grand Rapids: Zondervan, 1978.

Ellul, Jacques. *The Presence of the Kingdom.* New York: Seabury Press, 1948.

Foster, Richard J. *Celebration of Discipline.* San Francisco: Harper & Row, 1978.

───────── *Freedom of Simplicity.* San Francisco: Harper & Row, 1981.

Fowler, James W. *Stages of Faith.* San Francisco: Harper & Row, 1981.

Friedmann, Robert. *The Theology of Anabaptism.* Scottdale: Herald Press, 1973.

Gerber, Vergil. ed. *Discipling Through Theological Education by Extension*. Chicago: Moody Press, 1980.

Hadidian, Allen. *Successful Discipling*. Chicago: Moody Press, 1979.

Hanks, Billie, Jr. and Shell, William A. ed. *Discipleship*. Grand Rapids: Zondervan, 1981.

Henrichsen, Walter A. *Disciples Are Made—Not Born*. Wheaton: Victor Books, 1974.

Henry, Carl F. H., ed. *Revelation and the Bible*. Philadelphia: Presbyterian and Reformed Publishing Company, 1958.

Holmes, Urban T., III. *A History of Christian Spirituality*. New York: Seabury Press, 1981.

Ignatius, St. *Spiritual Exercises*. English translation by Anthony Mottola. Garden City, NY: Image Books, 1964.

Isabell, Damien O.F.M. *The Spiritual Director*. Chicago: Franciscan Herald Press, 1976.

Jeschke, Marlin. *Discipling the Brother*. Scottdale: Herald Press, 1972.

Kelsey, Morton T. *Adventure Inward*. Minneapolis: Augsburg, 1980.

_____ *Discernment*. New York; Paulist Press, 1978.

Kurz, Albert L. *Disciple-Maker Workbook*. Chicago: Moody Press, 1981.

Leech, Kenneth. *Soul Friend*. San Francisco: Harper & Row, 1977.

Marshall, Catherine. *Adventures in Prayer*. New York: Ballantine Books, 1975.

Martin, John R. *Keys to Successful Bible Study*. Scottdale: Herald Press, 1981.

McGavran, Donald A. and Arn, Win. *How to Grow a Church*. Glendale: Gospel Light Publications, 1973.

Miller, Paul M. *Peer Counseling in the Church*. Scottdale: Herald Press, 1978.

Moore, Waylon B. *Multiplying Disciples: The New Testament Method for Church Growth*. Colorado Springs: Navpress, 1981.

O'Connor, Elizabeth. *Eighth Day of Creation*. Waco: Word Publishers, 1971.

Ortiz, Juan Carlos. *Disciple*. Carol Stream, Ill,: Creation House, 1975.

Richards, Larry and Wakefield, Norm. *Basic Christian Values*. Grand Rapids: Zondervan, 1981.

_____. *First Steps for New and Used Christians*. Grand Rapids: Zondervan, 1981.

_____, *Fruit of the Spirit*. Grand Rapids: Zondervan, 1981.

_____ *The Good Life*. Grand Rapids: Zondervan, 1981.

Roy, Paul, S.J. *Building Christian Communities for Justice*. New York: Paulist Press, 1981.

Scott, Waldron. *Bring Forth Justice*. Grand Rapids: Eerdmans Publishing Company, 1980.

Smith, Wilbur M. *Profitable Bible Study*. Boston: W. A. Wilde Co., 1953.

Snyder, Howard A. *The Community of the King*. Downers Grove, Ill.: InterVarsity Press, 1977.

Stott, J. R. W. *Basic Christianity*. Grand Rapids: Eerdmans, 1958.

The New International Dictionary of New Testament Theology. Vol. 1. Grand Rapids: Zondervan, 1975.

Trueblood, Elton. *A Place to Stand*. New York: Harper & Row, 1969.

————— *The Company of the Committed*. New York: Harper & Row, 1961.

Wallis, Jim. *The Call to Conversion*. San Francisco: Harper & Row, 1981.

Watson, David. *Called & Committed*. Wheaton: Harold Shaw, 1982.

Wenger, John Christian. *Introduction to Theology*. Scottdale: Herald Press, 1954.

————— *Separated unto God*. Scottdale: Herald Press, 1951.

Articles Related to Discipleship and Spirituality

Howard, Richard H. "Doing Theology and Living Our Lives." *Sojourners*, Vol. 6, No. 8. August 1977.

Kingsbury, Jack Dean. "The Verb *Akolouthein* ("To Follow") as an Index of Matthew's View of His Community." *Journal of Biblical Literature*, Vol. 97, No. 1. March 1978.

Martin, John R. "Discipling Disciplers." *The Seminarian*, Vol. 10, No. 5. May 1980.

McCarty, Shaun. "On Entering Spiritual Direction." *Review for Religious*. Vol. 35, 1976.

Nouwen, Henri. "A Self-Emptied Heart." *Sojourners*, Vol. 10, No. 8. August 1981.

————— "Temptation." *Sojourners*, Vol. 10, No. 7. July 1981.

————— "The Selfless Way of Christ." *Sojourners*, Vol. 10, No. 6. June 1981.

Scaer, David P. "The Conflict over Baptism." *Christianity Today*, Vol. 11, No. 14. April 1967.

Snyder, Howard. "Holding a Mirror to the Contemporary Church." *Christianity Today*, Vol. 26, No. 15. September 1982.

The Author

John R. Martin is registrar, associate professor of church ministry, and director of field education at Eastern Mennonite Seminary, Harrisonburg, Virginia.

He received the BA degree from Eastern Mennonite College in 1954. From Goshen Biblical Seminary, he received the ThB in 1955 and the BD in 1960. In 1971 he completed the first unit of clinical pastoral education at Lancaster General Hospital, Lancaster, Pennsylvania. He earned the ThM from Eastern Baptist Theological Seminary in 1972, and the Doctor of Ministry degree from Lancaster Theological Seminary in 1983.

During early seminary studies, he served as a mission pastor at Walkerton, Indiana. This was followed by a three-year pastorate (part-time) in a mission congregation in Washington, DC. From 1961 to 1971, he pastored the Neffsville Mennonite Church, Neffsville, Pennsylvania. During most of this time, he also served as an area overseer in his conference district. In 1971, he joined the Bible faculty at Eastern Mennonite College and taught there until 1978 when he joined the seminary faculty.

Martin has served as executive secretary of National Service Board of Religious Objectors, Washington, DC, director of 1-W Services for Mennonite Board of Missions, Elkhart, Indiana; a member of the board of trustees of Eastern Mennonite College; and president of Mennonite Broadcasts, Inc., (now Media Ministries), Harrisonburg, Virginia. He is currently president of the Mennonite Board of Congregational Ministries.

He is author of *Divorce and Remarriage: A Perspective for Counseling, Keys to Successful Bible Study,* and of numerous articles.

A native of Harrisonburg, he was married to Marian Landis, Blooming Glen, Pennsylvania in 1956. The Martins have three children.